79

Mike
To a good
friend the best
of the Holiday Season

Basic
Cabinetmaking
by Peter Jones

RESTON PUBLISHING COMPANY, INC.

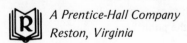

A Prentice-Hall Company
Reston, Virginia

Photographs by Stephen Helfland.
Woodgrain photographs pp. 46–52, courtesy
U.S. Forest Produce Laboratory, U.S. Department of Agriculture.

Library of Congress Cataloging in Publication Data

Jones, Peter,
  Basic cabinetmaking.

  Includes index.
  1. Cabinet-work. I. Title.
TT197.J65   684.1'6   78-10172
ISBN 0-8359-0369-9

10 9 8 7 6 5 4 3 2 1

Printed in the United States of America

Contents

Preface

Basic Cabinetmaking is intended as a guide for the student of cabinetmaking. The student presumably already possesses a skill in woodworking, although he need not have formal training as a professional cabinetmaker. He may, for example, be an accomplished carpenter who has simply decided that there must be some more creative outlet for his skills than building walls or hanging bookshelves.

What the student needs, however, is dedication. He must be passionately involved with his materials and must have a keen sense of pride in his work. He must have a profound desire to go beyond basic carpentry and create for himself—as well as others—truly fine articles of furniture.

The chapters throughout this book logically progress from the point at which an idea for a piece of cabinetry is first conceived, to the cutting, assembling, and ultimate finishing stages. Each chapter includes a visual record of a small veneered buffet which was constructed during production of the book to demonstrate the steps in cabinetmaking discussed in the text.

Although any number of persons interested in fine woodworking will find this text both enlightening and useful, it remains the reader's feeling about wood and workmanship that is most important to his success as a cabinetmaker. To engage in cabinetmaking is to be involved in a world-wide industry that extends from the production of lumber to the manufacture of such diverse materials as metal, glass, ceramics, and plastics. It behooves the cabinetmaker, be he private or professional, to keep abreast of the new products that continuously reach the marketplace. The reading that every cabinetmaker must do, therefore, should not end with this book. Learning must become a never-ending habit and technical journals, trade catalogs, and personal research can be truly valuable sources of information to the aspiring cabinetmaker.

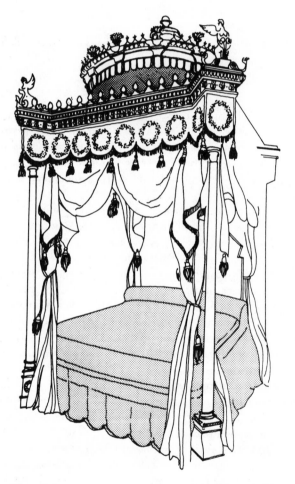

Figure 1-1.   Adams—18th century English.

Chapter 1

From the Love of Wood

Wood is like no other material in the universe. It has its own unique texture, hue, and fragrance. It is older than mankind itself. For centuries craftsmen have dedicated their lives to working with it, to understanding it, shaping it, and using it to meet their needs.

Down through the centuries, these artisans have invented unique tools, even machines, to make the physical part of their labors easier; they have devised systems, procedures, and time-honored techniques for transforming towering trees into decorative and useful objects. They have invented fasteners that will hold their pieces of wood together. They have concocted countless potions that when applied to a wood surface enhance its beauty, as well as protect it from the ravages of time and the elements.

CENTURIES OF CRAFTSMANSHIP

Precisely when the first wooden furniture was made and by whom, is lost in the unwritten annals of prehistory. Certainly among the Assyrians and Babylonians there were all manner of woodworkers, but the most notable craftsmen of antiquity were the Egyptians. Not only were they adept at assembling wooden objects with such joints as the mortise and tenon, rabbet, and dowel (which they invented), but they also developed the art of inlay and veneer. The principles and procedures attending both joinery and veneering were thus established in the Western Hemisphere more than 3,500 years ago, and in essence they have not changed or even been very much improved upon since that time.

Equally important contributions were made by other ancient cultures. The fluting so prevalent in Greek and Roman architecture has been repeated end-lessly on furniture as a decorative motif, a motif that prevails in much of the Mediterranean and Italian provincial furniture manufactured today. Beading, coves, and scrolls also originated with the Greeks and Romans as well as such geometric forms as the square, rectangle, and circle. All had a tremendous impact on furniture design and the art of cabinetmaking.

1

It was not until the Renaissance, beginning in the fourteenth century, that carpenters were faced with an overwhelming public demand for fine woodwork both inside and outside the home. Before the reign of Queen Elizabeth I (1558–1603), there was no distinction between a cabinetmaker and a carpenter; both had a comprehensive knowledge of all things wooden. Now, the cabinetmaker emerged as a specialized artisan and by the 18th century, cabinetmaking in Europe had attained its golden age as far as furniture design and construction were concerned. It was an age typified by four famous English cabinetmakers: the Adams brothers, Robert and James, Thomas Chippendale, George Hepplewhite, and Thomas Sheraton. Furniture making had become an art, but one that would endure only a few decades; for soon after this great period of creativity came the Industrial Revolution of the 19th century.

Figure 1-2.   Chippendale—18th century English.

Many of the protéges and apprentices of the "big four" emigrated to America to establish their own shops. The best known among the American craftsmen was Duncan Phyfe, who employed as many as a hundred cabinetmakers. Phyfe and his men, as well as their competitors were capable of doing everything from felling a tree to making it into a finished piece of furniture.

But there were other forces at work in America. There were carpenters and joiners and millmen who could hew trees, strip them into lumber, and build homes. In the process they did every kind of decorative work on-site, including moldings, windows, and door frames. Many of these journeymen became so adept at their trades and so skilled in decorative carving (known as *millwork*) that they opened their own mill shops. Now they provided their brethren in the building trade with all manner of premilled moldings and trim, and for a few cents per running foot they saved the carpenters and cabinetmakers considerable time and effort.

As millwork grew into a separate industry, a variety of woodworking machines were developed that could not only mold, cut, shape, and plane, but also could be run by unskilled laborers. With the machines came new production methods which separated many of the cabinetmaker's tasks into machine-performed operations, each of which could be completed by men who com-

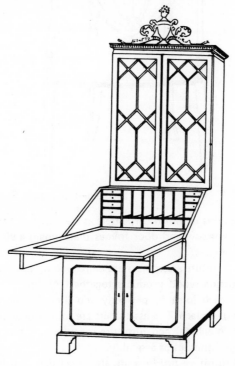

Figure 1-3.   Hepplewhite—18th century English.

manded lower pay for their lesser skills. Within a few years industry had little need for the skilled cabinetmaker who could painstakingly create an entire piece of furniture by hand. These men had to adapt to the industrial age or go without work. Yet, it is a sign of the need men have to work with wood that the business of cabinetmaking has not vanished; it has indeed become more of an art in the twentieth century than ever before.

OPPORTUNITIES FOR A LIVELIHOOD

Today, in the building trade, there are several million *rough* carpenters who cut and assemble studs, beams, and other unseen lumber in nearly every structure.

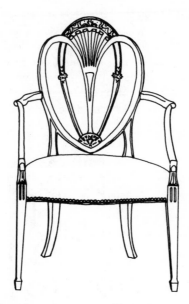

Figure 1–4.   Sheraton—18th century English.

There are millions of *finish* carpenters as well, who put together the moldings and trim, the window and door frames that remain a visible part of every store, office, and home.

Cabinet and furniture *assemblers* are employed by furniture manufacturers as specialists in putting wood products together. Assemblers are the men and women who make each joint fit perfectly and then fasten every piece of the product into its proper place. The assemblers are fully acquainted with the many processes involved in cabinet and furniture manufacture, but they have chosen to specialize in the techniques of assembly.

Cabinet and furniture *finishers* are also specialists, but in the finishing of wooden objects. They understand pigments and how to blend, as well as apply, them. They understand varnish and how to use it to produce any desired finish, from a hand-rubbed matte texture to a high gloss.

Beyond the assembly and finishing work there exists a whole range of skilled and semiskilled jobs in the cabinetmaking field. Both the production and the custom furniture manufacturers, as well as millworking plants, employ men and women with a variety of specialized skills and talents. And they need the services of cabinetmakers.

THE CABINETMAKER

Today, there are perhaps a million qualified cabinetmakers in the United States. They are employed in millwork plants, and in custom and production furniture companies as boatbuilders and modelmakers. They possess a broad-based knowledge of wood, woodworking procedures, and machines that qualifies them as master craftsmen.

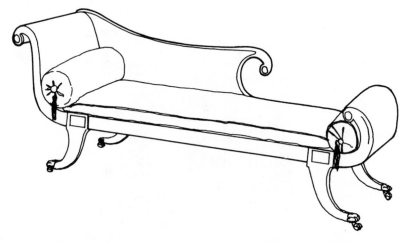

Figure 1-5.   Duncan Phyfe—19th century American.

The cabinetmaker constructs and repairs all manner of wooden objects, including furniture. He works with both natural and man-made woods and is adept at matching the color, grain, and texture of woods. He has a full knowledge of how best to use hand and power tools including joiners, molders, shapers, drill presses, lathes, and saws. He must be proficient in the techniques of joinery and must be capable of applying the proper finish to his project; a finish that will enhance and preserve the wood.

Background Training and Patience

Most woodworking is performed indoors, is a relatively noisy occupation, and sometimes a hazardous one because of the sharp tools involved. Physically, only medium strength is necessary, but all woodworking does require considerable bending, kneeling, reaching, and handling. The training necessary for any of the woodworking jobs available in industry is generally the same. Woodworkers must be competent with both hand and power tools and knowledgeable enough to do algebra as well as interpret technical literature, blueprints, and drawings.

The physical hardships are easily endured and skills can be developed through formal schooling and apprenticeship. But to achieve the level of *master craftsman,* the woodworker must also have a compelling appreciation for detail and a fathomless reservoir of patience.

Figure 2-1. A Colonial design buffet and china cabinet. The colonists used only the woods they found in America and worked with simple tools.

Chapter 2

The Hows and Whys of Furniture Design

Every piece of furniture represents the solution to a specific need. Eons ago, in the very dawn of mankind, one imagines that the only criterion for the furniture used by cavemen was that it satisfy a specific physical need. Thus, a chair or table could be made by piling rocks in front of the cooking fire. But mankind being what it is, soon devised a longer list of requirements that had to be satisfied before a piece of furniture could be considered successful: comfort, convenience, sturdiness, ease of maintenance, and finally, appearance. Design any furniture that is comfortable, convenient to use, solid, easy to take care of, and pleasing to the eye, and you most probably have constructed an object that will be deemed well designed.

But there are no simple rules for furniture design, no specific list of points that can be checked off on a piece of paper and thereby guarantee that a given piece is, indeed, well designed. Good furniture design depends on taste which can change according to the times and can vary from place to place. Unfortunately for anyone trying to define it, taste is a matter of personal or generally accepted preference. This is the reason there have been so many different trends (i.e., tastes) in furniture design throughout history.

PURPOSE

From the caveman to the present time, the purpose, or function, of any piece of furniture has remained the only constant element of design. The question that always must be asked and then answered is, "What need does this object satisfy?" A table must have one height for eating, another for some other purpose. An easy chair must be comfortable, but to achieve that comfort, the angle between the seat and the back will vary. A chest of drawers is to store things. But the kind of objects that will be stored has a great deal to do with its overall size, as well as its shelf and drawer dimensions.

MATERIALS

Given the specific purpose of a piece of furniture, the materials to be used in its construction must also be considered. The various kinds of woods that go into a piece ultimately account for its overall design qualities—the look of the piece—and they should be chosen carefully with the final appearance of the project well in mind.

There are more than 25,000 species of wood in the world today and easily 250 of these are available to the cabinetmaker, to say nothing of numerous man-made materials. The hardwoods used in furniture offer both durability and beauty, but for many kinds of furniture, plywood is an equally acceptable material and can become every bit as attractive. For special purposes, there are also numerous nonwood materials such as plastic laminates, tile, ceramics, metal, glass, textiles, and cane. Each of these materials must be considered and evaluated for its useful and attractive qualities in terms of the particular piece to be constructed.

ASSEMBLY

Obviously, if a well-designed piece of furniture is to meet the criterion of stability, then it must be soundly constructed. From time immemorial, sound construction had relied on proper joinery, and even twentieth century techniques, tools, and fasteners do not replace the need for well-fitting joints; they only make those joints a little easier to create and perhaps a bit more durable.

Quality in furniture means long lasting, durable, and sturdy construction. But in modern terms, quality does not necessarily mean that the most complicated, hardest to achieve joint is the one to use. A mortise and tenon, for example, has always been considered one of the strongest of all joints. But it is also a difficult joint to make with precision, and under the best of circumstances with the best of tools, its construction is time consuming. Nor is it any better, really, than doweling which is infinitely easier to do and almost as strong. Thus, if durability is the ultimate aim and two methods are available, both equally capable of assuring that durability, it is acceptable by modern standards to use the simpler, more efficient joint or method.

APPEARANCE—STYLE

Every piece of furniture, every cabinet constructed, in the final analysis, must be esthetically pleasing and a joy to use. Perhaps the best standard to follow when choosing a design to construct is to base your selection on your own preferences, if only because people have different tastes. Because of all these different tastes, the history of furniture making is speckled with a procession of styles ranging from the elaborate decor of the Greeks and Romans to the elegance of French provincial, to the ponderousness of Mediterranean, the informality of Contemporary, or the security of Traditional.

There are whole encyclopedias devoted to furniture which offer detailed descriptions of the many designs invented and used by mankind, past and present. At some time or other each of the designs presented has, or is, receiving popular acceptance, if only for a few years or in one small corner of the world. A few years ago the American public widely embraced only three basic design classifications: Early American, Traditional, and Modern. Today, there are all kinds of style mixtures, and the evolution in public taste has lengthened the list of acceptable designs to include Early American (Colonial), Traditional, Contemporary, French provincial, Italian provincial, and Mediterranean (Spanish).

Early American

Often called Colonial, Early American furniture is anything that looks like it was made in the United States between the years 1608 (when Jamestown was founded) to 1830. The Early American designs are a function of the limitless supply of wood which the early settlers found abounding in America, and the limited number of hand tools they had for working with that wood. The settler's needed sturdy, durable furniture that could be worked up with a minimum of basic tools.

By the time of the American Revolution, new settlers were arriving from Europe bringing with them a few of their most prized pieces, and native cabinetmakers had begun to make more ornate furniture. They seem to have relied heavily on the foot-powered lathe which was used to produce all kinds of spindly legs and fine turnings. Still, the Early American pieces were modest in decorative effects and always remained, first of all, functional. They always were made with woods indigenous to America—maple, oak, pine, and birch.

Traditional

During the 18th century in England there stepped onto the stage of furniture making four great designers, and so began the golden age of cabinetmaking. Chippendale, Sheraton, Hepplewhite and the Adams brothers brought to the world of furniture design tremendous versatility. They enhanced their work with intricate carvings as well as the use of simple, straight lines. They applied delicate fretwork and fine moldings, and adapted many of the classic designs inherited from ancient Greece and Rome. Most of their furniture was made of mahogany, primarily because it is an excellent material for carving. The work of these English cabinetmakers is still revered and highly valued today, and it is classified by modern furniture experts as Traditional.

Contemporary

The march of machines at the turn of the nineteenth century took away many opportunities for old-time cabinetmakers to earn their living. Hand-carved scrolls for desk fronts and multicurved chair and table legs were far more expensive to make and unprofitable to market than solid furniture assembled by unskilled or semiskilled laborers operating machines.

At first, modern furniture design was square and harsh, boasting few eye-appealing curves. This resulted from the clumsy, forthright machinery that was engineered to cut straight lines but not curves. The designers of Contemporary furniture were concerned with production costs and multiple sales. Unlike other furniture styles that developed gradually over a period of years, Contemporary burst upon the buying public like a tidal wave.

Figure 2-2.   The great advantage of contemporary furniture is that it can often be assembled into different pieces and can be used in any room.

Contemporary was garish at first, but gradually the designers began to evolve a style and a few distinctive qualities; to add different materials such as ceramics and cane, plastics, metal and glass. Today, Contemporary evidences a versatility that makes most pieces suitable for any room in the house and even permits the assembling of various units to create still new pieces. Thus, flexibility and informality have become the guide words of today's contemporary designs. Modern furniture is functional, space saving, and usually finished in a color close to the natural hues of whatever wood is used in its manufacture. It has, in fact, even reached out to embrace some of the features belonging to the other popular styles.

French Provincial

French provincial takes its inspiration from the old French traditions and is characteristically filled with dainty curves and graceful lines. Originally, while the eighteenth century French monarchs Louis XIV and XV commissioned elabo-

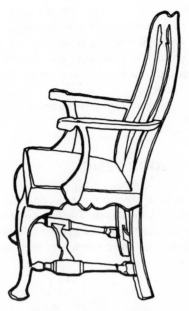

Figure 2-3.   Rich in curves, the French provincial style is best noted for its use of the cabriole, S-shaped leg.

rately decorated furniture, the rural population of French clung to simpler designs which were less ornate and more useful on a day-to-day basis. The woods that were accessible to provincial French cabinetmakers were walnut and the fruitwoods, and their local markets wanted fewer frills on their furniture and more stability. Nevertheless, the royal taste imposed itself on everyone so the cabriole (cab-ree-ol) leg, shaped with a double curve and studded with various styles of carved feet, universally became a part of French provincial furniture, as did at least some amount of scrollwork, fluting and/or carvings. But none of these decorative flourishes were anything like the ornate objects d'art that found acceptance in Versailles.

Today, French provincial furniture is usually made of cherry or mahogany and if it is not finished in a natural wood color, it is likely to be painted black or white and trimmed with gold. The most notable feature of the French provincial finish is the tiny scratches in the wood surface known as a *distressed finish*. The distressing is added by modern manufacturers as an imitation of the original French Provincial furniture.

Italian Provincial

In the provinces of 18th and 19th century Italy the cabinetmakers set about imitating the furniture so popular during the height of the Roman Empire. The local artisans were not so ornate in their designs as their forebears had been. They simplified their basic structures, eliminated much of the ornamentation, and often adapted the simple, unadorned straight line. Nevertheless, they continued the Roman tradition of fine inlays and overlays, recesses and fluting, particularly in the leg designs of their tables and chairs. They created interesting patterns in their well-proportioned paneling and framed it with molding, all of which makes Italian provincial furniture resemble traditional designs more closely than the French.

THE ELEMENTS OF GOOD DESIGN

Line, shape, and mass exist in every cabinetmaking project; they are the cornerstones of all furniture and cabinet design. The first problem that confronts every cabinetmaker when he approaches a new project is whether or not all of the basic elements are properly balanced relative to each other and to the entire piece.

Line

Lines can be straight or curved, S-shaped, circular, or spiral. Their purpose is to give a feeling to the object, be it the severity of an angular Contemporary chest or the graceful curves of a French provincial chair. The line is an easy thing to put on paper, but put enough of them together and a unique shape evolves. Suddenly those easily rendered little pencil marks become a series of problems for the designer—each of which must be confronted and dealt with.

Shape

Squares, rectangles, circles, triangles, diamonds, eclipses, hexagons, pentagons, and octagons are all shapes that appear in table tops and drawer pulls, chairs, chests, and end tables. The way the shape of a piece is presented to the viewer, and the combination of other shapes and forms that appear as part of the design, become the essence of how the entire piece looks. It is the combination of many shapes within a given piece that produces its mass.

Mass

Lines make up the shape, and shape makes up the mass; this gives the object its three-dimensional appearance and qualities. All furniture has height, width, length, and depth. Moreover, all materials come in a variety of shapes that also have height, depth, width, and length. When considering the mass of a piece of furniture, the designer must consider not only its square footage, but also the cubic area of the unit.

Proportion and Balance

Essential to the design of every piece of furniture is the balance or proportion of its components. Proportion is defined as "the relationship of the parts of an object to each other and to the total object." A square, or a cube, by the nature of their sides all having the same length, have balance; this balance can be either formal or informal. *Formal* balance is produced when all the parts of an object are symmetrically arranged, such as the straight legs of a table or chair when they are placed under each corner of the top. *Informal* balance is created when dissimilar parts of an object are arranged so that while they are stable in appearance, they are not symmetrical. A chair, for example, might appear to be quite stable, except that it has an unusually high back which is out of proportion to the legs and seat.

The Golden Mean Rectangle

When we go beyond the square or cube to consider the rectangle, the question of proportion becomes more complicated. A square is always in balance and so is a cube, a circle, or an equilateral triangle. But when is a rectangle balanced? That is, when are its dissimilar sides in proportion? A 3/4" X 1 1/2" X 20' board is a rectangle. But are its dimensions balanced? It is generally agreed among designers that a properly proportioned rectangle has a ratio of 1 to 1.618 between its shorter and longer sides. At some other time and place in history, men may come to agree that the ratio should be 1 : 2, or 3 : 8, or anything else, but for the present, the experts consider 1 : 1.618 as the ideal.

Discovering the specific dimensions of a given golden mean rectangle can, of course, be done mathematically. But adding up a column of 1.618s and translating their sum into inches and feet or meters is somewhat tedious. Almost as tedious, but at least a little more fun, is to work out the ratio of a rectangular project with a ruler, square, and compass.

Developing a Golden Mean Rectangle

1. Begin with the smallest square that equals 1 unit per side and find the center of the bottom side. Mark the center x.
2. Open the compass to a distance between x and the upper right corner of the square; strike an arc (R.A.) until it intersects with line ab when it is extended.
3. Now complete the rectangle. It will measure 1 unit high by 1.618 units wide and is therefore a golden mean rectangle.
4. To draw the next larger golden mean rectangle, use a for the center and open the compass to the length of line ab, then strike an arc until it intersects line ac when it is extended.

5. Complete the rectangle; it, too, will have a ratio of 1 : 1.618.

6. The arcs can continue to be struck, always using the right angle opposite the arc as the center point, and the long (1.618) side of the previous rectangle as the radius until a rectangle of the desired dimensions has been reached.

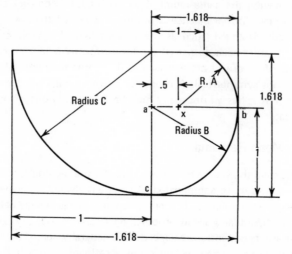

Figure 2-4.   When developing the Golden Mean Rectangle keep making the rectangle larger and larger until it reaches the dimensions you want.

A project, any project, always begins with a need, which in turn gives rise to the idea of the object to be made. From the idea springs a design and then must come an orderly procedure which progresses from a planning stage through construction and prefinishing, to completion of the piece. The steps taken are nearly always the same, but as the craftsman proceeds through each phase he must keep his mind open to the possibilities of change, of improvement upon his original plans. The following work flow chart can be used with any cabinetmaking project:

I. Planning

  A. Sketch the project
   1. Include all unique features
   2. Decide on a finished appearance
  B. Assemble materials
   1. Make formal drawings
   2. Estimate plywood and stock requirements
   3. Decide on hardware and type of finish
   4. Make a complete bill of materials

II. Construction

    A. Lay out and cut parts

        1. Measure and mark all plywood parts and stock

        2. Cut all plywood and stock

        3. Dado, miter, rout, shape; sand for assembly

    B. Assembly

        1. Make subassemblies

        2. Combine subassemblies

        3. Make and install drawers

            a. Measure and cut all drawer parts

            b. Dado, rout, join and sand parts

            c. Assemble drawers

            d. Install drawers

        4. Make and fit doors

            a. Measure and cut all door parts

            b. Dado, rout, join and sand parts

            c. Assemble doors

            d. Install doors

        5. Add molding and trim (except areas to be veneered)

III. Prefinishing

    A. Fill all cracks, dents, holes

    B. Sand

    C. Veneer (optional)

        1. Flatten, measure, and cut all veneer pieces

        2. Glue all pieces

        3. Roller and trim veneer

        4. Clamp

        5. Repair dents and blisters

    D. Add molding and trim

    E. Apply sander-sealer and sand lightly

IV. Completion

    A. Apply undercoats and sand

    B. Apply final coats and sand

    C. Oil rub or polish (if varnish finish is used)

    D. Attach all hardware

Planning

Start with the size of the piece that you plan to build and measure it exactly in your mind—its depth and width and height. Try to imagine it in space with all its components neatly in place. Then mentally begin to rearrange the parts. Add and subtract and change the shape of each major element until you arrive at a design that pleases you.

After the design is generally the way you imagine it should be, in your mind's eye begin detailing the supports, the sides, the legs, the horizontals. You can start doodling on paper at this point, getting down a gridwork of verticals and horizontals, so you will not forget what has come to mind.

When you have as many of the basics of the project as you can think of for the moment, sketch the front of it, then show yourself how it will look from the back, the top, the sides. How large should it be? What molding will be most compatible with its design? What kind of hardware most complements the design? Should the piece be veneered, varnished, or painted?

It takes time to do the drawings. Sometimes a project even causes a few restless nights before it is settled in your mind. Somehow, new ideas like to occur in the dead of night; so take your drawings to bed with you and jot down any new thoughts that strike so hard they wake you up. That sounds outlandish, but the value of any project is directly proportional to how much of yourself you put into it; how much care, attention, and *feeling* you give it.

Materials

When you have a rough sketch of what it is you are about to create, do the formal drawings. One helpful approach at this point is to use grid paper, which can be purchased at any stationery store. The grids are usually 1/4″ squares so 4 of them equal an inch, equals a foot. You can mark off 8″ × 16″ squares in the form of a rectangle and immediately have an accurate, scaled outline of a 4″ × 8″ plywood panel. Play around with the rectangle, fitting as many pieces as possible into it, until you have determined how many panels you will need, and how you will cut each of them. At the same time you can estimate how much stock the project will require, the amount of molding and trim needed, even the hardware that should be used. Finally, count it all up and make a complete shopping list, or bill of materials. The BOM should include everything: wood, hardware, nails and screws, glue, and finishing materials. If cost is a concern, call your local lumberyard and ask for current prices. Wood prices these days are written on bouncing rubber balls and last month's lumber bill will not necessarily have any relationship to this week's prices.

Lay Out and Cut Parts

When all of the materials are in your workshop, rule off the plywood panels, marking each cut to be made. Bear in mind the width of the saw kerf (probably

1/8"), and that the first cut or two in each panel should be aimed at reducing the pieces to manageable size. Mark off the stock, and everything you can cut except the parts for drawers and doors. The door and drawer subassemblies are better left until their frames have been put together and they can be built to exact measurement. Now cut up everything in sight. When that is done, complete whatever joinery and shaping must be done on each of the pieces.

Assembly

First put together the subassemblies, the basic structure, the frames for drawers and doors, and so on. Then unite the subassemblies using whatever glue-nail-screw combinations you have elected to hold the project together.

Drawers and Doors

Once their frames exist, drawers and doors can be made to fit inside them. Measure and cut all their pieces, do the joinery work, and then assemble them. When they are properly installed, you can attach any trim or molding that will not interfere with the area you are planning to veneer.

Prefinishing

Fill in all cracks, dents, gouges, and loose joints before sanding. Sanding should start with medium grits and work down to the super fine. Of course, the sanding is minimal in those areas that will be covered by veneer.

Veneering

Measure and cut all veneer pieces. Glue and roller, then trim the edges and clamp the veneer to dry. Repair any imperfections in the veneer. Attach the molding and trim. Give the project a final, light sanding, then a coat of sealer-filler. Sand the sealer.

Completion

Apply the various undercoats and sand after each application. Put on the final coats with sanding in between, and finally give the entire project its oil rubbing. Now put on all the drawer pulls and catches, latches, knobs, and casters.

A QUESTION OF TASTE

It is unquestionably easier to create a cabinet by using only straight lines. Who can question your taste if everything about a project reflects an angular simplicity? But the moment a curve appears, an army of "experts" arrive who nod their heads disapprovingly and loudly proclaim that the curves in the door panels are too broad and the molding is not ornate enough. There is always someone who arrogantly suggests that the cabinetmaker was influenced obviously by Italian provincial, trained by Neo-Greeks and confused by Louis XIV, or he would never have assembled so many ill-fitting, unharmonious curves in one piece.

Let the critics enjoy themselves; it is their nature to be arbitrary judges. Whatever you have elected to do, for whatever reasons, the choices *you* make are the correct ones. They can only be correct because it is your project, conceived by you, executed with your hands. If you deem that a cabinet is enhanced by the particular joinery, trim, and finish you give it, then the choices are perfect for that particular project. If someone else makes a similar cabinet, then that becomes *his* project, and however he sees the different components are perfect for what he is doing. Let that cabinet be his business. Yours is the business of making your own cabinets in your way, to stand as you have envisioned them.

Review Questions

1. What is the importance of purpose in furniture design?
2. Using a compass and ruler, find the dimensions of a golden mean rectangle which measures 20″ along its short sides.
3. List all the steps required to complete a furniture project.
4. What advantages do professional cabinetmakers have over nonprofessionals? What advantages do nonprofessionals have?
5. List some of the elements of good design.
6. What is the difference between formal and informal balance?
7. What is a bill of materials? How is it useful?
8. How does material selection affect a piece of furniture?
9. Why is patience important to furniture making?

Chapter 3

Sketching, Planning, and Estimating

Cabinetmakers almost always work from some sort of blueprint, be it a full-sized drawing of their project or a freehand sketch that shows only the outside dimensions and a few rough lines. Because everyone in the cabinetmaking business is confronted by various types of drawings on a daily basis, it is a necessity that you not only be able to read prints and plans, but make them as well.

BLUE AND WHITE PRINTS

In the building trades, most work is done according to a *blueprint.* These are normally made by architects, designers, or draftsmen and are then printed as white lines on blue paper so they will not fade when exposed to sunlight. Blueprints are extremely detailed and very accurate, and it is the tradesman's job to follow them exactly.

White prints are the cabinetmaker's version of blueprints. These are likely to be just as concise, but they are printed with black ink on a white background so pencil marks show up better on them than on blueprints. They also may not be as detailed as a blueprint. For example, a white print might only provide the overall size of a project, plus detailing one or two parts that have unusual aspects. But exactly what joints must be used, or which fasteners are best, is often left up to the cabinetmaker's good judgment.

In a furniture factory an architect, draftsman, or designer might well draw the original white print, but just as often the cabinetmaker will make it himself. That is why you too, must know how to create a white print.

DRAWING ELEMENTS

Every plan is comprised of lines, dimensions, symbols, abbreviations, and notes, and is usually drawn to some kind of scale. *Lines* are used to show the shape of the project and details of its construction. *Dimensions* are the little numbers next to each line that denote how long the line will be in its final form. In construction work, dimensions are given in feet and inches; in cabinetmaking they

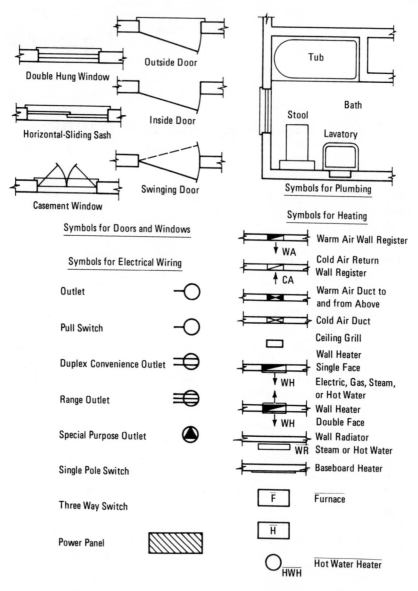

Figure 3-1   Symbols used in plans and sketches.

are always inches or centimeters. *Symbols* are used to express details that can not be drawn easily, such as cut stone, a wood grain, or a double-faced wall heater. The *notes* convey additional information that is more easily expressed in words than in pictures. Those occurring most frequently are as follows:

AP—Access panel
B&C—Bead and cove
BT—Bathtub
BASMT—Basement
BEV STKG—Bevel sticking
BR—Bedroom
BC—Between centers
BOM—Bill of materials
BLDG—Building
BL—Building line
BDY—Boundary
BRK—Brick
CAB—Cabinet
CASWK—Casework
CLG—Ceiling
CL—Center line
C to C—Center-to-center
CS—Cut stone
CUP—Cupboard
DSGN—Design
DET—Detail
DIN RM—Dining room
DVTL—Dovetail
DWL—Dowel
DS—Down spout
DWG—Drawing
DR—Door (or doors)
DRW (DRWS)—Drawer(s)
EL—Elevation
ENT—Entrance
EST—Estimate
EXT—Exterior
FAB—Fabricate
FIN—Finish
FL—Floor
FD—Floor drain
FRA—Frame
FDN—Foundation
FTG—Footing
GR—Gas range
GL—Grade line

RFG—Roofing
SC—Scale
SK—Sink
SB—Standard bead
S—Stile
STKG—Sticking
SYM—Symbol
T—Truss
VARN—Varnish
WD—Windows
WC—Water closet
GRV—Groove
1/2RD—Half-round
INSTL—Install
INSUL—Insulation
INT—Interior
KD—Knocked down
LAV—Lavatory
LIV RM—Living room
LOC—Locate
MATL—Material
MILWK (MLWK)—Millwork
ML—Material list
MLDG—Molding
MULL—Mullion
MUNT—Muntin
NWL—Newel
NO. (   )—Number
OA—Over-all
OC—On center
OG—Ogee (sticking)
OVO—Ovolo
PLAS (PL)—Plaster
QUAL—Quality
QTY—Quantity
RAB (RABT)—Rabbet
RAD—Radiator
REQD—Required
1/4RD—Quarter-round
RF—Refrigerator

Drawings must often be less than actual size, if only for the sake of convenience, so they are usually made to some kind of *scale.* The scale is not a measurement, but a ratio between the actual size of the finished project and the size of the drawing. The most usual scales follow:

6"   = 1' : half-size
3"   = 1' : one-fourth size
1 1/2" = 1' : one-eighth size
1"   = 1' : one-twelfth size
3/4"   = 1' : one-sixteenth size
1/2"   = 1' : one twenty-fourth size
3/8"   = 1' : one thirty-second size
1/4"   = 1' : one forty-eighth size
3/16" = 1' : one sixty-fourth size
1/8"   = 1' : one ninety-sixth size

A scale of 1/4" equals 1' is often used for drawing buildings and rooms, while details which show one part of a product are usually scaled 3/8", 1/2", 3/4", or 1 1/2" equals 1'.

DRAWINGS

There are four basic kinds of drawings used in woodworking: perspective, cabinet, isometric and multiview.

The perspective drawing, or rendering, is a photographic view of the project which shows the finished look of the piece.

Figure 3-2   Perspective drawing of a three-drawer, two-door buffet.

Cabinet drawings are used for such rectangular objects as a buffet or bookcase and simply outline the object's shape, usually with the front of the piece shown in exact scale and proportion. The top and sides then slant back at some angle around 45°. Although the side lines may be out of scale, their proper dimensions are usually given on the drawing.

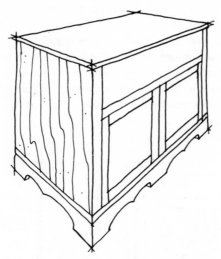

Figure 3-3   Cabinet drawing of the buffet.

Figure 3-4   Isometric drawing of the buffet.

Isometric means "having equal angles," so an *isometric* drawing is always constructed around three lines that are exactly 120° apart. To achieve these proportions, a center line is drawn vertically and the two lines that join it each form 60° angles. All other lines are then kept in parallel with the initial configuration.

Multiview drawings are not as pictorial as the other three types. They are the real working drawings and the most common type used in cabinetmaking. They show the top, front, and one side of the project in flat, straight lines, all of which are labeled with their proper dimensions. Sooner or later, with every project you build, there should be a multiview drawing which lays out each of the sides of the project. In may also include a *section view* of some interior part of the piece. Or there may be *auxiliary views* which explain the true shape of an angled surface that does not show accurately in one of the top, front, or side views.

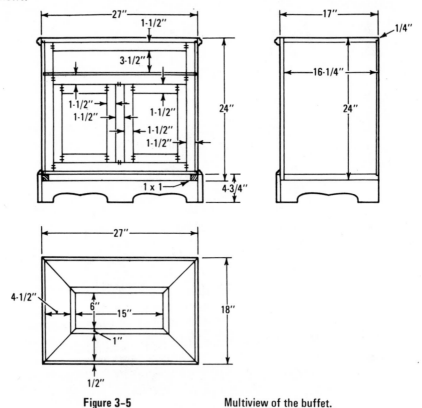

Figure 3-5   Multiview of the buffet.

The drawings used by furniture companies are usually made full-sized with three basic views: the front, or elevation view, the top, or plain view, and the right side view. From these drawings come detail drawings made to scale for each part to be manufactured. But furniture and cabinet drawings do not always follow standard drafting practices; several kinds of drawings may be included. For example, there may be a front view and then a perspective or an isometric view of the project. With multiview drawings, the top view is supposed to be positioned directly above the front view, and the side view directly opposite the front view, but they are not always arranged that way. Many drawings do not include *all* of the information a cabinetmaker must have to build the project, so he is often left with decisions to make for himself. Such details as proper joinery, for example, or the final dimensions of a drawer width, will not be resolved until the project is constructed.

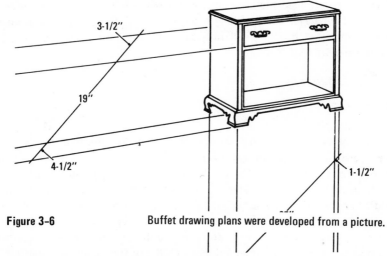

Figure 3-6   Buffet drawing plans were developed from a picture.

CADGING PLANS FROM A PICTURE

You probably see pictures of furniture every day and think, "I'd like to make that." If there are no dimensions given with the picture, you have to arbitrarily give it some, but often the height, depth, and width of the piece are noted somewhere in, or around the picture. If the picture gives you that much information, you can determine all the dimensions just by sitting down with a T-square and a ruler. The procedure is this simple:

1. Attach the picture to one side of a piece of paper.

2. Extend the top and bottom lines on the same plane outward from the drawing, using a ruler.

3. Suppose you are extending the front lines of a buffet that measures 20″ deep by 30″ high by 56″ long. After the top and bottom lines are extended, select a scale that has 30 units (millimeters, inches, 1/16″, anything that adds up to 30) and can be fitted *diagonally* between the horizontal lines. Spot the first unit at the top line and the last unit at the bottom line. It does not matter at what angle the scale is placed, so long as it is not 90°

4. Now extend all of the other lines in the picture to intersect your diagonal and mark off the units between each line. With the buffet, for instance, you will find that the drawer heights are 6″, 6″, and 5″, with 2″-rails between each.

5. In order to determine the widths of the buffet doors, the vertical lines must be extended, then a scale of 56 units is angled between them. By also projecting the door lines and measuring the distances between them, you find that both the doors and the drawers are 18″ wide, with 1″ stiles between them.

Having determined the essential measurements of the buffet, you are now free to make whatever design changes appeal to you. Or, you might go on to develop a shop sketch which will provide a construction plan for building the unit as it is pictured.

SKETCHING

A *shop sketch* is just a drawing. You could make it on a drafting table with T-squares, rules, and French curves. You can also use the back of an old lumber bill and a carpenter's pencil. The most important element of any sketch is the accuracy of its dimensions. If you are doing something like constructing a built-in, and can take on-site measurements, do it. Then make your sketch. If you are designing a piece of furniture, you are, of course, inhibited only by the ultimate size you wish the piece to become. You will find that it is also easier and quicker if you do not use the back of an old lumber bill, but find some ruled paper that is squared off in 1/4″ squares. With this, you have an automatic 1/4″ = 1′ scale and it is easier to sketch the correct shape, size, and scale of your project.

When making a sketch, first decide what views are needed. Obviously, if both the right and left sides of the buffet are identical, there is no need to draw both of them. But you will want both a top and a front view. Second, decide what scale to use. If you are using squared paper in which each square is 1/4″, the squares can equal any length you wish. Finally, take all measurements very carefully. If you are working on a built-in, measure the windows and doors that are in your way, as well as trim, pipes, and any other obstructions that must be taken into account during final construction.

LAYOUTS

Having developed working drawings of your project, there are still several steps to go through before you are ready to begin construction. There must be a BOM, or *bill of materials,* also known as a *stock bill* or *materials list.* How you arrive at this bill of materials is a procedure known as *stock billing.* The BOM should always include: (1) the name of each part; (2) the number of pieces; (3) finish sizes in terms of their thickness, width, and length; (4) all of the materials needed; and (5) the rough cut sizes of each part.

TABLE 3-1 BILL OF MATERIALS FOR THE BUFFET

Number of Pieces	Part Name	Material	T	Finish Size W	L
5	Frame Stiles	Cherry	3/4"	1 1/2"	24"
1	Frame Door Post	Cherry	3/4"	1 1/2"	16"
4	Door Frame	Cherry	3/4"	1 1/2"	16"
4	Door Frame	Cherry	3/4"	1 1/2"	8 1/2"
1	Base Front	Cherry	3/4"	1 1/2"	28 1/2"
2 sides	Base 2 sides	Plywood	3/4"	1 1/2"	18"
1	Cabinet Top	Plywood	5/8"	16 1/4"	27"
2	Cabinet Sides	Plywood	5/8"	16 1/4"	24"
1	Dust Cover	Plywood	5/8"	16 1/4"	26 5/8"
1	Shelf	Plywood	5/8"	16 1/4"	26 5/8"
1	Bottom	Plywood	5/8"	16 1/4"	26 5/8"
2	Door Panels	Plywood	1/4"	9"	13 1/2"
1	Cabinet Back	Plywood	1/4"	3 1/2"	24"
2	Drawer Sides	Oak	1/2"	3 1/2"	16"
1	Drawer Front	Plywood	5/8"	3 1/2"	24"
1	Drawer Bottom	Plywood	1/4"		
	Veneer	Honduras Mahogany	1/42"	18"	72"
2	Base Supports	Oak	1"	1"	17"
1	Base Support	Oak	1"	1"	27"

All of the pieces in a project are listed in order of their thickness, width, and length, but it really does not matter in which order you list the parts. The rough cut size may not be necessary unless you are buying rough lumber which you intend to surface yourself, in which case allow between 1/16″ to 1/8″ waste per side finished, and add about 1″ to the length of solid lumber. For the man-made materials such as plywood, hardboard, and particleboard, the finished and rough cut sizes are, of course, the same.

Some points to remember when you are stock billing:

1. Finish sizes are normally given in the order of their thickness, width, and length.

2. Any tenon, whether it is a tiny dovetail or a full-blown mortise and tenon joint, will require extra wood. Allow enough lumber for the length of the tenons.

3. The rough cut size is the amount of wood cut from a standard piece of lumber. Make sure you allow enough wood for machining.

4. Always list plywood, particleboard, and hardboard as separate items in your lumber order. Hardwood and softwood should also be listed separately.

5. Write all sizes in inches and fractions of inches, not feet.

A LUMBER AND MATERIALS ORDER

Once you have determined the rough cut sizes of each piece in a project you can then determine which sizes of material to buy. Lumber must be purchased in certain standard sizes and you want to buy only as much as the project requires. First, look down your BOM and identify how many materials are the same thicknesses. If, for example, you will need four pieces that are 3/4″ hardwood, add up the lengths and try to buy one piece that can be cut into all four pieces. Actually, with solid stock you may have to group the pieces according to both their widths *and* their thicknesses. Thus, you might have to buy a 10′ board 1/2″ thick by 5 1/2″ wide for two pieces and a 6′ board 1/2″ X 7 1/2″ for the other two pieces.

It is also useful to make a cutting diagram of all the pieces that will come from one of the man-made panels such as plywood. By sitting with a piece of paper and your thinking cap on for a while, you can save considerable money when you get to the lumberyard.

How Wood is Sold

Lumber is processed and sold according to some long accepted standards. The standards are so well known that people in the lumber business assume *everybody* knows the rules they live by. But, in truth, hardly anybody knows what possesses lumbermen, so here are some of the industry's best-known secrets.

TABLE 3-2 LUMBER AND MATERIALS ORDER FORM

Number of Pieces	Dimensions T	W	L	Material	Total Cost
1 Veneer		15″	8″	Honduras Mahogany	
2	3/4″	9 1/2″	24″	Cherry	11.90
1	3/4″	9/12″	36″	Cherry	8.85
1	1/4″	4′	8′	Plywood Panel	11.50
1	3/4″	4′	8′	A-D Ply	21.75
1	1/2″	1 1/2″	24″	Oak	5.25

SUPPLIES, FASTENERS, AND HARDWARE LIST

Item	Quantity	Size	Unit Cost	Total Cost
Dowels	100	3/8″		1.60
Polyurethane	1 qt.			3.75
Hinges	4	2″	1.75	7.00
Door Pulls	2		1.00	2.00
Drawer Pulls	2		1.50	3.00
#10 Screws	24			1.00
Contact Cement	1 qt.			3.75

Board Feet

The most common lumber measurement is the *board foot* (Bd. Ft.). It is best known because lumber dealers always talk about board feet, but what outsiders do not realize is that the shape of a board foot can differ considerably. *One board foot is 144 cubic inches.* It could measure 1″ thick and be 1′ square. But it could also be 2″ thick by 6″ wide and 12″ long. Whatever it is, a board foot comes out to 144 cu. ft.—approximately.

When lumber is sold by the board foot the size is computed according to its rough cut dimensions, *not* the real measurements it has on the day you buy it. Thus, a 1″ × 6″ × 10′ board would be sold as 5 board feet. But if the board has been dressed it will measure 3/4″ X 5 1/2″ X 10′ and be **3.43** Bd. Ft. Stock that is thinner than 1″ when you buy it is always counted as an inch. If it is more than an inch its actual thickness is always figured, unless you are buying hardwood that is between 1″ and 2″ thick, in which case the thickness is always figured to the nearest 1/4″. All this notwithstanding, here are three ways of computing board feet:

1. Bd. Ft. = thickness in inches times width in feet, times length in feet. So the 1″ X 6″ X 10′ board would be figured $\frac{1''}{1}$ (thickness) X $\frac{1''}{2}$ (width) X $\frac{10'}{1}$ (length) = $\frac{10}{2}$ = 5 Bd. Ft. If converting the width inches into a percentage of a foot is difficult for you, there is an alternative:

2. Bd. Ft. = $\dfrac{\text{T (inches)} \times \text{W (inches)} \times \text{L (feet)}}{12}$

   $$\frac{1'' \times 6'' \times 10'}{12} = \frac{60}{12} = 5 \text{ Bd. Ft.}$$

3. Or, Bd. Ft. = T (inches) X W (inches) X L (inches) divided by 144.

   $$\frac{1 \times 6 \times 120}{144} = \frac{720}{144} = 5 \text{ Bd. Ft.}$$

Lumber is priced at so much per 1,000 board feet. So if **1,000** board feet cost $300, one board foot would cost 30¢.

Lumber Sizes

Most lumber is dried and surfaced (dressed) at the saw mill. However, some wood can be purchased with rough surfaces, in which case you will have to run it through a surfacer or planer before you can use it. As noted, the surfaced size is always smaller than the rough, or *nominal* size. American Lumber Standards for softwood provide that a 2″ X 4″ board shall measure 1-1/2″ X 3-1/2″ if it has 19 percent or less moisture content. If the moisture content is over 19 percent, the wood can only be dressed to 1-9/16″ X 3-9/16″ (because it will shrink when it dries). The standard for a 1″ thick piece of softwood is 25/32″ (3/4″ when dressed); a 1″ hardwood when surfaced is reduced to 13/16″.

Softwoods are always cut to standard thicknesses, widths, and lengths. The nominal widths increase every 2″ from 4″ up to 18″ and standard softwood lengths range from 8′ to 20′, at 2′ intervals. Hardwood is usually available in the standard thicknesses, but because it is more expensive, the widths and lengths are often cut according to whatever size is most economical and convenient for the mill to produce.

Lumber Grading

The National Bureau of Standards of the Department of Commerce has established the American Lumber Standards for softwoods as a guide for different lumber producers when grading their products. The essential element of the Standards is to divide all softwood lumber into two groups for grading purposes: *Dry* lumber must have 19 percent or less moisture content. *Green* lumber has a moisture content in excess of 19 percent. Beyond these two divisions softwood is classified according to its intended uses.

Classification of Softwood Uses

Structural lumber is always at least 2" or more in nominal thickness and width, and is used wherever strength is required.

Factory and *shop lumber* are selected primarily for remanufacturing purposes.

Yard lumber is intended for general building purposes and is divided into *finish* (select) and *common* grades. The finish grades are labeled A, B, C, and D. Grade A is almost clear wood. B has only a few imperfections. C and D have increasingly more checks, knots, splits, and so on, but are still suitable for painting.

The primary differences between the different grades of common lumber are in the number of knots and amount of pitch found in the stock. Common lumber is graded from 1 to 5. Numbers 1 and 2 can be used totally with almost no waste, while numbers 3, 4, and 5 will have a certain amount of waste because of knots or pitch in the wood. In some locales No. 1 is considered *construction grade;* No. 2 is *standard;* No. 3, *utility;* and No. 4 is *economy.*

The manufacturers also have their own classifications:

Rough lumber is sawed, edged, and trimmed, but not dressed (surfaced). Saw marks show on all of the surfaces.

Dressed (surfaced) lumber has been planed smooth on its longitudinal surfaces and is marked with the letter S (for both surfaced and side) and/or an E (for edge). You are likely to find boards marked like, S1S—one side surfaced, or S2S1E—two sides and one edge surfaced.

Worked lumber is not only dressed, but it is matched, shiplapped, or patterned.

Matched lumber has a tongue along one edge and a groove along the opposite edge so that pieces can be interlocked. They can also be *end matched* with tongues and grooves on each end.

Shiplapped lumber is rabbeted on opposite edges.

Patterned lumber is shaped to a pattern or a molded form as well as being dressed, matched, or shiplapped.

Hardwood Grading

The National Hardwood Lumber Association has established gradings, primarily for use in the furniture industry. The entire grading system is complicated, but you need not bother to understand all of it in order to select the kind of wood you want. With all lumber grades wood is divided according to its number of defects. But bear in mind that people, not computers, sort and grade lumber. So there can be errors. Furthermore, a piece might offer enough clear cuttings to almost qualify it for the next higher grade, or not enough clear cuttings to almost put it in the next lower grade. So there is a wide range of quality within each grade and what the smart cabinetmaker does is hand pick his lumber, always looking for the maximum amount of clear face cuttings he can get from each piece—and never mind what the grade is. There are, nevertheless, several grades of hardwood to choose from.

FAS (first and seconds) are the Rolls Royces of hardwood. They must be at least 6″ wide and over 8′ in length, and on an average will produce 90 percent clear cuttings. FAS grades are selected according to the condition of their *worst* side, so the better side is sure to have fewer defects, if any at all.

The *select* grade is good enough for almost any furniture project that requires only one good side. Select boards must be at least 4″ wide and more than 6′ long, but are chosen from their best side, which generally should meet the minimal standards of first and seconds.

No. 1 common and *No. 2 common* are the least expensive hardwoods because they are narrower and shorter. They must be a minimum of 3″ wide and 2′ long, and are graded from their poorer side. They will produce around 67 percent clear cuttings and are often used for smaller furniture parts.

Some Hints About Ordering Lumber

When you sit down to devise a lumber order, *be very specific* about what you want, especially when ordering hardwood. You may have to accept random lengths of hardwood because it is not readily available in the 8′, 10′, and 12′ lengths you might like to have. So whenever possible, ask for random lengths.

Always specify the rough thickness of the wood and then explain how much of it you want surfaced. Your specifications should include the thickness, width, and length (in that order) of every piece you wish to purchase, along with the grade, the wood species, and the seasoning (air dried or kiln dried), and to what percentage. You should also use the terms generally accepted and understood throughout the lumber industry. The most common of these are as follows:

AD—Air dried	BDL—Bundle
AL—All lengths	BEV—Bevel
ALS—American Lumber Standards	BM—Board measure
AV—Average	BTR—Better
B&B or B&Btr—B and better	C/L—Carload
BD—Board	CLG—Ceiling
BD FT—Board Feet	CLR—Clear

COM—Common
CSG—Casing
CU FT—Cubic Feet
DF—Douglas fir
DIM—Dimension
DKG—Decking
D/S, DS—Drop siding
D&M—Dressed and matched; center
D&CM—Dressed and center matched
   matched unless otherwise specified
D&SM—Dressed and standard matched
E—Edge
EB1S—Edge bead one side
EG—Edge (vertical) grain
FAS—Firsts and seconds
FG—Flat or slash grain
FCTY—Factory lumber
FLG—Flooring
FT—Foot
FT BM or FBM—Feet board measure
FT SM—Feet surface measure
GR—Green
H&M—Hit and miss
HDWD—Hardwood
HRT—Heart
HRTWD—Heartwood
IN—inch or inches
JTD—Jointed
KD—Kiln dried
LBR—Lumber
LGTH—length
LIN—Lineal
LIN FT—Lineal (or linear) foot
M—Thousand
M BM—Thousand (ft.) board measure
MC—Moisture content
MLDG—Moulding or molding
MR—Mill run
N—Nosed
OC—On center
OG—Ogee
P—Planed
PC—Piece

QTD—Quartered, when referring to
   hardwoods
RDM—Random
REG—Regular
RGH—Rough
RIP—Ripped
R/L, RL—Random lengths
RND—Round
R/W, RW—Random widths
RWD—Redwood
SAP—Sapwood
SD—Seasoned
SDG—Siding
SEL—Select
SF—Surface foot; that is, an area
   of one square foot
SG—Slash grain
SH D—Shipping dry
SM—Surface measure
SQ—Square
SQRS—Squares
STD—Standard
STD M—Standard matched
STK—Stock
STRUCT—Structural
SYMBOLS
"—Inch or inches
'—Foot or feet
X—By, as 4 X 4
4/4, 5/4, 6/4, etc.—Thickness
   expressed in fractions of an inch
S&E—Side and edge
S1E—Surfaced one edge
S2E—Surfaced 2 edges
S1S—Surfaced one side
S2S—Surfaced two sides
S4S—Surfaced four sides
S1S&CM—Surfaced one side and
   center matched
S2S&CM—Surfaced two sides and
   center matched
S4S&CS—Surfaced four sides and
   caulking seam

S1S1E—Surfaced one side, one edge
S1S2E—Surfaced one side, two edges
S2S&SM—Surfaced two sides and
   standard matched

VG—Vertical (edge) grain
WDR—Wider
WT—Weight
WTH—Width
T&G—Tongue-and-grooved, center
matched unless otherwise specified

Estimating

The cost of materials can be ascertained as easily as making a phone call to your lumberyard. But in addition to this cost you should also allow about 35 percent more for waste, spoilage, and pieces built or machined incorrectly. You can allow for this waste simply by adding a specific percentage to the cost of the materials, or by raising the cost per board.

Labor costs must also be accounted for. Not only your own salary, and whatever you have to pay other workers must be figured in, but also such items as social security tax, pension-funds and supervisory labor. As a rule of thumb, the hourly wage earned by every worker should be increased by 15 percent to 25 percent in your computations—and that includes you, even if you are the boss or just working for yourself.

On top of all the above costs, there is also a matter of overhead and profit. Overhead is the cost of running a business, whether it is a one-man shop or an entire furniture factory. The overhead includes depreciation of all your machines, monthly utility bills, rent, office expenses and so on. Generally, a furniture factory will add as much as 50 percent to the cost of manufacturing a product to cover its overhead and profit. Although that may seem high if you are a self-employed cabinetmaker, bear in mind what a consumer would pay if he went to a larger company for the same work you are providing.

Review Questions

1. What are the different uses of blue and white prints?
2. Name 25 common abbreviations used in cabinetmaking.
3. What is a scale?
4. Draw a cabinet using both perspective and isometric views.
5. Find a picture of a cabinet you would like to build. Determine all of the necessary measurements for constructing the cabinet.
6. When ordering finish lumber, what are three elements to remember?
7. What are three common grades of hardwood? Of softwood? How do the grades differ?
8. If a board is 8' long, 1" thick, and equals 3 Bd. Ft., how wide is it?
9. What does S1S1E mean?
10. When estimating the costs of building a buffet, how much money should you allow for labor, overhead, and profit when you bill your customer?

A   Cambial Zone
B   Inner Bark
C   Outer Bark

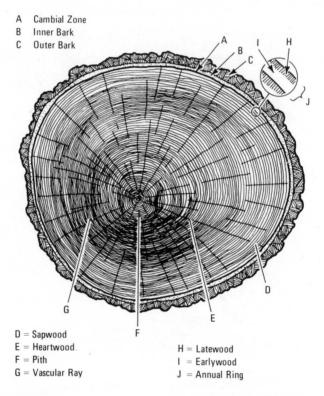

D = Sapwood
E = Heartwood
F = Pith
G = Vascular Ray

H = Latewood
I = Earlywood
J = Annual Ring

Figure 4-1   Anatomy of a tree (cross-section).

Chapter 4

Selection of Wood

After the cabinetmaker has settled on a project and completed its design, his next step is the selection of the woods he will use in its construction. In many cases the choice of wood is a simple one based on what the project is and what woods are available. Thus, a craftsman may quickly resolve to construct a kitchen cabinet out of pine, which is the most readily available wood in America (but not Europe), or from plywood, which abounds at nearly every lumberyard. But the selection of building material could be made from any of the 25,000 known species of trees in the world and the more than 100,000 different varieties of these species which are used commercially.

In general, cabinetmakers tend to use the woods most readily accessible in their locale and only on rare occasions do they take up a wood with which they are unfamiliar. But that reluctance is purely a human trait; aside from the inconvenience of having to wait for lumber to be shipped from a distant part of the country, there is no reason why any cabinetmaker cannot use any of the exotic or merely unfamiliar woods available on the American market today.

Various woods have experienced a rise and fall of popularity at different times during history. During the early colonial years only native American woods (primarily pine, oak, maple, birch, walnut, and cherry) were used in this country. It does not matter what woods you use, as long as they are compatible. The furniture makers of eighteenth century England became renowned for their ability to match the woods and veneers they used, and it is to them that we owe the idea that all of the woods used in a given piece of furniture must in some way enhance each other if the piece is to achieve a standard of craftsmanship and good taste.

IDENTIFYING TREES

Because no two trees are ever exactly the same, numerous categories have been established for identifying wood. The best known of these categories are *softwood* and *hardwood*. All of the conifers, or cone-bearing trees, such as spruce, fir, pine, and cedar, are known as softwoods. Everything else, that is, all of the flowering trees, such as oak, maple, and mahogany, are hardwoods. But this broad division of the world's trees has its shortcomings if only because many softwoods are considerably harder than balsa, a tree classified as a hardwood. Consequently, the absolute classification of any tree involves an evaluation of its color, odor, taste, texture, grain, growth rings (if any), resin ducts, figure, etc. And to complete all that classifying you must have a well-equipped laboratory and the scientific knowledge of a systematic botanist or a taxonomist (a scientist who specializes in trees). Even then, it is not easy to accurately identify a given piece of wood.

If you acquire a piece of wood that you want to identify, the best approach is to send a sample of it to the United States Government's official wood identification agency, the Forest Products Laboratory, in Madison, Wisconsin. This laboratory has the equipment and the scientifically trained personnel to accurately identify your sample; and the service is free of charge.

ANATOMY OF A TREE

Under a microscope it is evident that every tree is an unbelievably complex structure. It has cells, tissues, chemicals, and minerals; crystals of calcium oxalate, sugars, starch grains, oils, fats, resins, latex, tannins, dyestuffs, and alkaloids. In its center is the *pith,* which is the soft core of the tree, usually darker in color than the wood around it. Radiating from the pith are *vascular* (or wood) rays that slash across the layers of wood as far as the bark of the tree. The rays are made up of soft tissues used for storing food. The wood at the center of a tree is known as the *heartwood,* and it is always darker, often a different color, than the wood nearest the bark. Heartwood is the real strength of most trees. Its cells are inactive and often clogged with waste materials which help it to resist decay better than the outer ring of lighter colored wood known as *sapwood.* Sapwood is composed of living cells, all of which conduct water and minerals from the root system to the leaves of the tree. The layer of sapwood normally varies between 1-1/2" and 2" in width but it can be as much as 6" in some species; as the tree adds new layers of sapwood each year, the inner edge of the sapwood ring becomes inactive and forms heartwood. Heartwood is the lumber you buy; most sapwood is too saturated with moisture to have any commercial value.

Surrounding the sapwood, and separating it from the bark of the tree, is a sheath of generative cells known as *vascular cambium.* The cambium endlessly produces new cells which in turn add more wood to the inside of the tree and new bark to the outside. The *inner bark* carries food to the living parts of the tree, while the *outer bark* is made up of dead cells that form a protective shield. It is the cambium that generates the growth rings, which in many climates are divided into two layers. The first one is formed at the start of the growth season and is known as *springwood,* or early wood. The second ring, formed at the end of the growth period, is called *summerwood,* or late wood.

GROWTH RINGS

There is a popular idea that the age of a tree can be computed by counting the annual rings that are exposed on the top of its stump. Counting annual rings works for trees that grow in temperate zones where the annual growth and production of the wood occur only once a year. Elsewhere, there may be several periods of growth each year, which produce several layers of wood and therefore more than one growth ring per year. In the tropics, where growth is more or less continuous all year long, the trees bear no rings at all.

THE SPECIFIC GRAVITY OF WOOD

Far more important than the age of a tree is the specific gravity of its wood, because specific gravity is an indication of the strength and hardness of the species. As a rule, the higher the specific gravity, the stronger the wood.

Specific gravity is a scientific measurement expressed as a ratio of the weight of the wood to the weight of an equal amount of water. For example, the specific gravity of a wood stated as 0.50 means that the wood weighs half as much as an equal amount of water. Thus, a light wood might have a specific gravity of 0.25 or 0.30, while a heavy species would be 0.70 or 0.80.

THE STRUCTURE OF WOOD CELLS

Moisture, known as *protoplasm,* moves from the roots of a tree to its leaves through countless channels in the sapwood. These channels, known as *cells,* are so numerous they account for roughly half the entire volume of the wood. When the wood is sawed the ends of the cells are exposed at the surface and form a distinct pattern, much like a human fingerprint, that can be used as part of the identification of the species. More importantly, it is this configuration of open spaces and cell walls that gives wood its strength as well as other properties.

THE APPEARANCE OF WOOD

Wood is always described in terms of its grain, figure, texture, color, odor, taste, and luster, although there is a widespread misuse of the various terms.

Grain

Grain technically refers to the direction or orientation of wood fibers, and that is *all* the term refers to. There are six broad categories of grain: (1) A *straight grain* occurs when the fibers run more or less parallel to each other along the length of the tree; (2) An *irregular grain* is one in which the fibers vary with the vertical axis of the log, usually in a small area of the wood, such as around a knot; (3) *Diagonal grains* are man-made and occur when a sawyer miscuts the wood at an angle to the grain; (4) A *spiral grain* twists itself around the tree, like the thread of a screw; (5) *Interlocked grains* come from a spiral going in one direction during one growth layer, then reversing itself to go in the opposite direction in the next layer; (6) A *wavy grain* has its fibers changing directions continuously until the grain looks bumpy while actually remaining flat.

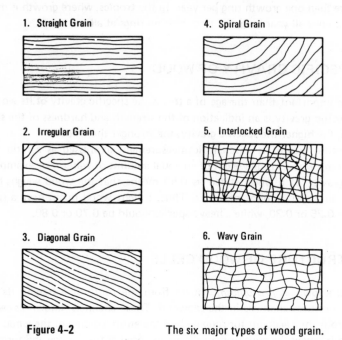

1. Straight Grain   4. Spiral Grain

2. Irregular Grain   5. Interlocked Grain

3. Diagonal Grain   6. Wavy Grain

Figure 4-2   The six major types of wood grain.

Figure or Surface Pattern

There is a considerable difference between the grain of a wood and its figure. Grain defines the direction of the wood fibers. Figure is the natural pattern in the surface of the wood. The figure is produced by a number of irregularities that occur in the growth rings, the vascular rays, the color patterns, and the grain as it swirls around knots, burls, crotches, and butts.

The grain has considerable effect on figure. An irregular grain can create a quilted figure, while interlocked grains often produce a ribbon, or striped figure; a wavy grain may generate a fiddleback figure. The names used to describe a figure are endless because lumber salesmen are forever inventing special appellations to describe a particular figure they have on hand. Some of the more usual figures are given such colorful titles as: mottle, plum pudding, curly, swirl, crotch, feather-crotch, moonshine crotch, finger-roll, birds-eye, pigment, and burl.

Texture

Texture means the *feel* of a wood and the feel is considered either *fine, coarse, even,* or *uneven.* The differences in texture depend on the size of the cells and the width of the vascular rays. If the cells are large and the rays wide, the texture is coarse (as in oak, ash, and chestnut). If the cells are small and the rays narrow, the texture is fine (as in fir, pine, and most softwoods). The grades of texture between fine and coarse include moderately coarse (walnut, mahogany) and very fine (European boxwood).

Color

The colors found in wood start at black, end with white, and include practically every shade in between. The color derives from the particular climate and soil content in which the tree grows, so it will vary considerably within the same species. Also, when the wood is exposed to light, air, moisture, or heat, its color may change and become either darker or lighter.

Fragrance

Many timbers also have a unique odor, particularly when freshly cut, although this often disappears as the wood dries. There are, of course, such trees as cedar, sandalwood, pine, and camphorwood which retain their unique aroma for years after they are sawed into lumber.

Taste

Taste is also a distinguishing feature of wood and because of it special woods must be used by certain industries. Food must be stored in wooden containers that do not impart their odor or taste to their contents. Some whiskies and many wines are improved by being aged in casks made of wood, while clothes closets and chests are often made of cedar because the taste and smell of that particular wood repels insects.

Luster

Finally, there is the luster of wood. Luster comes from the way in which the cells reflect light. How they reflect light is determined by how they are sawed. As a rule, a quartersawed surface is more lustrous than a flat-sawed one; if figures such as a fiddleback or stripe exist in a quartersawed board, it is likely to be even more lustrous.

HOW TREES ARE SAWED

Sawmills use two methods for cutting a tree into lumber. If a hardwood log is sliced parallel to its vascular rays it is *quartersawed.* If the log is a softwood, the same cut is known as *edge-grained*. When a hardwood log is cut perpendicular to its rays it is *plain-sawed*. If the log is softwood, the cut is called *flat grained*. How any board was cut can be determined simply by looking at the growth rings on its ends. If the rings form more or less parallel lines, the board was quartersawed (edge-grained). If the rings appear as a series of *Vs*, the board was plain-sawed (flat grained).

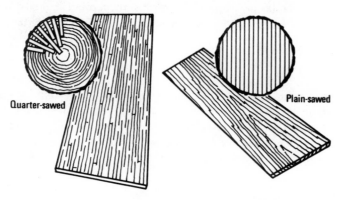

Quarter-sawed

Plain-sawed

Figure 4-3   Trees may be quartersawed or plain-sawed.

SEASONING LUMBER

Sawmills do not just cut up logs, they also season the lumber. Every log has an amazing amount of moisture content, ranging anywhere from 30 percent to 300 percent. Much of this moisture is *free water* held in the cell cavities, but there is also an *absorbed water* content, which is water that has soaked into the fibers of the wood.

Moisture in wood can be reduced through two different seasoning processes. The first is to *air dry* the lumber by stacking it outdoors with spaces left between layers so that air circulates freely around each piece. Air drying is obviously economical, but it takes a year or so, and in humid, wet, or cold climates the drying time can be considerably longer. The alternative is *kiln drying*. Kilns are huge ovens in which the temperature, humidity, and air circulation are fully controlled. In theory, if the kiln process is done properly, the wood will lose its moisture without warping, twisting, crooking, bowing, checking, or splitting. But anybody who has examined the stock in his local lumberyard knows how far apart theory and reality can be.

Lumber is carefully stacked in the kiln and steam is applied at a low heat. Gradually the steam is reduced as the heat increases, drawing moisture out of the wood. After the free water is removed from the cells in a piece of lumber, most of the absorbed water still remains and the wood is considered at its fiber-saturation point. For most woods, that means 30 percent of its weight is still moisture. But as this final 30 percent moisture content is reduced, shrinkage, or seasoning begins to take place, *across* the grain of the wood; as the board dries it becomes considerably narrower, but not much shorter. The drying process is stopped when there is still about 10 percent moisture content in the wood, but if the lumber is destined to be used as cabinet wood its moisture content should be reduced to less than 7 or 8 percent.

NOMINAL SIZES

After the wood is dried it must be smoothed and this is where nominal sizes come into being. When it is first sawed, the lumber is cut in thicknesses of say, one or two inches, but the heavy blades needed to reduce a ten-ton log to lumber leave the surface of the boards too rough to be workable, so they must be planed. The process of planing takes approximately 1/8″ to 1/4″ off each side of the board so that by the time it reaches your lumberyard it is nominally 1″ X 8″, but in reality it has been reduced to 3/4″ X 7-1/2″.

DEFECTS IN LUMBER

Grain, figure, texture, color, odor, taste, all of the characteristics of wood must be considered by the scientist when he classifies a tree. The cabinetmaker need only choose which of the 25,000 known species he shall use in a given project, and generally that choice is based on his personal preference, together with the woods available locally. Presumably, the more important the project the more carefully the cabinetmaker will make his wood selection, and the more anxious he will be to acquire "near perfect" stock.

Selecting a perfect piece of wood from the supply offered by your local lumberyard amounts to looking carefully at each piece and discarding any that has defects that could mar the appearance of the finished project. It is not important to your skill as a cabinetmaker to know the terms used to describe the defects found in lumber, but it is handy to have a name or two to describe your reasons for refusing to purchase an otherwise excellent piece of wood.

Bark pocket is a piece of bark trapped in the fibers of the wood. Sometimes it can be cut out of the board, sanded off, or positioned in the project so that it will not be seen.

Check is a crack in the wood that runs with the grain. If it is deep or too long it may not be repairable; it may also be the result of a warped, twisted, or cupped board, so look at the entire piece of wood before buying it.

Decay (rot) can show itself as a streak of degenerated wood fibers that are anything from barely soft to outright rotted. If it is a small decayed area, it can be scraped clean and filled. Otherwise it may present insurmountable problems.

Heart pith is the spongy center of the tree. When it appears on the surface of a board, skip the board because not much can be done to repair or obscure it.

Shake is a crack that runs parallel to (and between) the annual rings. Like a check, it may be repairable or simply cut out of the board.

Stain is, logically enough, a discoloration of the wood and may come from any number of sources, including the way in which the board was stored. The problem with stain is that it usually penetrates the wood and therefore cannot be sanded off. It may also be so heavy it will show through several coats of paint.

Wormholes come from insects and may be very tiny, or more than 1/4" in diameter. They can be filled and covered, or possibly used to advantage as part of the decor of the project.

Knots come in all sizes and shapes. They are part of a limb of the tree and may be partially or wholly locked into the fiber structure. They may also be loose in their holes but not loose enough to be pushed free. Or they may just fall out of the wood. If the knot is objectionable, or if it cannot be eliminated during construction of the project, do not buy the piece of lumber.

Pitch is a resin, usually soft and often sticky, that appears on the wood surface. If it is not too large a pocket, it can be removed and the pocket filled.

Wane means there is some bark—or some wood absent—at the corners of a board. Typically it does not take up much of the board so the piece can usually be trimmed square.

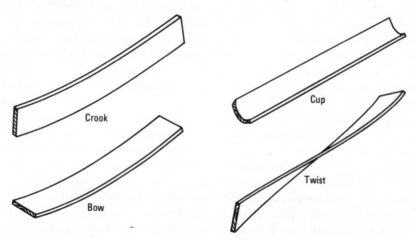

Figure 4-4   A "warped" board may be crooked, bowed, cupped, or twisted.

Warp is a general term applied to any variation of the wood from its true shape. Specifically, a warp is termed a *bow* when the board curves along its widest surface. It is known as a *crook* when the board bends along its narrow surface. A *cup* describes another type of warping in which the wide surface of the board curls up at its edges. A *twist* occurs when the board is simultaneously warped in more than one direction. Often, the warp in a piece of wood can be eliminated or minimized by cutting the piece into smaller sections. But working with warped wood presents countless problems when cutting and joining, so if at all possible try to find a piece that is straight and true.

SOME OF THE WOODS USED IN CABINETMAKING

There is not space enough in this volume to comment on all of the 25,000 species of wood available to the modern cabinetmaker, so only a few of the more common woods in use today have been selected for discussion. It should be noted that generally the softwoods are not used in making fine furniture, although they are an excellent choice for cabinets, built-ins, and trim. At the same time, the hardwoods selected for cabinetmaking should be comparatively free of warp, excessive swelling or shrinkage, and be hard enough to resist indentation.

The Softwoods

Western Red Cedar

Thuja plicata (aromatic wood; folded, scalelike leaves). Also known as canoe cedar, giant arbor vitae, Idaho cedar, Pacific red cedar, shinglewood, and stinking cedar.

Grows primarily in moist soil from southern Alaska to northern California and as far east as Montana and Idaho.

Description. Moderately soft and limber with a high resistance to decay. It has low resistance to nail withdrawal but can be glued. It is easily worked with all tools and holds any finish well. The heartwood is reddish or pinkish brown to a dull brown and emits the characteristic cedar odor.

Uses. Shingles, millwork, boatbuilding, poles, posts, and house siding.

Douglas Fir

Pseudotsuga menziesii (false hemlock; after its discoverer, Archibald Menzies). Also called Douglas spruce, fir, yellow fir, red pine, red spruce, red fir, Oregon pine, and dozens of other names.

The Douglas fir thrives throughout the western states, from Texas to Canada.

Description. Moderately heavy, strong, and stiff. The heartwood is dense, relatively hard, and has a moderate resistance to decay. The color ranges from yellow to light tan with brownish streaks. It is more difficult to work with handtools than pine but holds fastenings well and can be glued satisfactorily. It does not hold paint well and will not absorb preservatives.

Uses. Douglas fir is a primary veneer for plywood and is used extensively in the manufacture of sashes, doors, boxes, lumber, and millwork.

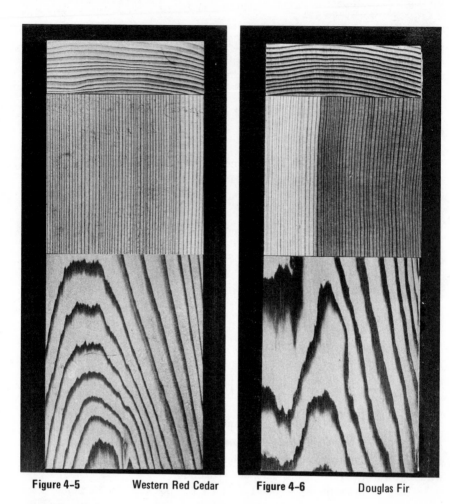

| Figure 4-5 | Western Red Cedar | Figure 4-6 | Douglas Fir |

Ponderosa Pine

Pinus ponderosa (the Latin species name; heavy). Also called big pine, bird's-eye pine, knotty pine, lodgepole pine, Oregon pine, pitch pine, pole pine, and prickly pine.

Ponderosa pine grows from Alaska to California at elevations as high as 12,000 feet.

Description. The lumber seldom warps and is moderately light, weak, and resistant to decay. The heartwood is yellowish to light reddish or orange brown.

Uses. Popular for cabinetwork, general millwork, sashes, doors, moldings, fences, and crates.

Western White Pine

Pinus monticola (Latin name for the species; of the mountains). Other names include Idaho white pine, mountain pine, and silver pine.

Found all over the Northwest from Idaho, Washington, and Oregon to British Columbia.

Description. Moderately soft, stiff, and low in decay resistance. Its coloring ranges from a light cream to reddish brown which darkens with age. It works easily with tools, glues readily, and does not split easily.

Uses. Western white pine is an all-purpose wood used in construction, millwork, boxes, and furniture.

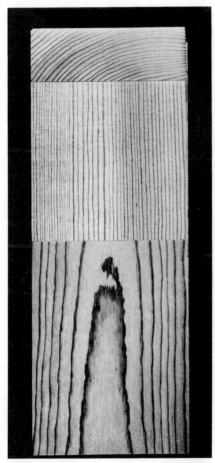 

| **Figure 4-7** | Ponderosa Pine | **Figure 4-8** | Western White Pine |

Redwood

Sequoia sempervirens (honoring the Cherokee Indian, Sequoyah; always green)

The giant redwood is found in only a 35-mile wide strip stretching 500 miles along the California coast.

Description. Lightweight, moderately hard, strong, stiff, and almost totally decay resistant. The heartwood is a uniform deep reddish brown and has no distinctive odor, taste, or feel.

Uses. House construction, millwork, outdoor furniture, trim and molding.

Engelmann Spruce

Picea engelmannii (pitch; after George Engelmann).

Found at high altitudes in the western mountains from Canada to New Mexico.

Description. Engelmann spruce is soft, weak, light in weight, and moderately limber with a low decay resistance. The heartwood and sapwood look very much alike and range in color from white to pale yellowish brown.

Uses. Used principally for lumber, crossties, subflooring, sheathing, and studding.

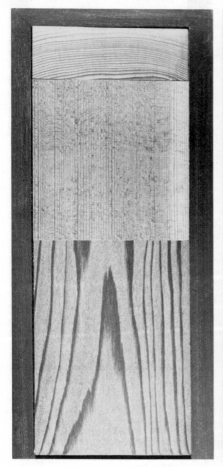 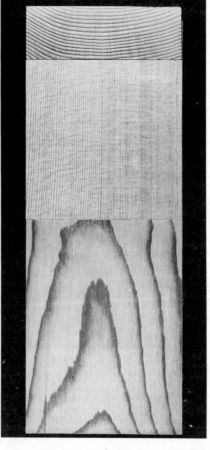

Figure 4-9   Redwood   **Figure 4-10**   Engelmann Spruce

The Hardwoods

White Ash

Fraxinus americana (Latin meaning ash; of America).
  Found in most of the states east of the Mississippi.
  Description. The wood is strong, stiff, and has excellent bending qualities. It is moderately easy to work with all tools. Although it has a tendency to split it will hold nails and screws well. The heartwood is brown to dark brown, occasionally with a reddish tint.
  Uses. Handles for baseball bats, shovels, forks, hoes, and rakes; used in furniture making as well.

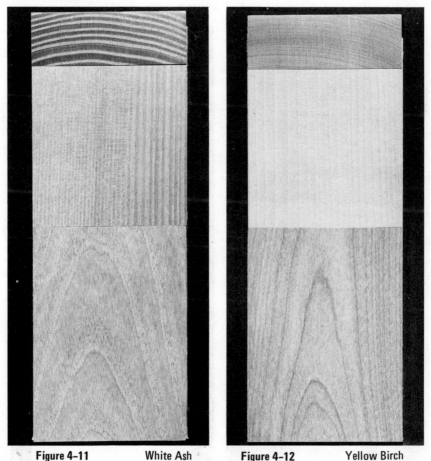

| **Figure 4-11** | White Ash | **Figure 4-12** | Yellow Birch |

Yellow Birch

Betula alleghaniensis (Latin name for birch; of the Allegheny Mountains). Also called gray birch, silver birch, and swamp birch.

Grows from Canada to the Great Lakes and New England and as far south as North Carolina.

Description. Creamy brown with tinges of red, the heartwood often has a prominent curly or wavy figure. It is heavy, strong, and stiff with a low decay resistance. The wood works easily with power tools and takes a nice finish.

Uses. Primarily used in furniture manufacture, general millwork, and woodenware. It is available as lumber, in plywood, and as veneer.

Black Cherry

Prunus serotina (peach; late maturing).

Also called choke cherry, whiskey cherry, rum cherry, and wild cherry.

Found all over the eastern half of the United States.

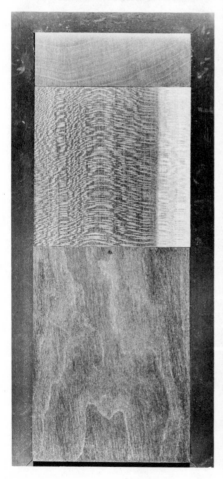 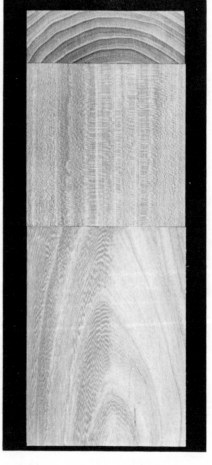

Figure 4-13   Black Cherry   Figure 4-14   American Elm

Description. The heartwood is a distinctive light to dark reddish brown. It is a heavy wood, considered hard, stiff, and strong. It sands easily and is capable of holding a highly polished finish.

Uses. The best logs are cut into veneers for cabinetmaking, furniture, and musical instruments, but it can also be purchased as lumber.

American Elm

Ulmus americana (Latin species name; from America).

Found throughout the Eastern states except in the Appalachians and southern Florida.

Description. A heavy, moderately hard wood, the heartwood is brown to dark brown, occasionally with shades of red. Although slightly below average in woodworking properties, elm has excellent bending qualities.

Uses. The lumber is used in making containers, furniture, and barrels. It is also manufactured as a veneer.

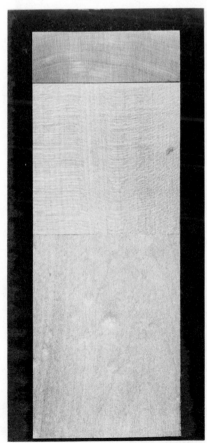

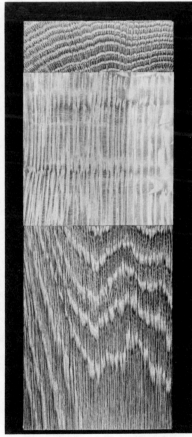

| **Figure 4-15** | Sugar Maple | **Figure 4-16** | White Oak |

Sugar Maple

Acer saccharum (Species name; sugary). Also known as black maple, hard maple, rock maple, sugar-tree maple, and white maple.

Sugar maples grow almost everywhere east of the Rockies.

Description. The heartwood is a very light tan to reddish brown; it is heavy, strong, and has an even texture. It can be glued, stained, and is capable of a high polish. While usually straight grained, various figures are obtained for veneers. Sugar maple is easy to work with tools and is excellent for turning.

Uses. Veneer, musical instruments, lumber, flooring, and woodenware.

White Oak

Quercus alba (Latin for oak; white). Also known as stave oak and forked-leaf white oak.

It is one of 60 species of oak indigenous to America. Found in eastern parts of Canada and the United States.

Figure 4-17   **Black Walnut**

Description. The heartwood is light tan to grayish brown. Oak is heavy, hard, and very decay resistant. It is above average in all machining operations except shaping.

Uses. Most white oak is used in flooring, general millwork, furniture, barrels, kegs, and boats.

Black Walnut

Juglans nigra (Latin for walnut; Jupiter's nut).

Grows in abundance throughout the eastern half of the United States.

Description. The wood is hard, strong, stiff, and resists decay. Heartwood is chocolate brown with dark, purple streaks. It works easily with hand-tools and holds paints and stains well. Black walnut also polishes exceptionally well.

Uses. As veneer, walnut produces butt, crotch, burl, fiddleback, leaf, and straight figures; as lumber, it is the first choice of many cabinet and furniture makers.

VENEERS

Three thousand five hundred years ago the ancient Egyptians possessed bronze tools that could hold their sharpness, so they developed techniques for peeling strips of veneer, less than 1/4″ thick, from the surface of a log. Thus, the Egyptians are credited with establishing the two basic steps in veneering; cutting thin sheets from logs and attaching them to the face of less attractive woods.

Centuries later the Greeks admired and practiced veneering, and later still the Romans invented both the hand plane and the bow saw. The Romans cut the veneers thinner than the Egyptians ever dreamed of doing and smoothed them even more. Veneering lost its popularity for the next 1,500 years or so, until the powered knife slicer was invented in 1880. From the slicer has come the modern equipment which peels sheets of veneer from 10-ton logs that are either 1/42″, 1/40″, or 1/28″ thick. Actually, today's machines are capable of producing thicknesses of 1/100 of an inch, which is thinner than the paper this book is printed on.

It would be impossible to use solid stock from many of the species that produce the highly figured woods used as veneers. In some cases the cost of manufacturing the solid wood is prohibitive. Then there are such woods as walnut burl which is a beautiful, but structurally weak wood that splits almost as easily as it warps. There are also woods like ebony, which is so heavy that a small table made from solid stock can barely be moved. But perhaps most important of all, the enchanting figures that exist as veneers could never be seen if they were left inside a piece of lumber.

Although veneering is an ancient art, it was not until the twentieth century that science and technology achieved really manageable ways of manufacturing veneers. Sharper sawing knives were attached to improved machinery and concise cutting and drying techniques were developed. Today there are four different ways of getting a veneer from solid stock.

How Veneer is Cut

Veneers can be sawed with an old-fashioned circular saw blade, but the saw wastes considerable stock and produces a veneer no thinner than 1/24″. Far more efficient and preferable are three methods of slicing off veneers using a sawing knife. A veneer can be produced by moving the log up and down against a stationary blade. Or the log can be placed on a huge lathe and rotated against a knife which "unwinds" the entire piece of wood. Finally, the logs can be cut in half, then sliced on a veneer lathe, with the flat side acting to "cut off" each sheet.

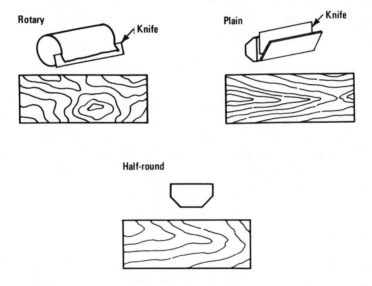

Figure 4-18 3 types of veneer "sliced" from a log in any of three different ways by modern machines.

How Veneers Are Dried

No matter how veneer is cut, each sheet must then be put in a dryer. The dryer has heated plates which move up and down, and squeeze the veneers between them. From the time they are cut, all of the sheets from a given log are carefully kept together so that the figures can be matched by the cabinetmakers who use them. As the sheets emerge from the drying machine, each is numbered and measured; then they are crated together for shipment.

TABLE 4-1 WOOD SPECIES SOLD AS VENEERS*

Name of Species	Origin	Description
Avoidre	Africa	White, yellow to gold; plain, striped, mottled
Benge	Africa	Light to dark brown with red brown stripes
Bubinga	Africa	Pinkish with wavy purple lines
Carpathian Elm Burl	England, France	Red to tan; circles and central eyes in pattern
Ebony, Gaboon	Africa	Black, little visible figure
Goncalo Alves	Brazil	Dark brown with tan streaks
Kelobra	Mexico	Brown with greenish cast; streaked, broad wavy lines
Lacewood	Australia	Pinkish flecked with brown
Makori	Africa	Pinkish to reddish brown; various degrees of ripple crossfire
Orientalwood	Australia	Greyish brown to pinkish; straight stripes
Padauk	Burma	Golden brown with red-violet stripes
Paldao	Philippines	Grey to reddish brown; wild irregular striped pattern
Primavera	Central America	Pale yellow to brown; wavy stripes, mottle has changing sheen that varies with light reflection
Rosewood	Brazil	Tan, golden brown to almost black; striped, wavy pattern
Rosewood	East India	Dark purple to ebony with streaks of red or yellow; straight stripes
Rosewood	Honduras	Orange brown to dark brown; irregular striped pattern
Saepele	Africa	Dark red brown; striped with crossfire flecks that sparkle

TABLE 4-1 WOOD SPECIES SOLD AS VENEERS* cont'd

Satinwood	Ceylon	Gold to deep yellow, straight, wavy, rippled, mottled, bee's wing mottle
Tamo	Japan	Tan with wavy brown grain; leaf, narrow wavy stripes plus a small peanut shell pattern
Thuya Burl	Africa	Golden to reddish brown with dark brown streaks; twists, swirls, numerous eyes
Zebrawood	Africa	Straw color; straight dark brown stripes

*There are more than 250 species from all over the world and they offer a complete range of colors, figures, and patterns. Those listed here represent only a few of the imported or more exotic woods.

Storing Veneers

Veneers will remain in good condition indefinitely, provided they are stored flat under a weight. Should you store some veneer in your shop and discover it has buckled, dip a whisk broom in water and sprinkle each of the veneers. Then stack them under a heavy weight. When they have dried, they will probably be flat and ready for use.

The Secret to Buying Veneer

Today veneers are produced with advanced cutting, handling, gluing, clamping, and repairing techniques. The veneers available are thinner and more even. Many of them are manufactured with a backing that makes their natural brittleness extremely manageable. So the biggest problem anyone has with veneer is deciding which one to use. More than 250 woods are sold as veneers and each species is likely to produce anything from straight stripes to bee's wing, rope, curly, mottle, burl, peanut, leaf, flake, quilted, circles, waves, bird's-eye, waterfall, or any number of exotically named figures. Moreover, no two veneers are ever the same, even when they come from the same tree.

Face veneers are cut either 1/40″ or 1/42″ thick and the length and width of each piece is determined by the size of the tree it came from. Veneers that have no particular figure are marketed as "crossband" in thicknesses between 1/28″ and 1/8″. Crossband is a stable backing that is glued behind the more fragile face veneers. Although any straight-grained wood may be used, the most frequent choices are poplar, sycamore, and mahogany.

In general, veneer costs between twenty-five cents and one dollar and fifty cents a square foot. Thus, a cabinet measuring 56″ X 30″ X 20″ can have its top, sides, door panels, and drawer fronts decorated with the most expensive veneer possible for under $40.

The Secret to Selecting Veneer

When choosing a face veneer always consider how the grain and color will look when finished. You should also take into account the shock resistance and warping tendencies of the wood itself, the effect of light reflection on the surface, and the pure design of the figure. A complete scientific knowledge of woods is invaluable when choosing a veneer, but all of that knowledge becomes irrelevant the moment you are smitten by the looks of a particular figure. So just buy the veneer you like best; worry about working with it when you get it in your shop.

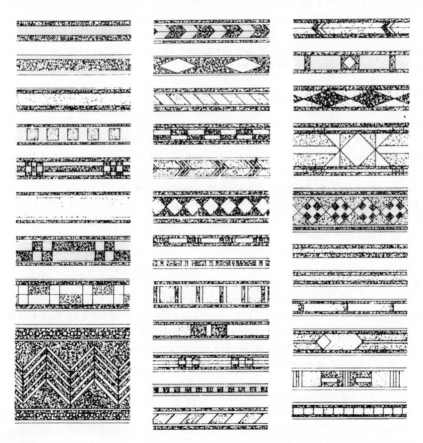

Figure 4-19   Inlay borders—made from a variety of woods glued together.

DECORATIVE INLAYS

Many of the magnificent inlaid borders found on old furniture are now manufactured in strips ready for gluing. The inlay market offers a variety of patterns and styles from which to choose. The strips are usually sold in 3-foot lengths and are 1/28" thick.

MILLWORK—MOLDING

Veneer all by itself can turn any box into a piece of furniture, but it will still be a box with straight lines. One way to give it some visual relief is to decorate it with molding. The kind of molding that is used, and exactly where it is placed, becomes strictly a matter of the cabinetmaker's personal taste. There are numerous shapes and sizes to pick from at almost any lumberyard. None of these need be used alone, but can be assembled in a multitude of ways to create still new designs. But if you cannot find an already milled piece that suits your particular purposes, you can shape your own with a molding head and blades and/or router with a complement of bits.

Molding Patterns and Where to Use Them

There is a tremendous number of molding patterns on the market today, all of which can be nailed, stapled, glued, or screwed to a cabinetmaking project. The following list is by no means complete, but is offered here as a general breakdown of the pattern types and their purposes. Bear in mind when choosing a molding that you are making a selection based on the visual effect the pattern will have on a specific project. Just because the molding was milled for one purpose does not limit its use elsewhere.

Crown and bed moldings have their tops and bottoms angled at 45° so they can bridge the right angle where two surfaces come together (i.e., the joint between a wall and ceiling). But they can also be used around the top of a tall chest or under the lip of a table.

Coves are concaved in a variety of ways but are smaller and more delicate in design than crown moldings. They also have a right-angled back so they can be used as a decorative strip under anything that overhangs, such as a table top.

Casings, bases, and base shoes are supposed to be for trimming doors and windows, or used as baseboards. They can also form a cabinet skirt or furniture baseboard.

Stools are designed to fit on the inside of a window sill and form a joint with the sash, but they can have a similar application on cabinets.

Rounds can be half, quarter, or full, and their uses as decorative additions to furniture and cabinets are endless.

Balusters are the decorative verticals that hold up stair railings. They can also hold up tables or chair backs, and adorn the front of something like Mediterranean-style furniture.

Battens are used to cover butt joints or other breaks in flat surfaces.

Glass beads are supposed to hold panes of glass in their frames. That is the least of it. They will fit into any right angle and provide a very handsome curved detail.

Stops are made for holding window sashes in their channels, but their simplicity is such that they are applicable to all sorts of cabinetwork.

CROWN MOULDING Softens the sharp lines where two planes meet, usually at the break between wall and ceiling, or under exterior eaves.	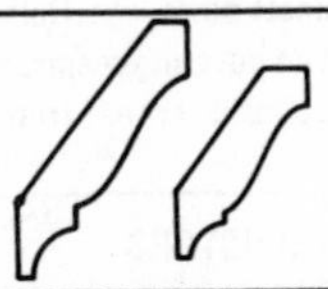
BED MOULDING Like Crown Mouldings, these soften sharp lines where two planes meet, usually between wall and ceiling, or under eaves.	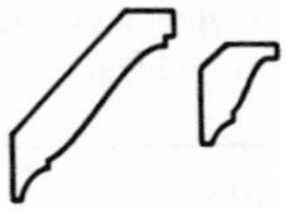
COVE MOULDING Except that this coulding has a "concave" face, it is used much the same way as are Bed and Crown Mouldings, above.	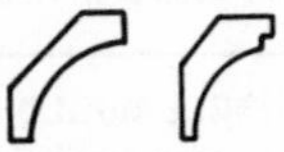
CASING and BASE These designs serve either as trim for doors and windows or as baseboard where wall meets floor.	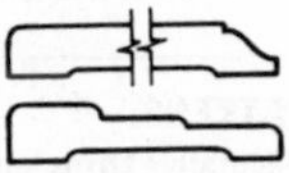
CASING Casing provides a decorative trim around a doorway or window or other opening, both inside and out.	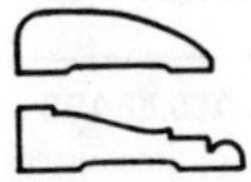
STOOLS Stools lie flat upon the inside of a sloping window sill and make a snug joint with the lowered sash.	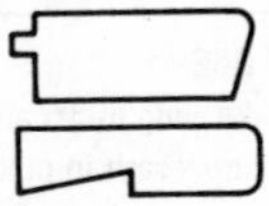
ROUND EDGE **CASING and BASE** This is available with one square edge for use as baseboard. With both edges rounded, this is door and window casing, and used for other trim purposes.	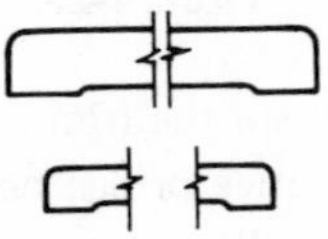

Figure 4-20   Examples of molding patterns.

CAP and BRICK MOULDING Caps top off wainscots and horizontal bases. Brick Mouldings provide a neat trim where brick or stucco meet wood in exterior walls	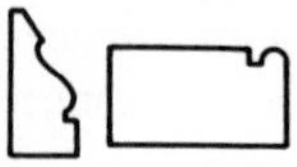
ROUNDS Full-rounds make curtain rods, bannisters, closet poles, etc. Half-rounds are decorative trim covering seams, etc. Quarter-rounds are inside corner trim.	
BALUSTERS Designed primarily as uprights in railings of all types, these handy squares find numerous other uses.	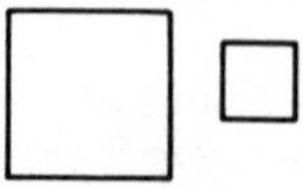
BANDS Top off baseboard and panel wainscot. Make good shelf cleats.	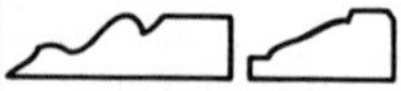
SHINGLE MOULDING Make neat, decorative joint where shingles or siding butt against window sills or eaves. Also used as bands or shelf cleats.	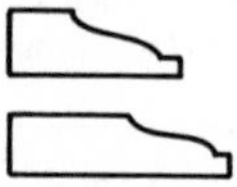
BATTENS Decorative strips applied over breaks in flat surfaces, such as over the cracks between boards in paneling or siding.	
GLASS BEADS Strips used instead of compounds to hold glass or other material in frames.	
STOPS Make snug joints and keep doors and window sash in place.	

Figure 4-20.　　　　　　Molding patterns cont'd.

Mullions are the trim that divides window panes. But any situation that requires an attractive bridge between elements (such as between door panels), is a candidate for mullion decoration.

Corner guards and back bands are used to cover an outside corner joint and are a particularly neat way of hiding a corner where one edge is exposed plywood.

MULLION CASING Decorative trim between windows when there is more than one in a series.	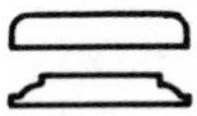
BASE SHOE Designed especially for use where the baseboard and the floor meet. However, it might be used in other trimming, too.	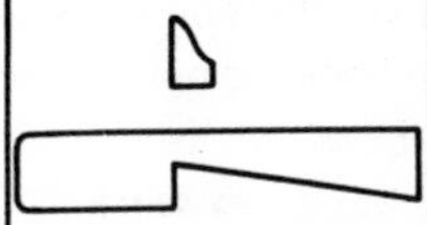
DRIP CAP Prevents moisture seepage into inside of walls when installed over exterior side of doors and windows.	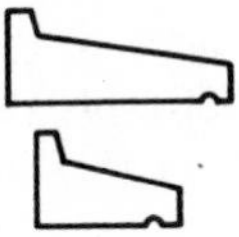
CORNER GUARD Designed for interior or exterior "outside" corners. Neatly covers as well as protects exposed corner construction.	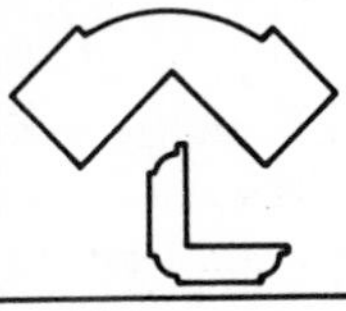
BACK BAND Caps baseboard and casings and is used in place of corner guards when only one edge is exposed.	
PICTURE MOULDING Primarily used as moulding around rooms on wall below ceiling. Design allows picture handing, hence the name.	
SCREEN STOCK Material shaped for use in window and door screens. Convenient shape makes it desirable for cabinet-work, too.	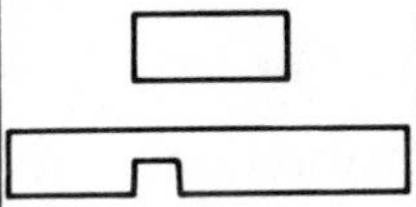
SCREEN MOULD Strips fasten over screen edges, hold screen firmly and neatly in place.	

Figure 4–20.   Molding patterns cont'd.

Picture moldings exist in all kinds of shapes and when they are not needed to go around a painting can be applied to all sorts of nooks, crannies, and flat surfaces in cabinetmaking.

Screen stock and screen beads are made to hold screens, but they can also be attached to furniture.

PLYWOOD

At the turn of the 20th century, men began gluing pieces of veneer together with the plies positioned so that their grains ran at right angles to each other. The plies got thicker, the boards grew bigger, and the glues that were used to hold them together became better and better, until the world was presented with a whole new form of lumber called plywood. From the beginning it was stronger, more durable, easier to work with, and unbelievably more versatile than solid stock. Plywood grew up slowly during the first three decades of the 20th century and in the 1940s came of age as the primary material for PT boat hulls. And by the end of the 1950s, plywood was just about everybody's choice for building practically everything, including furniture.

Advantages

When compared to solid stock, plywood demonstrates several tremendous advantages and very few drawbacks. It is, for example, equally strong in all directions, while solid wood tends to be weaker across its grain. There is almost no checking, splitting, or warping found in plywood. It will not swell or shrink to any noticeable degree during weather changes. It is easy to work with and to finish. Perhaps best of all, it comes in voluminous panels that permit large expanses of unjoined wood.

Disadvantages

There are two disadvantages to plywood: the raw edges of any panel are somewhat unsightly and require special techniques to cover. Care must also be taken when working close to the edges so that the thin-face veneer is not splintered or chipped.

Plywood Construction

Plywood is manufactured with either a veneer core or with a lumber core. *Veneer core* is assembled by gluing three, five, seven, or nine thin plies together, each with its grain going at right angles to the plies above and below it. Veneer core is available at almost any lumberyard for general construction. *Lumber core* is usually made with five plies. It has a center of solid lumber strips or particleboard sandwiched between two crossbands and two veneers. Lumber core is used primarily in cabinetmaking since the solid center helps to hold such joints as dowels, splines, and dovetails.

In both assemblies, the key to a balanced construction is to have all of the plies of the same shrinkage and density properties and the same moisture content. Also their grains should run at right angles to each other on either side of the core. This does not mean that the same species of wood must be used for every ply. In fact, it is an economic necessity that the hardwood-face veneer on a plywood panel be backed by less expensive woods.

Manufacturing Plywood

Plywood is manufactured in specific plywood plants, where the first step is to cut the logs into sections called *flitches.* The flitches are then soaked in hot water or steam to soften them for cutting with one of two types of machines.

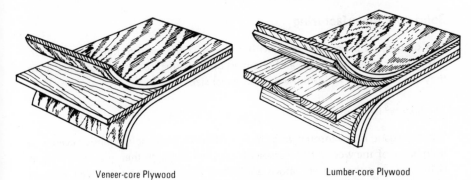

Veneer-core Plywood   Lumber-core Plywood

Figure 4-21   Veneer-core plywood may have as many as nine very thin plies glued together. Lumber-core plywood has a solid wood or particleboard center with four plies (two on each side) glued to it.

Cutting

The *rotary lathe* is used to cut more than 80 percent of all the veneer made in the United States. Essentially, it is an enormous lathe that rotates the flitch against an extremely sharp knife blade, allowing it to peel off a continuous sheet of wood.

The *veneer slicer* cuts the face veneers for such hardwood panels as oak, mahogany, cherry, and walnut. The flitch is merely held securely against a razor-sharp knife which slices off the veneer sheets. Like the cutting of any veneer, the face sheets are always kept in numerical order, so that it is possible to purchase consecutive hardwood panels.

The veneer sheets are then trimmed to size by an automatic clipper that reduces them to their best possible size and eliminates the majority of their natural defects.

Drying

The veneers are now sent through a 100-foot long oven heated to a temperature of around 350°F, which is hot enough to cook a roast, as well as reduce the moisture content of the wood to less than 4 percent.

Edge Bonding and Repairs

The next step is to join the strips of veneer by gluing their edges together in a tapeless splicer. Enough strips are bonded to achieve the required panel width; then the sheets are closely inspected and any defects such as cracks, knotholes, or checks are repaired.

Solid-core Manufacturing

The solid-cored panels are made with either particle-board or kiln-dried lumber. The lumber must be planed and trimmed until its surfaces are uniform and then they are edge-glued to form the desired panel size.

The Second Gluing

The crossband is put through large glue spreaders which apply adhesive evenly to both sides of the wood. The crossbands are then laid with their grains running at right angles to the veneers above and below them, and the assembled wooden sandwich is placed in a hot press that provides 250° F as it exerts an even 200 to 300 pounds per square inch of pressure on the panel. The result is a permanently bonded plywood panel which is then sanded and packed for shipping.

Types of Plywood

Plywood is manufactured in two types, exterior and interior. The exterior type is bonded with 100 percent waterproof glue which allows the panel to withstand all kinds of weather changes and conditions. Any project that may be subjected to the out-of-doors should be built with an exterior plywood, but you will have to specify "exterior" when ordering the panels. Interior type panels have highly moisture-resistant glues which can withstand occasional wetting, but should not be permanently exposed to the elements.

Plywood Grades

Besides being broadly categorized as either exterior or interior, plywood is also subdivided into several grades which are designated by letters. Each letter represents the quality of the front- or back-face veneers on the panel.

N Extremely smooth with no natural defects and capable of accepting any finish.

A Smooth, paintable, with neat repairs of minor surface defects.

B Smooth surface veneer with circular repair plugs and some knots.

C Knotholes of up to 1" in diameter and a limited number of splits.

D Knots, splits, and knotholes up to 2-1/2" in diameter.

Plywood panels are designated as A-B, or C-D, or any combination of the above five letters. The first letter always refers to the face of the panel and the second letter applies to the back.

Groups

There are over 70 different wood species used in the manufacture of the softwood plywood panels. The panels are divided into 5 groups numbered 1 to 5, which refer to the general strength of the panel. Group 1 is the hardest and stiffest, and group 5 is the weakest, with the other groups falling in between.

Thicknesses

Plywood is nearly always made of an odd number of plies and is sold in thicknesses of 1/8″, 3/16″, 1/2″, 5/16″, 3/8″, 5/8″, 3/4″, 7/8″, 1″, and 1-1/4″. Panel widths are 36″, 48″, and 60″, with lengths of 5′, 6′, 7′, 8′, 9′, 10′, 11′, and 12′, although the most common dimensions are 4′ X 8′.

Softwood and Hardwood Panels

Softwood, or construction, panels are primarily used in cabinetmaking for interior details, built-ins, kitchen cabinets, or paneling, as well as for the backing of fine veneers. Hardwood panels may have such face veneers as mahogany, birch, maple, or walnut, which make them excellent for making furniture.

Working With Plywood

No matter what plywood you are working with there are some rules to observe, most of them having to do with preserving the face veneers.

Cutting

Always use a sharp saw blade. If you insist on cutting up an entire 4′ X 8′ panel with a handsaw, be sure the saw has an all-purpose blade with 10 to 15 teeth per inch. Place the panel's good side UP and keep the saw blade as parallel to the wood as possible. Splintering can also be reduced if you nail a piece of thin wood to the underside of the panel and saw through that as well. But any way you do it, cutting plywood with a handsaw is long, hard work.

If you use a sabre or circular power saw, turn the good face of the panel DOWN. The teeth on both of these tools pull upward and will tear the edges of the top veneer. The radial arm and table saw blades rotate their teeth downward, so when cutting plywood with either stationary saw, keep the good face of the panel up.

Splintering almost always occurs when drilling plywood. The drill enters the panel smoothly, but chews up the last veneer as it exits. One way to avoid splintering is to drill halfway through the panel, then turn the wood over and drill through from the opposite side. Or clamp a piece of scrap against the back of the plywood to support the face veneer and prevent it from splintering.

Never forget how thin the face veneers on a plywood panel really are, and therefore how fragile they can be. Anytime you run a drill, nail, or screw through the back of that veneer, or scrape against its edges where it has a minimum of support, it will chip. This is particularly true when planing or sanding a plywood edge. Sanding or planing should always be done from the outside of the panel toward the center of the edge. Even with this precaution, use a sharp blade and take very shallow cuts.

Edges

Plywood face veneers rarely need sanding before applying primer-sealer but the edges are another story. In fact, the edges will appear very hard after only minimal sanding. Nevertheless, they will soak up paint like sponges unless they are first filled with spackle, wood putty, or wallboard compound.

There are several other ways of hiding plywood edges:

1. Tack a piece of molding or trim over them, using glue and nails.
2. Cut a V or groove in the edge and fit a shaped strip of plywood or molding into it.
3. When making a joint, the exposed edge can be rabbeted down to the back of the face ply so that it becomes a veneer for the overlapping edge.
4. Buy strips of veneer sold as edge banding and glue them along the edge. Some edge banding is sold with an adhesive already applied to it.

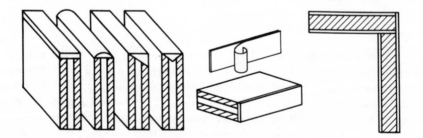

Figure 4-22   Covering the edges of a plywood panel.

Joints

Theoretically, you can make any kind of joint with plywood and hold it together with glue and nails or screws. With panels that are more than 1/2" thick, this is pretty much true. At best, the edge of any wood has minimum holding power;

plywood edges, if they are less than 1/2″ thick, have practically no grip at all. In other words, if the plywood is 1/2″ thick or less, add a corner block behind the joint and nail into it through the face of the plywood, or at least use a strong glue.

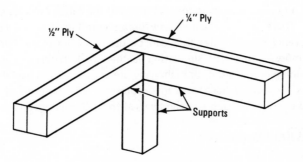

½″ Ply

¼″ Ply

Supports

Figure 4-23   Plywood panels 1/2″ thick or less should always be supported at their joints. Their edges do not have enough holding power for fasteners.

HARDBOARD

Hardboard is a manufactured wood product which has gained wide acceptance in cabinetmaking where it is used for drawer bottoms, cabinet backs, small sliding doors, and crossbands under fine veneer. Its advantages come from the fact that the size, shape, and working qualities are all man-made and therefore controllable.

Manufacture

Hardboard is made with wood chips that are refined (either mechanically or with steam) down to their individual wood fibers. The fibers are then treated chemically and compressed by a *felter* machine into one, continuous mat. The mat is called *wetlap* and it is fed into presses that dry and compress it under intense heat and pressure until it becomes thin, hard sheets which are then trimmed to their prescribed dimensions and packaged for shipping.

Sizes and Types

Hardboard is sold in three basic types as well as several specialty forms:

    Standard hardboard has high strength and is water resistant; it is primarily used in cabinetmaking because it will hold almost any finish without difficulty.

    Tempered hardboard has an added chemical/heat treatment which gives it an improved hardness and superior finishing properties.

    Service hardboard is a little less stiff and softer than the standard type, and it will not finish as well. But it is excellent wherever a lighter material is needed.

All hardboard types come with either one or both sides smooth and are manufactured in thicknesses from 1/16″ to 3/4″. The usual panel size is 4′ X 8′, although widths of up to 5′ and lengths of as much as 16′ are available.

Beyond the three basic types, hardboard is also produced in a wide range of finishes and sizes that serve specific needs of the cabinetmaking and furniture industries. There is, for example, *perforated* hardboard which comes with a series of evenly spaced holes that can be used to hold metal hooks or other fittings. *Embossed* patterns simulating leather, basketweave, or various wood grains including oak, walnut, or mahogany are widely used as panelling in homes and offices. *Acoustical* hardboard incorporates regular patterns of perforations which help to control sound and can be used to baffle ceilings and walls.

Working With Hardboard

Because hardboard has no grain, it is equally strong in all directions, but it should not be asked to span large areas without adequate support, and when joined at a corner, it should be backed by blocking. It can be dry-bent around a solid frame and fastened; for a tighter radius, dampen the hardboard and clamp it over heated forms until it dries. Tempered hardboard tends to bend more readily than the standard type.

Sawing

Hardboard can be sawed with any hand or power saw although the chemicals in the hardboard make carbide-tipped saw blades almost a necessity if a great deal of cutting is to be done.

Shaping, Drilling, and Nailing

Hardboard, since it has no grain, will produce a uniform machining with no splintering. Again, sharp molder blades or router bits should be used.

When drilling hardboard, the face side should be UP and the piece must be solidly supported if a clean edge is to be attained.

Either nails or screws combined with glue can be used with hardboard. Fasteners should be placed at least 1/4″ from the edge and be no more than 4″ apart. Begin fastening at the center of the piece and work toward the edges so that the panel will be absolutely flat. Any glue can be used with hardboard if it is applied according to the manufacturer's instructions.

Painting

Hardboard will accept most paints although the surface should be first sealed with a coat of shellac, enamel undercoater, or primer-sealer. Paint can be applied with a brush, roller, or spray gun.

PARTICLEBOARD

The 20 or so different kinds of particleboard on the market today not only have different commercial names, but are made up of different compositions as well. Essentially, all types of particleboard are concocted by blending wood chips and sawdust with a resin adhesive and compressing the mixture under intense heat. The result is a medium density, grainless panel that is very heavy, extremely stable, and rarely warps.

This kind of composition material has proven to be ideal for sliding doors, counter and table tops and as a core for veneer. It is too heavy for swinging doors because its edges have minimal holding power.

Flake board is the premier of particleboards. It is made with carefully cut flakes of wood, all cut with the grain, and is then bonded with a unique adhesive which gives the product better working qualities than any of the other types of particleboard.

How Particleboard is Manufactured

The properties of particleboard can be changed depending on the species and shape of the wood chips, the sort of adhesive used, and which of the two basic production methods are used in its manufacture.

The Mat-formed Process

Most particleboard is produced by flowing the wood particles and adhesive into the shape of a mat and then drying it in a hot press. What makes the difference between products is whether the panel is single layered, multilayered, or variable layered. *Single-layer* particleboard is made with shavings that are all the same kind and size. *Multilayer* has larger shavings in the center of the board and appreciably smaller particles toward its edges. *Variable layer* has coarse splinters and chips at its center with gradually finer shavings toward its outside surfaces.

The Extrusion Process

This process is used less often than mat forming, and is simply a matter of forcing the adhesive and wood particles through a small opening to form the board.

Weights and Sizes

Depending on its composition, particleboard weighs between 30 and 50 pounds per cubic foot. The density is somewhat higher in flake board where it ranges between 40 and 50 pounds per cubic foot.

Particleboard is available in thicknesses of 1/4″ to 2″ and comes in panels that are from 2′ to 5′ in width and 4′ to 16′ in length. The most common sizes are 4′ × 8′ and between 1/2″ to 1″ in thickness.

The question of which particleboard is best suited for a given project is better answered by your local lumber dealer. Each of the particleboards on the market has special qualities and characteristics; your lumber dealer can explain the advantages and disadvantages of the varieties he carries in stock.

Working with Particleboard

Like hardboard, particleboard has no grain and the comments already made about hardboard can generally be applied to working with particleboard. However, when handling particleboard, remember that it is made with a considerable amount of very tough resin adhesive which will dull most blades and bits very quickly. So use carbide-tipped tools. Particleboard also tends to create a very fine dust when it is cut and if you do not have adequate ventilation and an excellent waste removal system attached to your power tools, wear a mask. It takes days to get the dust out of your lungs.

Nails and Screws

Particleboard can be butt joined, but its nail-holding capabilities are considerably less than solid wood. Although a finishing nail no larger than 4d is generally acceptable, annular-thread or cement-coated nails are better. Standard wood screws are better still, although sheet metal screws of the same size will provide the best holding power of all. Because there is no grain, any pilot holes drilled in particleboard should be as small as possible.

Gluing

Use glue wherever possible; particleboard will respond to most of the glues used in cabinetmaking. Because particleboard is grainless and very stable, it is often used as a core for ply panels or as a backing for wood veneer and plastic laminates. In which case, use contact cement applied according to the manufacturer's instructions.

Joinery

Providing you use carbide-tipped or very sharp tools, particleboard can be routed, shaped, or dadoed with neat, clean results. But because of the material's weak holding power simple rabbets and butt joints are really inadequate. It is a safer procedure to make tongue-and-groove, dowel, dovetail, or spline joints.

Review Questions

1. What are the most popular woods used in the manufacture of fine furniture?
2. Why are the veneers taken from a single log always numbered and kept in consecutive order?
3. What is the difference between veneer-core and lumber-core plywood construction?
4. What is meant by the *balanced* construction of plywood panels?
5. When buying plywood it is necessary to state the veneer quality you wish the face veneers to have. What condition would you expect the face veneer to be in if it were designated D? B? N? C? A?
6. List three ways of hiding a plywood edge.
7. How can you prevent the face veneer of a piece of plywood from splintering when you are drilling through the panel? When you are planing or sanding a plywood edge?
8. When sawing plywood with a handsaw, would the face or the back of the panel be up? Which side is up when cutting plywood with a stationary power saw? When using a saber or portable circular saw?
9. What is hardboard used for in cabinetmaking?
10. What is particleboard used for in cabinetmaking?
11. What are three of the best joints to use when joining particleboard? Why?
12. How far apart should the fasteners be when attaching hardboard to a frame?

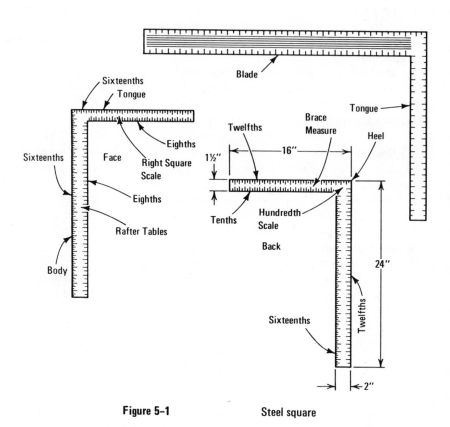

Figure 5-1   Steel square

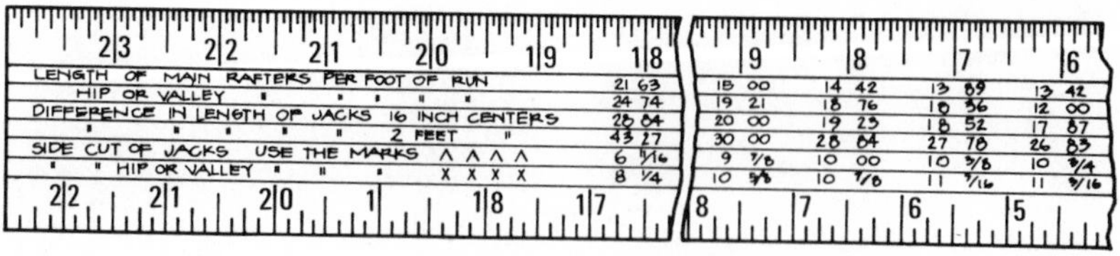

Figure 5-2   Roofing tables

Chapter 5

Measuring Steps

One of the big differences between an amateur woodworker and the professional cabinetmaker is the ability to measure accurately. There is an old adage that says, "Measure twice and cut once." Best you learn to follow it, for when a piece of material is cut too short, there is little you can do but take a new piece, measure it correctly, and cut it to its proper dimensions.

MEASURING A LUMBER DELIVERY

The first measuring you should do is on the lumber delivered for a project. The purpose, of course, is to make certain you have received the right species and grades. Then, when you know all that is in order, check to see that you have all the board feet you require to complete your construction.

TOOLS FOR MEASURING

You can use folding rules, steel-spring tapes, and yard sticks for measuring wood. But for laying out work on the wood you intend to cut, *the* tool to have is a *steel square*. Often called the *roofing square,* many people think of the steel square as something that belongs in the hands of a journeyman carpenter, and so it does. But cabinetmakers and finish carpenters have long used the steel square for determining many things other than the length or angle of a house rafter.

The steel square has two arms which come together at a 90° angle. The longer of the two arms is known as the *blade* or *body* and is normally 2″ wide and 24″ long. The other arm is the *tongue* and usually measures 1-1/4″ × 16″; the outer edge of the corner where the body and tongue meet is the *heel.* The *face* of the steel square is the side that is up when you hold the body in your left hand and the tongue in your right. If you forget, the face also has the manufacturer's name on it; the *back* is obviously the opposite side.

Scales and Tables

It should be noted immediately that by drawing a diagonal line from the outside corner of the body to the outside corner of the tongue, you will have a right triangle. Aside from this feature of the steel square, most of them come with an incredible number of scales and tables printed on both sides of both arms.

Face Scales

1. Along the outside edge of the body and tongue are inches and sixteenths.
2. Along the inside edge of the body and tongue are inches and eighths.

Back Scales

1. Along the outside edge of the body and tongue are inches and twelfths.
2. Along the inside edge of the body are inches and sixteenths.
3. Along the inside edge of the tongue are inches and tenths.

There is an additional scale on the back of many squares located near the heel, which is one inch divided into hundredths. The longer lines are placed every 25/100 of an inch; each shorter line represents 5/100 of an inch.

The scales on both sides of the square can be used for practically any measuring and layout work imaginable, but in between them all are several useful tables as well.

Tables

Besides the six roofing tables found on the face of the square and used to calculate the length of rafters, jacks, hips, and valleys, there is also a number of other woodworking tables that are particularly useful to the cabinetmaker.

The *octagon scale* (8-square scale) is a row of dots and numbers down the center of the tongue face. It is useful for laying out lines to cut an octagon from a square piece of wood. When converting, say, a 10″ square of wood to an octagon, first draw two lines at right angles through the center of the square. With a compass, count off the number of dots on the scale equal to the number of inches on one side of the square (10). This measurement is marked off on each side of the crossed lines with the result that you will have a perfect octagon.

The brace scale is along the center of the back side of the tongue and is used to determine the length of a brace between two members forming a right angle. You might use the rafting scales, since a brace is essentially a rafter, but usually the brace scale is easier.

Immediately under the edge figure 3″ are the numbers 18 over 24 and next to these is the figure 30. The numbers mean that any brace joining a frame which is 24″ on one leg and 18″ on the other, must be 30″ long. Farther along the scale,

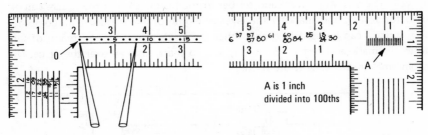

Figure 5-3 Octagon scale **Figure 5-4** Brace scale

A is 1 inch
divided into 100ths

under the edge number 12″ are the numbers 33 over 33 next to 46.67. These are read as a brace joining a frame which measures 33 inches each way must be 46 and 67/100 inches long. The 67/100″ can be measured off on the inch divided into 100 parts at the heel of the square.

The Essex board measure, or *lumber table* is found on the back of the blade and is used to find the board feet in a piece of lumber. The base number that determines everything on the scale is the 12″ mark on the outside edge of the blade. Directly under the base number is a column of numbers from 8 to 15. They indicate that a board 1″ thick and 12″ long will have 8 board feet if it is 8′ wide, or 9 board feet if it is 9′ wide, and so on.

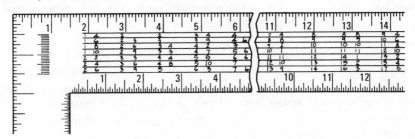

Figure 5-5 Essex-board measure

But suppose the board is 5″ wide and 14′ long. Follow the column under the base number 12″ down to the 14 near the bottom of the column. That is your length, 14′. Now follow the line to your left until you reach the column of numbers under the edge number 5″, which is the width of the board. You will find the numbers 5 and 10, which mean there are 5-10/12 or 5-5/6 board feet in the piece of wood. If your board were 2″, rather than 1″ thick, then you must multiply the 5-5/6″ times 2″ which would give you a total of 10-11/12 board feet.

Combination Square

The *combination square* has almost as many uses as the roofing square and is easier to handle, if only because it is smaller. It consists of a ruled blade 12″ long that is divided into different fractions along each of its four edges. The blade slides through a handle which not only has a 90° surface, but a 45° one as well. There is also a level and scriber in the handle so that the square can be used for testing and marking the level or plumb of any surface. The combination squares can be used to check either the inside or outside squareness of surfaces, to mark and test a 45° miter, and to mark lines all over the place. No cabinetmaker should be without one.

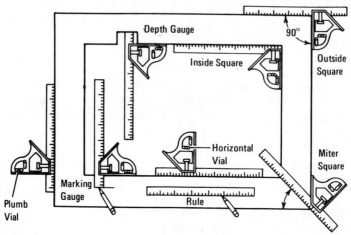

Figure 5-6 The combination square can perform eight different measuring functions.

Try Square

In the old days, no cabinetmaker was ever without a *try square,* but now it has been pretty well supplanted by the combination square, which can do all the same things and considerably more. The try square is a ruled metal blade fixed at right angles to a wooden or metal handle. It is good for marking lines across the face or edge of stock and testing for squareness.

Sliding T-Bevel

If you are putting up rafters and keep a protractor handy, the *sliding T-bevel* is a good tool to have. Its blade can be set at any angle to the handle, so you can either measure or transfer any angle from 0° to 180°, or check a miter cut. If you want to know what the angle is, however, you have to hold the bevel against a protractor.

Carpenter's Level

Carpenters' levels are rectangular wooden or metal frames with one or more level glasses set in them. The most useful levels have glasses that go vertically, horizontally, and at 45°, so they can be placed against any surface to determine whether it is level or plumb. Some levels have inches and feet painted on their edges which is a very useful feature, at least until the marks wear off.

Marking Gauge

The *marking gauge* is used to scratch a parallel line in wood grain. It consists of a wooden or metal head which can be locked at any place along a ruled beam that has a metal point fixed to its end. The head is pressed against the edge of the wood and the point is set at the distance inside the edge which is to be marked. Then the gauge is slid along the wood, allowing the point to scratch the surface.

Dividers

If you are going to deal with curves (and every cabinetmaker does) you will need a pair of *dividers*. The tool consists of two metal legs hinged at one end and pointed at the other. Good dividers have one leg that can be removed and replaced by a pencil. To set the dividers, place both points on the measuring lines of a rule and lock them in place. You can then lay out an arc or a complete circle, step off measurements, or divide distances along a straight line.

Flexible Tape Rules

Flexible tapes can be either cloth or metal rolled into a narrow case; they come in lengths of 6', 8', 10', 12', 50' and 100'. You can use them to measure either the inside or outside of irregular, as well as regular shapes. So far, you can only buy them marked in inches and feet.

Folding Rules

Woodworkers are probably evenly divided over which is best, the flexible, or the *folding*, rule. The complaint with folding rulers has always been that their sections break and the swivel pins at each end of the six-inch sections become loose. Now, some manufacturers are making their rules out of fiberglass and neither the pin arrangement nor the material is supposed to weaken or break. The six-foot folding rule is a little easier to carry and handle because it is narrower when folded up. But when it comes to marking off plywood panels, you will find it infinitely more convenient to have an eight-foot rule that reaches from one end of the panel to the other. The folding rules are usually divided into 1/16″ and so far they have not appeared on the market with metric calibrations.

THE METRIC SYSTEM AND YOU

The metric system is officially with us, as of 1977. Without question, it would be simpler if everyone in America did not have to learn a whole new system of measurement, but on the other hand, woodworking measurements are a lot easier to make in millimeters and centimeters, if only because you are always dealing with that nice, round number, 10.

The metric system consists of seven base units from which all other units are derived by multiples of ten. The seven units and their symbols are:

1. Meter: unit of length   m
2. Kilogram: unit of mass   kg
3. Second: unit of time   sec
4. Ampere: unit of electric current   amp
5. Kelvin (or degrees Celsius): Unit of temperature   K or °C
6. Candela: unit of luminous intensity   cd
7. Mole: unit of amount of substance   mol

The same prefixes are used for all seven types of measurements, so you can have a kilometer, kilogram, or a kilowatt. But with the prefix *kilo-* attached, the measurement will always mean **1,000** of something. The most common prefixes used throughout the metric system are listed in Table 5-1.

For all practical purposes, the easiest way to learn the metric system is to forget that your arm is a yard long and your thumb is an inch wide, and perhaps in time you will be able to do that. But for the moment, America in general and cabinetmakers in particular are faced with the problems of converting from one system to the other, which means not only learning different terms for length, weight, volume, liquid capacity, and temperature, but also a whole new set of symbols. Fortunately, there are not too many terms and symbols beyond those listed in Table 5-2.

TABLE 5-1 PREFIX SYMBOLS

Exponent or Power	Prefix	Pronun- ciation	Symbol	Meaning	Decimal Form
$= 10^3$	kilo-	kĭl′ ō	k	thousand	1.000
$= 10^2$	hecto-	hĕk′ tō	h	hundred	100
$= 10^1$	deca-	dĕc′ ā	dk	ten	10
$= 10^{-1}$	deci-	dĕs′ ī	d	tenth	0.1
$= 10^{-2}$	centi-	sĕn′ tĭ	c	hundredth	0.01
$= 10^{-3}$	milli-	mĭl ĭ	m	thousandth	0.001

Length

The yard as we know it today will be replaced by the meter rule which measures 39.37″. The meter rule is divided into 100 equal parts called *centimeters* (*centi-* meaning hundredth) and each centimeter is divided into 10 equal parts called millimeters (*milli-* meaning thousandth). In other words there are a thousand little lines on a meter rule and each one of them represents a distance that is ap-

TABLE 5-2 EQUIVALENT TERMS AND SYMBOLS OF MEASUREMENT

Unit	Customary Symbol	Metric Symbol
Length	feet = ' or ft. inch = " or in. fraction of an inch =	meter = m centimeter = cm millimeter = mm
Weight	pound = lb. ounce = oz.	kilogram = kg gram = g
Volume	cubic yard = yd.^{3} cubic foot = ft.^{3} cubic inch = in.^{3}	cubic meter = m^3 cubic decimeter = dm^3 cubic millimeter = mm^3
Liquid capacity	quart = qt. pint = pt.	liter = l milliliter = ml
Temperature	Fahrenheit = °F	degrees Celsius = °C

proximately halfway between 1/32″ and 1/16″. Since it is customary in cabinet-making to work pretty much around a tolerance of 1/16″, using millimeters will make everything you build just a shade more accurate. In fact, European crafts-men normally round off their work to either the nearest millimeter, or half milli-meter. They refer to the measurement as *bare* if it is more than half but less than a full millimeter or *full* if it is more than a millimeter but less than a millimeter and a half. The conversion of linear measurements to the metric system is shown in Table 5-3.

Weights

In the metric system the basic unit of weight is the kilogram, which equals 1,000 grams. Roughly 28 grams equal one ounce, so a kilogram becomes 2.2 pounds. The weights of such dry materials as plastic, cloth, and powders are, or soon will be, given in kilograms.

Volume

Volume, of course, is cubic measurement, and your standard neighborhood cubic meter is a little bulky, since it is around 30 percent larger than a cubic yard. However, one tenth of a cubic meter is a decimeter (*deci-* meaning a tenth) and that becomes the liquid capacity of a liter. Moreover, if the liquid is water, one decimeter will weigh one kilogram.

Liquid Capacity

A liter is about 6 percent larger than a quart, so three liters make up 3.8 quarts, or nearly a gallon. Since the liter and half liter are roughly the equivalent of quarts and pints, when buying paints, oils, and other finishing materials, you

TABLE 5-3 LINEAR–METRIC EQUIVALENTS

Linear	Actual	Referred to as:	Tool Sizes	Lumber Sizes	
				Thickness	Width
1/32"	0.8 mm	1 mm bare			
1/16"	1.6 mm	1.5 mm			
1/8"	3.2 mm	3 mm full	3 mm		
3/16"	4.8 mm	5 mm bare	5 mm		
1/4"	6.4 mm	6.5 mm	6 mm		
5/16"	7.9 mm	8 mm bare	8 mm		
3/8"	9.5 mm	9.5 mm	10 mm		
7/16"	11.1 mm	11 mm full	11 mm		
1/2"	12.7 mm	12.5 mm full	13 mm		
9/16"	14.3 mm	14.5 mm bare	14 mm		
5/8"	15.9 mm	16 mm bare	16 mm	16 mm	
11/16"	17.5 mm	17.5 mm	17 mm		
3/4"	19.1 mm	19 mm full	19 mm	19 mm	
13/16"	20.6 mm	20.5 mm	21 mm		
7/8"	22.2 mm	22 mm full	22 mm	22 mm	
15/16"	23.8 mm	24 mm bare	24 mm		
1"	25.4 mm	25.5 mm	25 mm	25 mm	
1-1/4"	31.8 mm	32 mm bare	32 mm	32 mm	
1-3/8"	34.9 mm	35 mm bare	36 mm	36 mm	

TABLE 5-3 LINEAR–METRIC EQUIVALENTS, Cont'd

Linear	Actual	Referred to as	Tool Sizes	Lumber Sizes Thickness	Lumber Sizes Width
1-1/2"	38.1 mm	38 mm full	38 mm	38 mm (or 40 mm)	
1-3/4"	44.5 mm	44.5 mm	44 mm	44 mm	
2"	50.8 mm	51 mm bare	50 mm	50 mm	
2-1/2"	63.5 mm	63.5 mm	64 mm	64 mm	
3"	76.2 mm	76 mm full		75 mm	75 mm
4"	101.6 mm	101.5 mm		100 mm	100 mm
5"	127.0 mm	127 mm			125 mm
6"	152.4 mm	152.5 mm			150 mm
7"	177.8 mm	178 mm bare			
8"	203.2 mm	203 mm full			200 mm
9"	228.6 mm	228.5 mm			
10"	254.0 mm	254 mm			250 mm
11"	279.4 mm	279.5 mm			
12"	304.8 mm	305 mm bare			300 mm
18"	457.2 mm	457 mm full	460 mm		
24"	609.6 mm	609.5 mm			
36"	914.4 mm	914.5 mm			Panel Stock Sizes
48" (4')	1219.2 mm	1220 mm or 1.22 m			1220 mm or 1.22 m width
96" (8')	2438.4 mm	2440 mm or 2.44 m			2440 mm or 2.44 m width

will discover that a can about the same size as a quart or pint covers a little bit more area. But when you come to the gallon sizes, they will cover less, simply because 3.8 liters is less than four quarts; except the metric gallon is considerably larger.

Temperature

The metric temperature scale is also devised around the base unit 1. It starts at 0 and goes up or down, with the boiling temperature of water being 100° Celsius. On the Celsius scale, 100°C equals 212° Fahrenheit; body temperature is 37°C, or 98.6°F; absolute zero is registered as –273.15°C and –459.67°F.

Conversions

It will be easier for everyone when the entire nation learns to just think in terms of metric, but until that time, we have a lot of multiplying to do every time we need to convert from our present system to metric, and vice versa. Here are the most common conversions and the numbers you have to multiply by to get them:

LAYING OUT SHAPES

As a cabinetmaker you will find yourself wrestling with the right angle ad infinitum but there are also all 360 degrees in the compass to worry about, and then there are curves. When you have the lumber before you and you begin marking it off for your initial rough cuts, there are likely to be all sorts of geometric configurations that have to be drawn, each of which has a procedure you can follow.

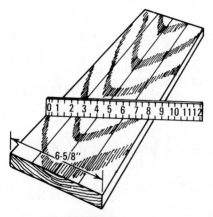

Figure 5-7   Use an acute angle to divide a board into equal parts.

TABLE 5-4 METRIC—LINEAR CONVERSION TABLE

Given Measurement	Multiply by	Result
Length		
inches	25.4	millimeters
feet	30.48	centimeters
yards	0.9	meters
miles	1.6	kilometers
millimeters	0.04	inches
centimeters	0.4	inches
meters	1.1	yards
kilometers	0.6	miles
Area		
square inches	6.5	square centimeters
square feet	0.09	square meters
square yards	0.8	square meters
square miles	2.6	square kilometers
acres	0.4	square hectometers
square centimeters	0.16	square inches
square meters	1.2	square yards
square kilometers	0.4	square miles
square hectometers	2.5	acres
Weight		
ounces	28.0	grams
pounds	0.45	kilograms
short tons	0.9	megagrams (metric tons)
grams	0.035	ounces
kilograms	2.2	pounds
megagrams (metric tons)	1.1	short tons
Liquid Volume		
ounces	30.0	milliliters
pints	0.47	liters
quarts	0.95	liters
gallons	3.8	liters
milliliters	0.034	ounces
liters	2.1	pints
liters	1.06	quarts
liters	0.26	gallons
Temperature		
degrees Fahrenheit	Subtract 32, then multiply by 5/9	degrees Celsius
degrees Celsius	Multiply by 9/5, then add 32	degrees Fahrenheit

Dividing a Board into Several Equal Parts

The practical application of dividing a line into several equal parts occurs when you want to split a board that is an odd width into equal parts. Suppose you have a board 6-5/8″ wide and you want to cut it into four equal strips. Instead of grabbing your dividers, protractor, and parallel rulers, lay a ruler diagonally across the board. The 0 end of the ruler is held against one edge of the board; the ruler is angled toward the opposite edge until the 8 touches the opposite edge. You choose the 8 because it is the first number easily divisible by four that will also provide an angle on the wood. But you could take 10, 12, or 24, any even number. Once the ruler is set, mark it off in four equal parts (every two inches). Now draw guidelines that are parallel to the edges of the board and intersect each of the four marks. A 6-5/8″ wide board divides into four strips each 1-21/32″ wide.

Bisecting Angles

You have an undetermined angle formed by two lines meeting and you want to divide the angle in half.

1. Open your compass to any width and place the pointer at the point of the angle.
2. Inscribe an arc that intersects both legs of the angle.
3. Adjust the compass to any radius that is more than half the distance between the two intersecting arcs.
4. Using the two intersecting arcs as centers, draw two intersecting arcs at a point opposite the angle.
5. Draw a straight line from the intersecting arcs to the point of the angle. This line will equally divide the angle.

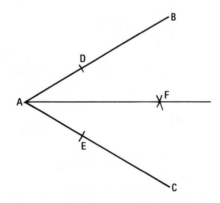

Figure 5-8   Dividing an unknown angle in half with a compass.

Rounding a Square Corner

Projects are forever demanding rounded corners. The plans will say, to give an example, 1-1/2″ radius or 3″ radius. Simply mark off the radius in both directions from the corner and draw lines at a right angle to the corner edges, until they intersect. The cross-over becomes the center of the circle. Set your dividers or a compass at the proper radius and place the pointer at the intersecting lines. Draw the arc around the corner.

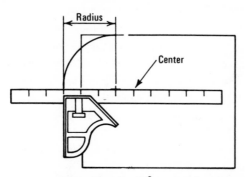

Figure 5-9   Rounding off a 90° corner, given the radius of the curve.

Rounding a Corner That is Not 90°

If you want to round the corners of, say, a hexagon, the same principle used in rounding a square corner is used, but you have to work a little harder.

1. Determine the radius of the curve and adjust your dividers or compass accordingly.
2. Draw a series of arcs at random points along each side of the angle.
3. Now draw straight lines across the top of the arcs (tangent to the arcs). The two lines will be parallel to the edges of the corner and will intersect in front of the corner to be rounded.
4. Use the point where the two straight lines intersect as the center and inscribe the arc without changing the compass or divider setting.

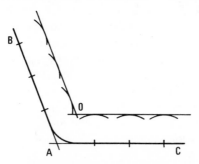

Figure 5-10   Rounding off a corner that is not 90° requires only one compass setting.

Drawing an Ellipse

An ellipse is a flattened circle, but in reality it has two different diameters. In order to accomplish the regular curve of the ellipse, you will need a straight ruler, three pins, a pencil, and a piece of string.

1. Establish the length and width of the ellipse by drawing one long line which is crossed at right angles to its center with the shorter line. These two lines are called the *major-* and *minor-axis* lines.
2. Set your dividers equal to one half of the longest line.
3. Using either end of the shorter axis line as the center point, inscribe intersecting arcs on either side of the center of the longer axis line.
4. Stick pins in each of the intersecting arcs and a third pin at one end of the shorter axis line. Tie a string around the pins.
5. Remove the pin at the end of the short axis line and put a pencil in its place.
6. Hold the pencil so that the string is always taut, and draw the ellipse around the pair of axis lines.

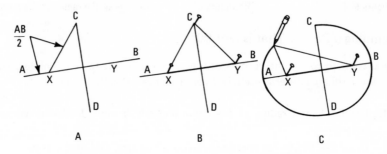

A　　　　　　　　　　B　　　　　　　　　　C

Figure 5-11　　　　　　　Making a perfect eclipse.

Transferring Irregular Designs

Every month new books and magazines arrive on the market crammed with cabinetmaking projects and the plans for building them. Often, these plans contain irregular parts which must be enlarged to full scale before they can be made. Usually, these irregular parts are drawn on grid squares with the dimensions of the full-sized squares noted. The note means that when you transfer the design, you will need to do it on a grid that has, for example, one-inch squares. You will also probably need the services of a French curve, which can be purchased at most good stationery or art supply stores.

The first step is to make the grid on a large piece of wrapping paper or better still, cardboard. Be very careful when ruling the squares that they are all really square and that their dimensions are accurate. You will find it convenient if you label the vertical lines A, B, C, etc., and the horizontal lines numerically, on both the original plans and your own grid. Then, using the numbers and letters, begin locating positions on the oirignal plan and placing them in their corresponding squares on your grid. Any point where a line crosses one of the grid lines is a point to be transferred and the more points you have to work with, the more easily the transfer can be made. When you have enough transfer points on your grid, sketch the pattern freehand, moving from point to point. Then use your French curve to produce smooth, even curves. When you are finished, cut out the design and use it as a pattern to trace on the wood it will be cut from. Or, if you have used a thin paper, you can place it over a piece of carbon paper on the wood and trace the lines onto the wood that way. If you have no carbon paper handy, blacken the back of the drawing with your pencil. The graphite will act the same way carbon paper does.

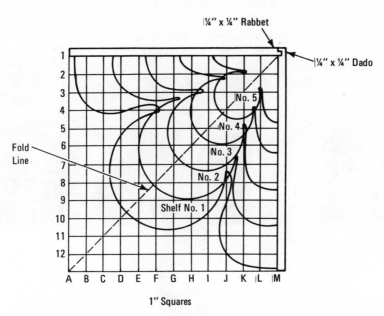

Figure 5-12   Transferring, irregular designs.

A Couple of Hints

1. If there are a number of parts which must be cut to the same pattern, put your initial transfer on a sheet of 1/8" or 1/4" stock and cut it out to be used as a template.

2. If the pattern is symmetrical, that is, has the same curves on both sides of its center line, you need only transfer one half of it. Then fold the paper in half and cut out the full pattern.

The Process of Measuring

The act of measuring and marking the pieces you intend to cut is normally done all at once so that when you bring the wood to your saws you can do all of your rough cutting at one time without stopping every few minutes to measure. But there are some inherent dangers in cutting everything all at once. The biggest problem is that you will end up with a stack of neatly cut lumber, none of which you can identify. So mark every piece on an edge, or on its back, and stack the pieces in some sort of order so that you know what they are when you pick them up. The best way to stack them is according to the joinery that will be done on them. Thus, all the pieces to be mortised will be in one pile and all the pieces to be rabbeted will be in another, and so on. Pieces that will require more than one joint are placed in the pile that will be worked on first. That is, if you intend to do all of the dadoes first, put all the pieces requiring dadoing together. Then, as the dadoes are made, repile the pieces to be rabbeted in the rabbet pile and the ones to be dovetailed in another pile, and so forth.

Figure 5-13   Marking plywood for cutting. Leave enough space between lines for your saw kerf.

Marking Plywood

Everybody always says, "Mark all the pieces to be cut from a plywood panel first, then cut them all." By and large this is reasonable advice, but beware of two critical factors: First, if you are marking out pieces which are adjacent to each other, *remember that your saw kerf will take up 1/8 inch.* You cannot blithely mark off four 3" strips of wood by laying a ruler across the wood and putting a pencil mark every 3". If you do that and then cut on each of those marks, only the first piece will be accurate. You have to give yourself the 1/8" space between lines. Second, as you lay out the piece to be cut from a panel, try to establish one or two long rough cuts through the center of the panel. Make these cuts first. Your problem is to reduce the 4' X 8' panel to manageable pieces as quickly as possible. Running a lot of narrow rips down one side or the other will not help. Even a 2' X 8' piece is difficult to rip accurately; any time you can get it down to something around 2' X 5' or 6' you will have an easier time making the remainder of your cuts. Above all, *always measure twice,* so you will need to cut only once.

Review Questions

1. Why should you bother measuring the wood in a lumber delivery?
2. Name four important tools needed for measuring.
3. Why is the steel square important in cabinetmaking?
4. How do you use the brace scale on a steel square?
5. How do you measure board feet with a steel square?
6. What are the advantages of a combination square over a try square?
7. What is a millimeter? A centimeter? A kilogram? A liter? Compare each to its equivalent in the linear system.
8. Make an octagon using a steel square. Make an octagon using a compass.
9. You have a board that is 6-3/16" wide. Divide it into 9 equal parts.
10. How do you transfer a curved piece in a set of plans onto the wood from which it must be cut?
11. Round a square corner to a 6" radius.
12. Round a 120° corner to a 9" radius.

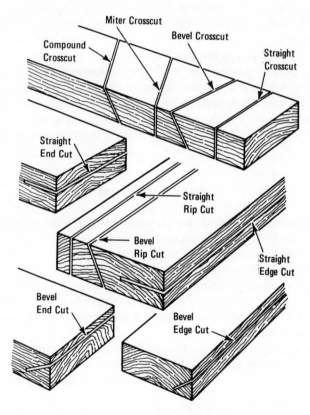

Figure 6-1   The ten basic saw cuts.

Chapter 6

The Techniques of Cutting Wood

There is a ritual to putting a saw blade to wood. It is a timeless procedure performed sometimes unwittingly but just as often with conscious consideration. It is, however, always performed to some degree by every person who approaches any piece of wood with a saw in his hand.

FROM A RITUAL OF CONTEMPLATION . . .

The ritual begins the moment a piece of wood is selected for cutting. That moment alone demands that a host of large and small decisions be made concerning the ultimate size of the piece of wood, the inherent strength of the material, and the purpose it will serve as part of a specific project. Then the look of the wood must be considered—its texture, the direction of its grain in relationship to its placement in the finished piece, and its color and touch. All involve, equally important questions to be resolved.

Cabinetmakers have been known to spend days, even weeks, pacing around a stick of fine grade lumber, talking to themselves, turning the wood over, squinting at it, memorizing its every feature, gradually arriving at an answer to each of the questions it presents.

When the cabinetmaker is satisfied with what he plans to do, he then sets up his cutting tools. He assures himself that his machine is in proper running order and the blade is precisely aligned. And at long last, the steel of the blade bites into the wood, and suddenly, he has irrevocably altered its shape forever, for better or for worse, but most certainly, forever.

IN PURSUIT OF THE RIGHT ANGLE

With one saw cut, there must always be two. The second cut may be an existing edge of the board, but someone, somewhere, made that cut and it has a relationship with any cut that is made near, or tangent to it. The angle between two intersecting cuts is always a function of $90°$. Indeed, $90°$ is the single most important angle in cabinetmaking. Even when a right angle is not specifically used, whatever angle is taken must be drawn from a point of reference and most often that point is 90° with something.

Creating any right angle is an elusive and awesome task. The best tool you can use is a perfectly aligned table saw, but even with that, there is no guarantee you can cut one absolutely straight line, let alone two lines that will intersect at exactly 90°

Consider the odds against making a perfect right angle. If the wood is slightly warped (and wood usually is), the board will lift as it travels past the saw blade, forcing an off-angle cut. There is also the human factor. It is nearly impossible for any man to exert constant pressure against a piece of stock as he pushes it past a saw blade. If it requires two minutes to rip an 8' board, that is 120 seconds and 96" of opportunity for the wood to drift away from the guide fence— and immediately distort the cut.

Lest you think that the fault of an imperfect right angle is all your own, it is not. Part of the blame can often be placed directly in the hands of the men who mill the wood you use. The millworkers have marvelous, huge, precision machines for cutting and planing logs into lumber. But the wood is always imperfect, the machines occasionally get out of line, and millworkers have bad days at the office like everyone else. So who is to guarantee that every freshly milled plank on sale at your local lumberyard is absolutely square to begin with? Measure a few of them. They are all pretty close, but they can also be as much as 1/8" off line. Even their thicknesses can vary. Today's 3/4" boards can be anything from 5/8" to 13/16"! Plywood panels are not so perfect, either. Most of them are warped these days and sometimes they are imported from countries such as Taiwan measuring 4'-1/8" X 8'-1/4". That happens to be a blessing; those extra fractions of an inch are grist for your saw kerf so that you can cut pieces that are exactly 4' X 4' or 2' X 8' instead of 4' X 3' 11-15/16", or 1' 11-15/16" X 8'. Therefore you should measure the wood you buy before you begin to cut it.

Every cabinet is only as true to its prescribed measurements as the cuts that were made to form each of its pieces. There is a myth among men who should know better, than an off-angle cut can often go unnoticed or that it can be hidden during the joining, assembly, or finishing stages. But that rarely happens. If a cut is wrong, it can sometimes be corrected with some arduous planing or sanding. If it is really off line it will have to be redone, if possible, or a new piece must be selected and then cut more accurately.

TEN SAW CUTS

There are only ten ways you can saw a piece of wood, including four crosscuts, two end cuts, two edge cuts, and two rip cuts. Obviously, the ten basic cuts can be combined in unlimited ways to create an infinite number of wood shapes and forms.

Technically, any saw can make all of the basic cuts, but mankind has spent a great deal of effort designing saw blades which are supposed to make the cutting of wood easier and leave the edges of the cut smoother. The differences in blades are most noticeable when you are using a hand saw and personally supplying all the power the blade needs to cut through a piece of wood. There are also different kinds of blades for use on the power saws, all of which the cabinetmaker should be familiar with.

Bearing in mind that any saw is capable of making all of the cuts, the following descriptions list only the preferred hand and power saws to achieve the best results:

Crosscut. A simple right angle cut across the grain, with the saw blade perpendicular to the wood. *Tools:* Radial arm saw, crosscut saw.

Bevel crosscut. Identical to a crosscut, except that the saw blade is at any angle to the surface of the wood other than 90°. *Tools:* Radial arm saw, crosscut saw.

Miter crosscut. A crosscut made at an angle across the grain, with the blade held at 90° to the surface of the wood. The term *miter* commonly assumes that the angle of cut is 45°, but technically it can be any angle except 90°. *Tools:* Radial arm, crosscut saw.

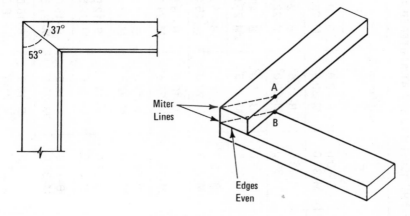

Figure 6-2

To determine a miter made of varying widths, place the narrower piece across the piece it will join, and align the outer edges. Mark the inside corner where the two pieces meet A. Draw a diagonal from point A to the outside corner of the wide piece. Put the wider member on top of the narrower one. Mark the inside corner B. Draw a diagonal from B to the oustide corner of the narrower piece. The two diagonals are the miter lines. When they are cut and joined, the two pieces will form a right angle.

Compound crosscut. Both the direction of the crosscut and the relationship of the blade to the wood are at any angle other than 90°. *Tools:* Radial arm, crosscut saw. Any closed structure with three or more sides (triangle, pentagon, or octagon) is likely to require several compound crosscuts. It should be

TABLE 6-1 CUTTING A COMPOUND ANGLE. YOU BEVEL AND SAW AT A MITERED ANGLE*

Pitch Of Side	Number of Sides							
	3	4	5	6	7	8	9	10
0°	B- 0.0° M-60.0°	B- 0.0° M-45.0°	B- 0.0° M-36.0°	B- 0.0° M-30.0°	B- 0.0° M-26.0°	B- 0.0° M-22.5°	B- 0.0° M-20.0°	B- 0.0° M-18.0°
5°	B- 3.5° M-50.0°	B- 3.5° M-45.0°	B- 3.0° M-36.0°	B- 2.5° M-30.0°	B- 2.5° M-22.5°	B- 2.0° M-22.5°	B- 2.0° M-20.0°	B- 2.0° M-18.0°
10°	B- 8.0° M-59.5°	B- 7.0° M-44.5°	B- 6.0° M-35.5°	B- 5.0° M-29.5°	B- 4.5° M-25.5°	B- 4.0° M-22.0°	B- 3.5° M-19.5°	B- 3.0° M-17.5°
15°	B-12.5° M-58.5°	B-10.5° M-44.0°	B- 8.5° M-34.0°	B- 7.5° M-29.0°	B- 6.5° M-25.0°	B- 5.5° M-22.0°	B- 5.0° M-19.5°	B- 4.5° M-17.5°
20°	B-18.5° M-57.5°	B-14.0° M-43.0°	B-11.5° M-34.0°	B-10.0° M-23.5°	B- 8.5° M-24.5°	B- 7.5° M-21.5°	B- 6.5° M-19.0°	B- 6.0° M-17.0°
25°	B-22.0° M-56.0°	B-17.5° M-41.5°	B-14.5° M-33.0°	B-12.0° M-27.5°	B-10.5° M-23.5°	B- 9.0° M-20.5°	B- 8.0° M-18.5°	B- 7.5° M-16.5°
30°	B-26.5° M-53.5°	B-21.0° M-40.0°	B-17.0° M-32.0°	B-14.5° M-28.5°	B-12.5° M-22.5°	B-11.0° M-19.5°	B- 9.5° M-17.5°	B- 8.5° M-18.0°
35°	B-31.0° M-51.5°	B-24.0° M-38.0°	B-19.5° M-30.0°	B-16.5° M-25.0°	B-15.0° M-21.5°	B-12.5° M-19.0°	B-11.0° M-16.5°	B-10.0° M-15.0°
40°	B-35.0° M-48.5°	B-27.0° M-36.0°	B-22.0° M-28.5°	B-18.5° M-23.5°	B-16.0° M-20.0°	B-14.0° M-17.5°	B-12.5° M-15.5°	B-11.5° M-14.0°

TABLE 6-1 Cont'd

45°	B-39.0° / M-46.5°	B-30.0° / M-33.5°	B-24.5° / M-26.5°	B-20.5° / M-22.0°	B-17.5° / M-19.0°	B-15.5° / M-16.5°	B-13.5° / M-14.5°	B-12.5° / M-13.0°
50°	B-42.5° / M-42.0°	B-33.0° / M-31.0°	B-27.5° / M-24.5°	B-22.0° / M-21.5°	B-19.0° / M-17.5°	B-16.5° / M-15.0°	B-15.0° / M-13.5°	B-13.5° / M-12.0°
55°	B-46.0° / M-38.0°	B-35.5° / M-28.0°	B-28.5° / M-22.0°	B-23.5° / M-18.5°	B-20.5° / M-15.5°	B-18.0° / M-13.5°	B-16.0° / M-12.0°	B-14.5° / M-11.0°
60°	B-49.5° / M-34.5°	B-37.5° / M-24.5°	B-30.5° / M-19.5°	B-25.5° / M-16.5°	B-21.5° / M-14.0°	B-19.0° / M-12.0°	B-17.0° / M-10.5°	B-15.5° / M- 9.5°
65°	B-52.5° / M-29.0°	B-39.5° / M-21.5°	B-32.0° / M-17.0°	B-26.5° / M-14.0°	B-23.0° / M-12.0°	B-20.0° / M-10.5°	B-18.0° / M- 9.0°	B-16.5° / M- 8.0°
70°	B-55.0° / M-24.0°	B-41.5° / M-17.5°	B-33.5° / M-13.5°	B-28.0° / M-11.5°	B-24.0° / M- 9.5°	B-21.0° / M- 8.5°	B-18.5° / M- 7.5°	B-17.0° / M- 6.5°
75°	B-57.0° / M-18.5°	B-43.0° / M-13.0°	B-34.5° / M-10.5°	B-29.0° / M- 8.5°	B-24.5° / M- 7.0°	B-21.5° / M- 6.5°	B-19.0° / M- 5.5°	B-17.5° / M- 5.0°
80°	B-58.5° / M-13.0°	B-44.0° / M- 9.0°	B-35.5° / M- 7.0°	B-29.5° / M- 6.0°	B-25.0° / M- 5.0°	B-22.0° / M- 4.0°	B-19.5° / M- 3.5°	B-18.0° / M- 4.0°
85°	B-59.5° / M- 7.0°	B-44.5° / M- 4.5°	B-36.0° / M- 3.5°	B-30.0° / M- 3.0°	B-25.5° / M- 2.5°	B-22.5° / M- 2.0°	B-20.0° / M- 1.5°	B-18.0° / M- 1.5°
90°	B-60.0° / M- 0.0°	B-45.0° / M- 0.0°	B-36.0° / M- 0.0°	B-30.0° / M- 0.0°	B-26.0° / M- 0.0°	B-22.5° / M- 0.0°	B-20.0° / M- 0.0°	B-18.0° / M- 0.0°

*The chart gives setting for each combination to the nearest 0.5°. B = bevel. M = miter.

noted that trying to draw a hand saw diagonally across the grain of a board while at the same time angling the blade at, say, 25.7° is no mean feat, especially if the identical cut must be repeated several times.

Straight rip cut. A right angle cut in the direction of the grain, with the blade held at 90°. *Tools:* Table saw, rip saw.

Beveled rip cut. Identical to a straight rip cut, but the blade is held at any angle other than 90°. *Tools:* bench saw, rip saw.

Straight end cut. A slice across the grain into the end of a board. *Tools:* Radial arm saw, crosscut saw.

Straight edge cut. Like an end cut, except that it is made with the grain. *Tools:* bench saw, rip saw.

Bevel end cut. A slice across the grain at any angle other than 90°. *Tools:* Radial arm saw, crosscut saw.

Bevel edge cut. A slice with the grain at any angle other than 90°. *Tools:* bench saw, rip saw.

TABLE 6-2 MITER AND BEVEL ANGLES*

Number of sides	Angle of miter or bevel setting
3	60°
4	45°
5	36°
6	30°
7	25.7°
8	22.5°
9	20°
10	18°

*To compute the miter or bevel setting for any closed construction, divide the number of sides into 180°. The result is the number of degrees that you set your saw blade.

CIRCULAR POWER-SAW BLADES

The blades used with all of the circular power saws are made of tempered steel or such tough alloys as chrome-nickel-molybdenum steel, which have the ability to hold a sharp cutting edge for hundreds of cuts before they must be sharpened. The various configurations of tooth arrangements on these blades have much to do with not only how they cut, but also the condition they leave the edges of the wood after they have done their job. Generally, the more teeth on the blade, the smoother the cut, assuming that the teeth are also sharp.

TUNGSTEN CARBIDE-TIPPED BLADES

A few years ago manufacturers came up with tungsten carbide-tipped blades. Tungsten carbide is a tough alloy that is cobalt bonded for strength, and then each point is individually brazed onto the blade. Then the points are diamond ground to a razor-sharp edge that will last many times longer than other blades before it has to be sharpened. Tungsten carbide-tipped blades cost about twice as much as regular blades so, although the initial layout is higher, there is a savings in sharpening bills and time lost while the blade is off its machine. There is another worthwhile advantage to tungsten carbide-tipped blades; they produce a more controlled and smoother cut than you can get with regular blades.

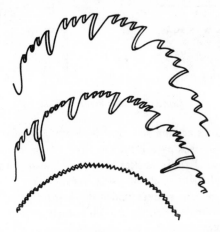

Figure 6-3   Circular power saw blades. A. Combination (48–72 teeth). B. Rip saw (30–36 teeth). C. Plywood/veneer (150–200 teeth).

TOOLS FOR CUTTING

A well-equipped cabinetmaking shop should include several handsaws, a bench and/or radial arm saw, and a band saw. Given one of the stationary saws and the band saw, you can accomplish any straight or curved cut in any material, but there will be times when a jig, or at least a sabre saw, and perhaps even a hand-power saw are handy to have around.

Handsaws

On occasion, a handsaw is necessary, but so far as your pursuit of the right angle is concerned, you will need the services of a plane or a joiner-planer to complete an absolutely accurate cut.

Crosscut saw. A high quality crosscut saw has between 7 and 12 precision ground teeth per inch which are able to slice sharply across the wood fibers. The lower the number of teeth, the faster the saw will work—but it will leave the edges of the cut rough. The more teeth you have, the slower the cut, but also the smoother its edges. As a rule, choose a saw with about 8 points per inch for finer work, and one with 10 points per inch for rough cutting. The teeth are alternately bent outward approximately 1/4 of the blade thickness. This results in a cut that is slightly wider than the thickness of the blade but allows the saw to cut freely.

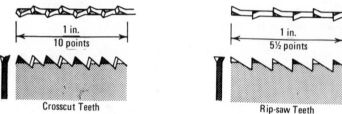

| 1 in. |
| 10 points |

Crosscut Teeth

| 1 in. |
| 5½ points |

Rip-saw Teeth

Figure 6–4　　　　　　　Crosscut blade.　**Figure 6–5**　　　　　　　Ripsaw blade.

To begin a cut, start the saw on the waste side of the marked line and begin with the butt, or back part of the saw (near the handle). Using your thumb as a guide, draw several short strokes to make a starting groove. Then use full strokes with the blade held at about a 45° angle. The crosscut saw cuts on both the forward and backward strokes under its own weight, so the pressure you have to supply is minimal. When finishing a cut always support the waste piece during the final strokes.

Plywood should always be cut with a crosscut saw no matter what direction the surface grain is going.

Rip saw. Typically, the rip saw has between 5-1/2 and 6-1/2 teeth per inch and the blade is 26″ long. Each tooth is shaped like a small chisel with its cutting edge crosswise to the blade. Thus, the teeth actually chop their way between the fibers of the wood. The teeth are also alternately bent, or set about 1/3 of the thickness of the blade to reduce friction during the cut.

To start cutting with a rip saw, use the front of the blade where there are 6 1/2 teeth per inch and pull a few short strokes to start the groove. Since the rip saw cuts only on the forward strokes, it is surprising that as many as 10 feet of pine board can be ripped in about a minute (but your arm will hurt a lot). If the saw drifts away from the guide line (and it will) steer it gradually back on course, do not bend it sharply. There are a couple of tricks to remember when ripping long boards: (1) Put a wedge into the starting end of the cut; (2) Clamp a strip of scrap along the guide line and keep the blade against it as you cut.

Backsaw. The backsaw has a rigid top edge and is between 10″ and 16″ long with 12 or 13 teeth per inch. It produces smooth cuts with, or across the grain; its longer 26″ cousin is customarily used with miter boxes. The purpose of the backsaw is to make the smooth cuts necessary in joinery, so it shows up in miter boxes all the time.

To use a backsaw in a miter box, first mark the wood for cutting, then line the mark up with the slots in the box. Cut on the waste side of the line and hold the wood firmly against the back of the box; start with a single backward stroke of the saw, with the handle lifted slightly. As you proceed, level the blade. The rigidity of the blade is such that it can be drawn across the surface of the wood absolutely parallel to the surface. You really *can* cut rabbets and dadoes with a backsaw but it is hard work and there are plenty of easier ways.

Coping saw. This has between 10 and 20 teeth per inch and its blade can be as narrow as 7/100″. It is used to cut circles or curves in delicate ornamental work or filigree, which makes it invaluable in any area that might be damaged by a power saw. The blades are replaceable and the slant of the teeth depends on how the work is to be cut. If the wood is held vertically in a vice, set the blade so the teeth are away from the handle. Otherwise, use the teeth slanting toward the handle so that they cut on the pull stroke.

Scroll, fret, and deep-throat saws are all coping saws with frame depths of 8″ to 12″ and blades mounted with their teeth slanted toward the handles.

Compass and keyhole saws. Both of these can cut curves, although the keyhole will saw out a smaller diameter hole. Compass saws have 12″ to 14″ blades with 8 to 10 teeth per inch. Keyhole blades are narrower and have 10 teeth per inch with 10″ or 12″ blades. Both will also make straight cuts so they are useful for working in tight places and cutting such things as holes in the back of a finished cabinet. When starting from a bored hole, use short, vertical strokes, then bring the saw to a 45° angle.

Hacksaws. These will cut almost any metal if you have the right blade. Blade choice depends on what is being cut and how thick it is, but in general, coarse teeth are used on thick metal with progressively finer teeth for thinner metals.

Blades should have: 14 teeth per inch for bronze, brass, copper, aluminum, cast iron, or machine steel over 1″ thick; 18 teeth per inch for cutting copper, aluminum, bronze, high-speed, tool, and annealed steel up to 1″ thick; 24 teeth per inch for 1/8″ to 1/2″ iron, steel, wrought iron, brass or copper tubing, drill rod or electrical conduit; and 32 teeth per inch for any of these metals less than 1/8″ thick. Use a wavy set of teeth for thin stock and a regular set for everything else.

The rule to remember with hacksaws is that at least two teeth must be in contact with the metal at all times. So when cutting thin material, hold the saw at an angle that prevents the teeth from hooking in the material and bending it. Always mount the work to be cut in a vice or jig. Make slow strokes at the beginning of the cut using moderate downward pressure on the forward stroke and no pressure at all on the back stroke.

Hand-Power Saws

There are chain saws and reciprocating saws but these would hardly be used in cabinetwork. There are also sabre saws and circular-power saws which men have been known to use as the only cutting equipment during the entire construction of a fine piece of furniture.

Sabre saws. Even with a full complement of band, jig, and table saws in a workshop, there are times when the portability and convenience of a sabre saw are indispensable. A sabre saw can be mounted upside down under a table and used for controlled fret work, but by far, the sabre is at its best cutting circles, curves, and even straight lines. A sabre saw with the proper blade will cut anything from hardened steel to Styrofoam; generally, wide blades are used for straight cuts and narrow ones are used for making curves. Blade lengths vary considerably (2-1/2″ up to 6″), but always choose the shortest blade that will do the job.

It is essential that the sabre saw be held firmly and flat on the work surface and guided slowly through the cut, or the blade will break. When straight cutting, always use a guide or fence. The fence is an accessory that comes with the machine and is attached to its base, but an equally good one can be made by using a piece of scrap clamped or nailed to the stock along the cut line.

	Teeth per Inch	Material	Uses
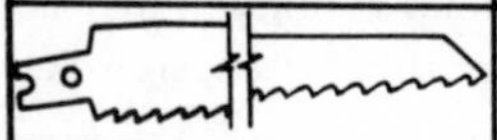	3	lumber	Fast, deep angle cuts in wood up to 6″ thick.
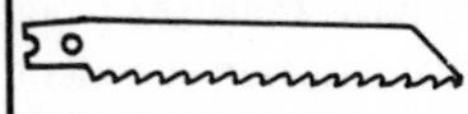	5	lumber	Rough, general cutting, ripping stock up to 2″ thick.
	6	lumber	Same as above, but makes a smoother cut.
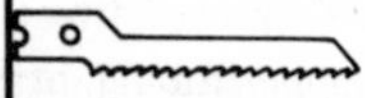	7, 8	lumber, insulation board	General purpose blades primarily for construction work, produces medium-smooth cuts.
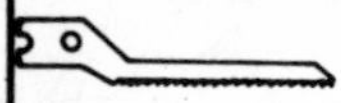	10	hardwoods, composition board, plastics	Scrollwork, finish cuts in plywood or veneer. Smoother cuts, but slower.
	12, 14	plywood, linoleum, rubber tile, hardboards, nylon, plexiglass, fiberglass	Smoothest possible cuts in plywood and fine scrollwork.

Figure 6–6   Sabre-saw blades (9).

	10	wood with nails, asbestos, laminates	The tempered steel this blade is made from helps it stand up to nails.
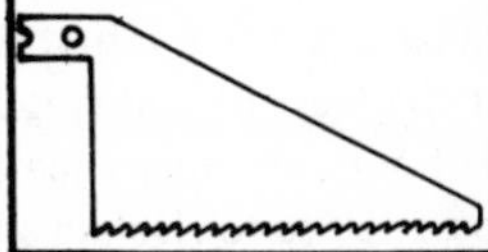	7 flush	lumber	The unusual shape of this blade brings the teeth in front of the baseplate so that it can cut through attached moldings or hard to reach surfaces.
	Knife Edge	leather, cork, cloth, paper, rubber, cardboard, Styrofoam	Be sure the material being cut is firmly supported.
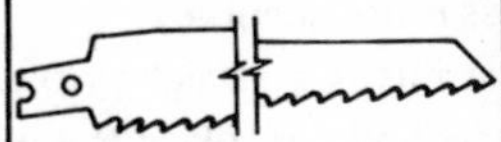	6	aluminum, copper, brass, laminates, compositions	Maximum cut in aluminum is ½"
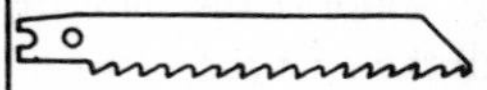	10	same as above	General cutting with a smoother finish.
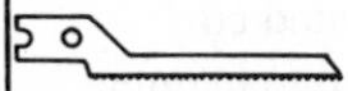	14	aluminum, brass, bronze, copper, laminates, hardboard, steel pipe	General cutting with a smooth finish. Maximum cut in steel is ½".
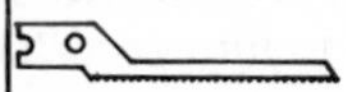	18	same as above	Generally this is best with the lighter metals with a maximum cut of 1/8".
	24	sheet metal, light guage steel, thin walled tubing, tile, all non-ferrous metals	This is wave-set (like a hacksaw blade) and does all the same jobs a hacksaw does.
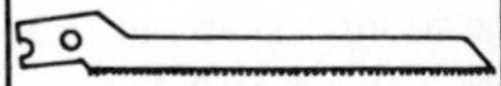	32	mild steel rods, pipe, sheet metal	Also wave-set.

TUNGSTEN-CARBIDE BLADES

These blades have no teeth. Their cutting edges are particles of tungsten-carbide fused to the blade, and they will cut practically anything. They come with fine, medium, and coarse grits and their cutting speed is somewhat slower than toothed blades. When used on wood, they leave an almost sanded cut and are excellent for cutting ceramic tile or slate, as well as produce a minimum of burring in sheet metal.

Figure 6-6. Sabre saw blades [cont'd.]

When sawing out an enclosed opening there are two ways of starting the cut. A hole large enough for the sabre blade can be drilled inside the waste area and then the cut started from there. An alternative method is to plunge cut. This is accomplished by resting the saw on the front edge of its base and turning it on. Slowly rock the saw back and forth until the blade digs through the wood and the saw can be brought back firmly on its base.

Portable power saw. This is the work horse of portable power tools and indispensable for on-site wood working. You need at least a minute to hand cut a 2″ × 4″, and then the cut will probably not be perfect. A circular saw requires seconds to do the same job accurately. Pick up a circular saw for the first time and you will quickly discover a dozen uses for it, not the least of which is cutting rabbets, dadoes, bevels, and miters. Given a few hours of experience and some shop-made jigs, you will be using a tool that comes close to rivaling all of the stationary saws.

The most dependable method of making a rip cut with a portable saw is to clamp or nail a guide to the work. It is possible to cut miters and crosscuts freehand, but a miter box or some kind of guide guarantees more accuracy.

Rabbets involve two passes of the saw. The first cut is a straight rip with the blade set to the depth of the rabbet. To make the second cut, place the work on end and clamp it against anything wide enough to support the base of the saw. The blade is then set deep enough to intersect with the first cut.

Dadoes can be produced with repeated cuts, unless you have a set of dado blades. With a normal blade, use a guide to make the two outside cuts; the material between them can be *routed out* freehand with repeated cuts.

The hand power saw can also be used as a table saw by clamping it to a board on each side of the saw's baseplate. Suspend the boards between saw horses with the blade facing up and tie the trigger in the on position. Then plug the saw into an extension cord with a switch, which is used to turn your "table saw" on and off.

Band Saws

Band saws use a flexible steel blade welded to form a continuous loop that will accurately cut any curve or irregular shape, as well as rip or crosscutting. The size of the band saw is determined by the diameter of the two rubber wheels that the blade moves over; the most common size range found in cabinet shops is between 14″ and 36″. Blades are made in widths from 1/8″ up to 1 1/2″ and in general, the narrower the blade, the more teeth it will have. The narrow blades are used for fretwork and cutting sharp curves; wider ones are better for large radius curves, straight cutting, and resawing.

When operating the band saw, stand facing the blade and slightly to one side of it. The upper blade guide should be between 1/4″ to 1/2″ above the work, and the wood is fed past the blade as quickly as it will cut. Unlike other stationary saws, feeding work too slowly into a bandsaw tends to burn the blade.

The most distinctive feature of the band saw is that it requires a certain amount of skill before it can be used successfully. You must watch the feed carefully and plan each cut ahead of time, because the stock will tend to swing and you may find yourself wasting time backtracking along the cut. Develop the habit of making all short cuts before any long ones so there will be a minimum of backing out, and whenever possible cut through waste stock rather than back-tracking. You can also save some trouble by drilling turn around holes at various places in the design, at the corners of a rectangular cut, for example. And try to divide complicated curves into a series of short, relief cuts, rather than fight your wat through the work with one continuous cut. Beeswax applied to the blade will sometimes assist in cutting hardwood or a piece that has an inordinate amount of pitch.

Most band saws are equipped with a tilting table for beveling, as well as a fence used for ripping and resawing; the fence is actually used only with the wide blades. The advantage of a band saw is that the blade is capable of cutting thicker material with a narrower saw kerf, and thus wastes less material. When ripping, either the fence or a guide can be attached to the saw table, or use your thumb to hold the stock on the cut line.

Resawing is the act of cutting stock into thinner pieces and it is here that the band saw excels. The most practical method of resawing is to clamp a pivot pin to the front of the table or use the guide fence. Resawing can be done at a 45° angle merely by tilting the table. Circles or curves are easier to cut freehand, but keep the cut at least 1/32" outside the guide line so there is ample stock to sand. There is no particular problem in cutting several identical pieces if you set up a jig or a patterned guide that forces each piece of stock to follow the same directions. Or, you can produce multiple pieces by cutting the shape out of thick stock and then resawing it to the correct thickness.

Jigsaw

The jigsaw, or scroll saw, is a smaller version of the band saw, used primarily for model or filigree work. It is capable of extremely small radial cuts and with the proper blade will cut plastics, metal, and, of course, wood. The table on most models can be tilted for making beveled cuts.

Blades for the jigsaw divide into three types: the fret or power-jig blade, sabre blades, and the jeweler's piercing blade. The jeweler's and fret blades are mounted both top and bottom, while the sabre blade is a thicker blade locked into the machine via the bottom chuck and used for ripping or cutting large in-side curves. All jigsaws are made to cut on the *downstroke* which means that the blades are always mounted with their teeth pointing downward. It also means that the adjustable hold down must lightly touch the stock, since the wood will tend to lift off the table with the blade as it rises in the upstroke. It should be remembered that this downward stroke will splinter the bottom veneer of a piece of plywood, so when cutting plywood always have the good face up.

Some tips on cutting. Always apply slight pressure to get the stock started in waste stock, i.e., a kind of working margin and then cut to the guide line. Never force the stock into the blade and never turn the stock too sharply when cutting a curve, or the blade may break. When making an internal cut, drill a hole large enough for the blade but not too close to the guide line. The blade must be released from its top chuck and inserted in the hole before cutting can begin. Straight cutting is normally done only on small pieces since it is difficult to follow long, straight lines on a jigsaw.

When cutting thin metal there is liable to be excessive blade breakage. A way of minimizing this is to sandwich the metal between pieces of thin wood, along with a sheet of waxed paper. Draw the cutting design on the wood and then saw the entire sandwich. The wax paper will help lubricate the blade and prevent it from chipping the metal.

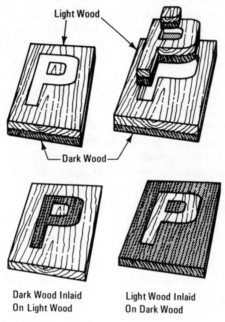

Light Wood

Dark Wood

Dark Wood Inlaid
On Light Wood

Light Wood Inlaid
On Dark Wood

Figure 6-7 Cut out an inlay and its hole at the same time with a slight bevel, to fit the pieces snugly together.

Bevel cuts can be made simply by tilting the saw table. But remember that the saw blade must always remain on the same side of the stock; if the material is swung around the blade, the bevel will change direction. A beveled cut is also an excellent way of hiding the saw kerf. If a simple inlay is being made, nail the stock used for the inset with the stock that is to accept it. Then cut out the inlay and its inset part at the same time, using a one- or two-degree bevel. The inlay will fit snugly into its hole and the kerf will hardly be visible. If you want the joint to bind even better, lightly sand the edges of both the inlay and the hole.

Table Saws

The table saw is the cabinetmaker's basic implement. With it, everything from rips, crosscuts, miters, bevels, compounds, chamfers, tapers, kerfs, and rabbets

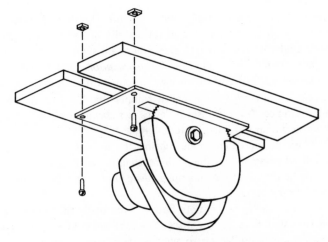

Figure 6-8   A portable handsaw can be clamped to the underside of a pair of boards to function as a table saw.

are all natural operations. Add dado blades and a molding head and almost any joint or contoured shaping becomes about as easy as pushing stock past the blade; devise a few special jigs and your table saw will even cut circles, turn wood, and make decorative designs.

True, a table saw will do all of the above. But it does them grudgingly. It screeches and snarls and fires pieces of stock back at you with astounding velocity. It is a dangerous beast poised with infinite patience, waiting for the opportunity to chew off the tip of any finger that passes too near its bared teeth. Table saws are built to cut with precision, but they will surely take their pound of flesh if you give them the least chance. So the best way of coexisting with your table saw is to always think, "safety" first.

The size of a table saw is determined by the diameter of its blade and these range from 8″ to 16″. The 10″ size is most commonly found in cabinet shops, although the 8″ is quite sufficient. The great advantage of table saws is that they have very few moving parts that can cause the blade and its guides to be out of alignment. Each saw comes equipped with a rip fence which is slid on rails toward the blade, and the table has two slots used for sliding the miter gauge needed when crosscutting. Depending on the model, the table is either tilted for bevel cuts, or the entire blade and motor assembly are moveable; the blade can also be raised or lowered.

The work is always fed into the blade with the operator standing to one side so that when errant pieces of stock are hurled back at him they will do no bodily harm. Whenever possible the safety guard should be used over the blade, although there are numerous instances when the guard is a hindrance, particularly when cutting small pieces. The danger is that the smaller the piece, the closer your fingers must come to the blade. So when doing close work always reach for some kind of support that will keep the saw in line and your hands attached to your wrists.

Ripping anything is the table saw's long suit. The stock is slid along the rip fence and although it will try to pull toward the blade, it can usually be kept pretty much under control. Nevertheless, there are some accessories that are invaluable when ripping on a table saw. A *roller support* can be built in your shop and stood at the outfeed end of the saw to support the cut stock. When ripping narrow stock, use a *push stick* which is thinner than the distance between the blade and the fence. Another useful device is a *spring board* which is merely a piece of wood which has been kerfed along a 45° angle. The "feather" end of the piece is flexible and when applied against the edge of a board being ripped, it will help to hold wood against the guide fence either vertically or horizontally. A second spring board can also be clamped vertically to the fence to hold the stock firmly down on the table.

Any stock that is 5″ or more between the blade and fence is considered *wide stock;* less than 5″ is *narrow stock.* The problem with most table-saw fences is that they cannot be relied on to tighten down at an exact right angle to the blade. There are tightening knobs at both ends of the fence to make certain that when it is in position it will stay there, but you should always measure it to be sure it is true. To be sure the rip fence is parallel with the blade, raise the blade to its fullest height and measure the desired distance from the back of the blade to the fence, then from the front of the blade. Or lay a roofing square along the front edge of the table and the fence, then measure the distance from the blade to the fence. When the fence is set at the proper distance from the blade, lower the blade until it is no more than 1/8″ or 1/4″ above the stock. The wood can be pushed through the blade as rapidly as the saw will cut it.

When sawing narrow stock, always use a push stick. Or saw through half of the wood, then pull it back from the blade and turn it over to saw the other half. In either instance, the object is to keep your fingers away from those hungry blade teeth.

Crosscutting on a table saw always requires the use of the miter gauge, which can be set at any angle and also bolted to a longer piece of wood to provide more stability for all types of cuts. The gauge is normally used in the left slot with the slide forward, and the stock held firmly against the gauge. Be careful to hold the stock very tightly, particularly when cutting an angle, and feed the work through the blade slowly or the stock will tend to slip backwards and result in a less than perfect cut.

The table saw will serve its user day in and day out, cutting bevels, miters, rips, and crosscuts. But with the addition of several specialty jigs it will do even more. Aside from the standard push stick and spring board, you can construct such useful jigs as an adjustable trough for handling narrow work that has to be resawed or molded. The step jig is an alternative to the kind of taper jig which can be purchased (or made). In either case, the jig is slid past the blade as it holds the work in position.

Tenoning jigs come in many forms. Any design is good as long as it holds the work firmly and provides a measure of safety. No matter how you make it,

Figure 6-9

The table or bench saw.

be certain that the vertical guide is at right angles to the saw table and never try to hold the work against it when it can be clamped. A V-shaped jig is useful for working on circular stock, whether you are shaping it, routing it, or rounding off the curve with a regular blade. Another way of cutting a circle is to clamp a board to the table top, then drive a pivot nail through the center of the circle. The blade depth must be such that it cuts no more than 1/16″ as the stock is rotated very slowly. Raise the blade 1/16″ at a time until the circle is completely cut. This same technique can be used with a dado blade or molding head, to perform a variety of routing, dadoing, rabbeting, beveling, and chamfering. Still another method for working on the edge of a circle is to pin it against a vertical support.

Tips on making jigs. Table-saw jigs must always be constructed so that every angle is precisely what it is supposed to be. When designing a jig, remember that its primary purpose is to give you a wider margin of safety and to support the work so that you can cut it as accurately as possible. Always consider putting blocks on the bottom of every jig which fit in the miter gauge slots; and add a lip or two to the jig that will allow you to clamp the jig to the fence or table.

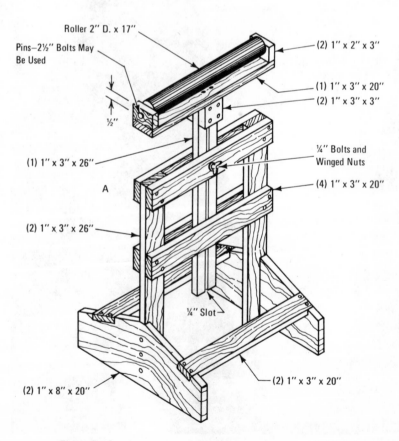

Figure 6-10 Plans for a simple roller support.

Radial Arm Saws

The cuts that a table saw has difficulty performing, the radial arm does without effort, and vice versa. Crosscuts, miters, and compounds which demand involved setting up and even jigs on a table saw are automatic operations with a radial

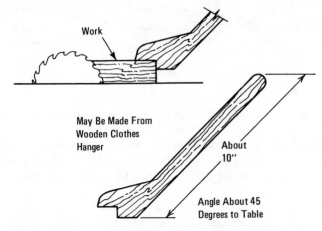

Work

May Be Made From
Wooden Clothes
Hanger

About
10"

Angle About 45
Degrees to Table

Figure 6-11   A push stick made from scrap wood.

arm. Dadoing, shaping, and molding are easier with a radial arm; ripping is easier and more accurate with a table saw. Because most radials have a chuck accessory that fits on the back of the motor shaft, the machine can also act as a drill press or router, two functions the table saw does not offer.

The radial arm also has a great many moveable parts, so that the arm can rotate $360°$ and the motor can do complete somersaults. All those parts involve a ton of screws and bolts, any of which will loosen at any time, which means the blade alignment must constantly be checked. Nevertheless, the radial is certainly easier and just as accurate as a table saw when crosscutting or mitering, since it is the saw blade you move, not that $20'$ board.

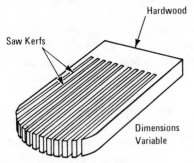

Hardwood

Saw Kerfs

Dimensions
Variable

Figure 6-12   Spring boards.

The advantage of holding your work stationary when crosscutting with a radial arm vanishes with ripping operations. When ripping on a radial, you must feed the work from one side of the saw, then reach around the motor to hold the stock after it passes the blade. With large boards that is not too much of a problem, provided there is support for the work on both sides of the saw. But smaller work has a tendency to pull away from the fence.

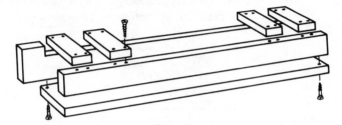

Figure 6-13   A trough used for holding narrow work.

The radial and its accessories. There are numerous designs of radial arm saws. Typically, the motor and blade ride back and forth on an overhead arm which in turn can be rotated 360°. The size of the saw is determined by the

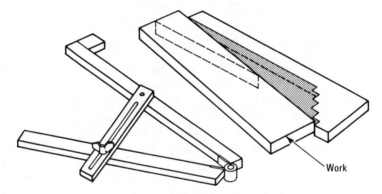

Work

Figure 6-14   Both the taper and step jigs must be pushed past the saw blade as they hold the work.

blade diameter and the horsepower of its motor; the common sizes used in cabinetmaking are 10″ and 12″. The accessories that can be purchased for a radial arm saw begin with dado blades, molder heads, and sanding disks, then go on to a chuck for the back of the motor shaft that allows the machine to be used as a drill or router.

Cutting. Everything done on a radial arm requires a different setting for the motor and arm. When crosscutting, the blade is pulled toward the operator while the stock is held firmly in place against the guide fence. If you want to miter, the arm is swung to the left or right and locked in place at 45° (or whatever angle you require); then the blade is pulled toward the operator at that angle. To make a bevel cut, the motor and blade assembly are tilted to the required angle. Then the motor is pulled through the stock. Crosscutting is done

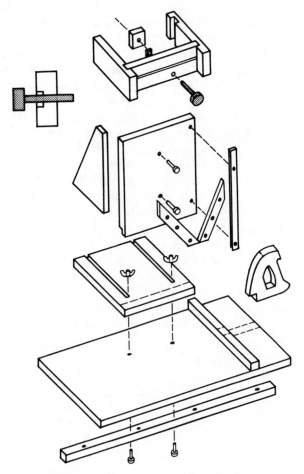

Figure 6-15   Tenoning jigs.

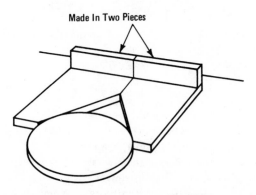

Made In Two Pieces

Figure 6-16   The V-jig.

by rotating the motor 90° until it is parallel with the guide fence and then locked in position on the arm at whatever distance from the fence you wish. The wood is then pushed past the blade as it is on a table saw.

In some cases, ripping, molds, dadoes, and rabbets are easier to do with a table saw. But even then, the dado blades or molding head can always be seen on a radial saw, which means you never have to "work blind;" you have better control over where they are going.

The radial has some added capabilities such as drilling, routing, and sanding. Circular sanding discs can be used on either saw, although with the radial it is mandatory that an elevation table be used.

The radial arm can also cut arcs and circles with the slight advantage that because the blade is cranked down into the stock 1/8" at a time, you are again, never working blind. A useful accessory when working with curved pieces is a V-jig. As with any stationary tool, never hesitate to spend the time inventing a special jig as the need arises. A pair of elevation tables that can be positioned on either side of the motor and used for end cutting, sanding, shaping, or molding are a useful addition to a radial saw. A nail driven through the center of the work and the saw table will permit you to cut out circles, as well as do routing and shaping. As an alternative, set up a V-jig.

The ideal arrangement, of course, is to have both a radial arm and a table saw. You set one up for ripping and the other for crosscutting, minimizing work time and errors.

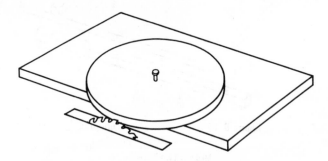

Figure 6-17   A pivot nail for cutting circles.

CUTTING

Plan your cutting so that you will have a minimum number of blade changes or jig set ups; the jigs should be anticipated and constructed before you begin any sawing in earnest. Whenever possible, if a number of identically-sized pieces are to be cut, clamp a stop block to the saw table so that every piece held against it will be cut with exactly the same dimensions without having to measure each piece. As a matter of reality, a stop block is quicker and more accurate than measuring every individual piece.

Figure 6-18   The radial-arm saw.

Plywood

Plywood must always be given special consideration. If you are using either a band, table, or radial-arm saw, the face veneer must be up, because the blades on all three machines come down on top of the wood. But with a hand power saw, always cut with the good side down. Plywood in its panel size of 4' X 8' (or 12') is a mean material to deal with until it has been reduced to manageable pieces. Try to position your first cut or two with this end in mind.

If you are faced with cutting a plywood panel on any stationary saw without a helper, your first cut or two should be just a rough rip that divides the panel in some manner. Even with full support on both sides of the saw, it is difficult to feed a full panel accurately past the blade. If that first dividing cut must be precise, the best approach is to nail two straight edges on either side of the guide line to form a channel for a hand power saw. Even with this there will be some planing, or at least sanding to be done afterward.

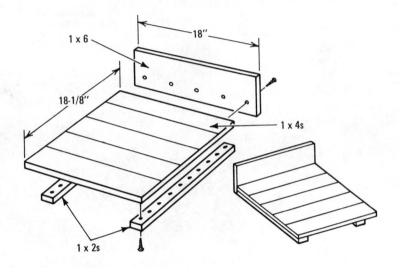

Figure 6-19   Elevation tables for a radial-arm saw.

The cutting procedure should go from all of the short cuts to all of the long cuts (whenever possible). If there is any beveling or mitering to do, reset the saw and then do all of it at one time. If you are making drawers and doors, their parts can be cut and assembled as separate projects so the stack for these can be kept aside until the basic unit is assembled. Or they can be constructed first and then the cabinet built around them.

Sawing is a form of engineering, while joinery is more of an art. It should be approached with care, this act of dividing nature's bounty into bits and pieces. Be inaccurate with your saw, and 99 times out of 100 the entire project will be inaccurate.

Presuming the tools that you use are accurately aligned, any errors that arise are *your* fault. They result when you do not position the wood properly, or hold it firmly enough, or demand too much of the saw. They result from a lack of attention on your part, not from any machine malfunction. People like to say, "The computer made a mistake." Computers are never wrong; only the people who run them make errors. Every power-cutting machine is a computer. If it is in proper working condition, if it is correctly aligned, in almost every instance the mistakes it makes will be the direct result of your inattentiveness to the minutiae of precision.

Figure 6-20   Rough cut lumber stacked according to the joinery cuts.

Review Questions

1. What saws can you use for cutting curves?
2. Which saw will cut a 4′ × 8′ plywood panel in half with the least amount of effort and the most accuracy?
3. Compare and contrast the radial arm saw with the table saw.
4. When would you use a compound crosscut?
5. Determine the miter angles in a pentagon.
6. What is the single most important angle in cabinetmaking? Why?
7. List the human, mechanical, and natural factors that must be overcome when you are cutting a right angle.
8. Why is a band saw considered the best tool for resawing?
9. What is the difference between a sabre saw and a jigsaw?
10. If you could possess only one power saw, which one would you choose? Why?

Dado blades and sets.

Chapter 7

Joinery

As a cabinetmaker you must be thoroughly familiar with all of the more than 100 joints well-known in the craft and be able to evaluate which of these joints offers the best union of pieces in a specific given project. Your choice depends on several factors, not the least of which are the need for strength at each point in the piece, the appearance you wish the joint to have, and the equipment available to you for making the joint you elect to use.

By definition, a joint is "the securing or fastening together of two or more *smooth, even* surfaces." Generally, it is wisest to opt for the simplest joints that will provide the necessary strength. Inevitably, your decision may also be determined by the cost of the materials used, equipment available, and the amount of time and work needed to perfect the joint. Thus, while the mortise-and-tenon is regarded as perhaps the strongest of all joints, furniture manufacturers often substitute it for a dowel and butt union, because doweling is quicker, wastes less material, and has been proven to be every bit as strong.

THE ELEMENTS OF JOINERY

There are some fundamental principles to observe when making joints:

1. Take all of your measurements from the same starting point, such as an edge or the center of one of the pieces.

2. Always use the method of superimposing one piece of wood on top of another when laying out a joint. For example, the width of a rabbet or dado is determined by holding the edge of the piece to be fitted in the dado against the piece to be cut, and then tracing it. This method is more accurate than measuring.

3. Always mark all duplicate parts at the same time, and cut them together whenever possible. Thus, if the stiles of a frame are to be doweled, clamp the pieces together and mark all of them. Then drill all of them before the clamps are removed.

Figure 7-1   Marking joints to be cut.

4. When working with solid wood, remember that it constantly swells and shrinks. Always allow space for the fitted part to change its size in the joint. The surfaces of the joint, in most instances, should fit snugly, but the ends can be slightly undercut to allow the fitted part space to expand. The shelf in a cabinet should fit snugly in its dado, but make it a fraction narrower than the width of the case so that it can expand without splitting the sides of the dado or the cabinet.

5. Always use the simplest joint that will provide the strength needed.

Figure 7-2.   A spiral grooved dowel.

Fastening Joints

Most joints are fastened with glue, and sometimes screws; nails are rarely used in any exposed surface of fine furniture, although they can be used in glue blocks, drawer guides, or other hidden parts of the project. But aside from the metal fasteners, there are other ways of strengthening and fastening glued joints.

Dowels

The dowel is a pin or peg, made of wood, plastic, or metal, that is inserted into the matching surfaces of a joint. Wooden dowels are normally made of hickory, birch, or maple and their diameters range from 1/8″ to 1″. You can buy wooden dowels in lengths of 3′. You can also purchase individual dowel pins made of wood or plastic with a spiral groove and pointed ends. The grooves permit the glue to move freely around the dowel when it is inserted in its holes, and actually provide more gluing surface. Right angle, spiraled plastic dowels are also sold for use in miter joints.

Always store wooden dowels in a warm, dry place, since the dryer they are, the better they will work. A dry dowel will absorb moisture from the glue, swell, and form a tighter union in its hole; a dowel with more than a 5 percent moisture content will eventually dry and shrink, causing the joint to fail.

Dowel sizes. The diameter of a dowel should be between one third and one half the thickness of the wood into which it is being inserted, and its length should be from 1/8″ to 1/4″ shorter than the combined depth of the two holes

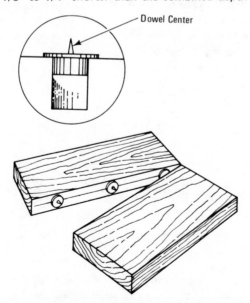

Figure 7-3 Hole alignment for dowel joints. The pin in the middle of a dowel center ensures accurate positioning for the second hole.

that hold it. One dowel should never be used alone. Dowels are always placed in at least pairs to provide maximum strength to the joint.

Making a dowel joint. A good dowel joint depends on precise hole alignment, and on the holes being exactly at right angles; if the holes are not properly drilled, the matching surfaces cannot line up correctly. The best way of making certain the holes are both straight and in line is to drill them on a drill press or with a radial-arm saw, while they are held tightly in a jig or clamped to the guard fence.

You can also drill dowel holes freehand with a hand borer or electric drill, but still clamp the work. The best way of lining up the holes is to drill the holes in one of the two matching surfaces, then insert metal dowel centers in them. Dowel centers can be purchased in a variety of diameters to fit snugly in whatever size hole you drill. The face of the center has a sharp prong on it which pokes into the matching surface when the two gluing faces are brought together. The holes made by the dowel centers become the center of the holes to be drilled. But you still have to drill everything perpendicular to the wood surfaces.

Splines

A spline is a thin piece of solid stock, plywood, hardboard, metal, or plastic which is inserted in a matching groove in the two surfaces of a joint. Splines are most often found in miter joints, although they are excellent for strengthening an edge-butt joint, where two boards are joined along their length. Typically, the grooves are about 1/8" wide and 1/2" deep and can be cut with a dado blade or a regular saw blade on either a radial arm or table saw. They should be positioned down the center of the wood in an edge-butt joint or a flat miter. With a corner miter, the spline is placed close to the inside corner. The spline should be cut so that its grain runs in the same direction as the grain of the joint.

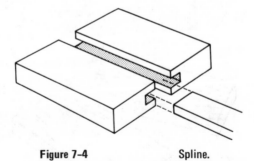

Figure 7-4   Spline.

Key or Feather

A key is a small piece of wood inserted in the center of a joint to give the joint added strength. It is, essentially, a pint-sized spline, and is most often inserted across the outside corners of a miter joint. The grooves are cut with a dado or regular circular saw blade and all of the rules observed when making a spline are applicable to cutting and assembling keys.

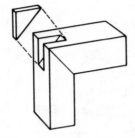

Figure 7–5   Key or feather.

Glue Blocks

Glue blocks are small, triangular, or square pieces of wood which are glue-nailed/
screwed behind a joint to support the adjoining surfaces. They are placed wherever the cabinetmaker feels there should be added strength in a given project,
but are commonly found under the bottoms of drawers, table tops, and furniture legs.

Figure 7–6   Glue blocks.

Corner Blocks

Corner blocks are normally too large to be solid pieces of wood that fit neatly
into a corner. More often, they are set against the corners of, say, a chair at a
45° angle to span the back of the leg, thereby forming a triangle. The ends of a
corner block are mitered and fastened with screws and glue. Or, the ends may fit
into dadoes. There are, however, numerous metal corner blocks that can be purchased, all of which serve the same purpose of strengthening the leg corners of
any piece of furniture.

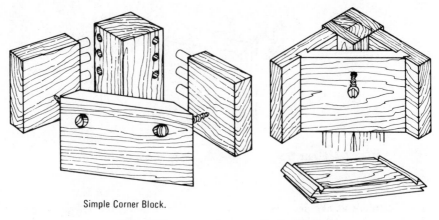

Simple Corner Block.

Figure 7-7   Corner blocks.

Joint-cutting Tools

The tools that are used for cutting joints include planes, chisels, hammers, jointer-planers, routers, shapers, files, rasps, and perhaps most important of all, dado blades. Making any joint with hand-tools is hard, time-consuming, and imprecise work. Anytime you can avoid it, shun the hand-tools. Your task, when cutting a joint, is to produce two matching surfaces that are both even and smooth. You have consistently better chances of perfection if you can use a power tool to do the cutting. Even with that, you may have to sand the gluing surfaces, but at least the basic cuts should be even.

Dado Blades

Any cabinetmaker who intends to make a lot of joints ought to have a dado blade or dado set. Dado blades will cut dadoes, rabbets, grooves, tenons, and lap joints, which combine to make up about 90 percent of all the joinery cutting you will ever do. (See Figure 7-8, and Chapter 7 frontispiece)

There are several single unit dado heads available. You can adjust one of these merely by setting a dial which angles the blade on the saw arbor so that it will cut any width groove from 1/8″ to 13/16″. Many of these one-unit blades have carbide-tipped teeth; all of them produce a straight, smooth slot in the wood and are somewhat easier to use because they do not have to be taken off the saw to be reset.

You can also buy dado sets which consist of two outside blades and several inside cutters, or chippers. By assembling the chippers on your saw arbor between the cutters, you can cut the same groove widths as you can with the one-unit blades. However, the outside cutters are manufactured 1/16″ larger than the chippers, so that any groove the assembly cuts will have two 1/8″ wide grooves extending along its corners to act as troughs for excess glue. The dado sets

Figure 7–8   Dado blades and sets.

require a lot of time to change the cutters and chippers on the saw arbor, and they do not have carbide tips, which means they must be sharpened more often.

The dado blades can be used on a hand-power saw as well as on a radial arm or table saw. In any case, the blade is treated the same way as a standard blade, except that it rarely is used to sever the wood, so it never extends beyond the saw by as much as the thickness of the stock being cut.

Cutting dadoes. Dadoes are grooves or slots cut at right angles to the wood grain and because they are crosscuts, they are most conveniently done with a radial-arm saw. The dado can be any depth but should be wide enough so that the stock to be inserted in it fits snugly.

Grooves or ploughs are dadoes that run with the wood grain. Since they are essentially rip cuts, you might think that it would be easier to make them on a table saw. That may be true in many instances but controlling stock on a radial arm as it is being ploughed is not as difficult as normal ripping. And with the radial arm you have the advantage of seeing where the blade is going.

Routers

A router can make fancy edges, trim plastic laminates, and cut a host of joints. The cuts produced by a router rarely need any smoothing. However, the portable router is, of necessity, so powerful it will literally get out of hand and go roaring off in all directions unless you keep it firmly in check. Thus, almost every one of the router accessories you can buy is oriented toward some way of keeping the machine in control. Even so, unless you are using a specific free-hand accessory such as a laminate trimmer or a jamb and door butt template, it is best to clamp at least one, and preferably, two guides to your work. Better still, if you have a drill press or radial-arm saw, use them with your router bits for as much of the work as you can.

While you can buy router bits that will make a variety of joints, the router's most important contribution to joinery is the *dovetail template.* The template costs about thirty dollars but is the only sensible way of making dovetail joints; it will, in fact, let you make dovetails by the hundreds without a single error.

Joints

There are more than 100 joints known to woodworkers, but most of them are variations and combinations of ten basic ways of joining wood, each of which has different advantages and uses.

Butt Joint

Description. When two pieces of wood come together they form a butt joint. They can meet side by side on the same plane or form an angle. Since only two flat surfaces meet, the butt is weaker than most joints and should have some added form of support. Butts are normally glued and nailed or screwed.

Uses. Right-angled butt joints are typical in framing, boxes, or molding. Straight butt joints are used when two or more boards are joined to each other along their edges.

Assembly. Because the butt joint is inherently weak, it is best to support it with some kind of backing such as glue blocks. The matching edges must be smooth and touch at all points, and the glue should be spread evenly over the entire surface.

Tools. A butt is made with any saw. Sanding or planing may be necessary to assure absolutely even gluing surfaces.

Variations. The edge butt is strengthened appreciably when used in conjunction with a spline or dowels.

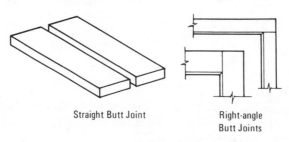

Straight Butt Joint

Right-angle
Butt Joints

Figure 7-9   Butt joints.

Dado

Description. One of the stablest and strongest of all wood joints. It is a square trough cut in a piece of wood which is wide enough to accept a second piece fitted into it. The dadoed stock is weakened only until the slot is filled and glued. Dadoes cut along the grain are known as *ploughs.*

Uses. Dadoes are invariably used in shelf assembly, since they both hold the shelf and help the entire project attain its right angles. Dadoes are also used when recessing hardware, such as hinges, and as slots (or ploughs) for the panels in frame and panel construction.

Assembly. A dado is always glued. Screws or nails may be toed into the filling member or driven through the outside of the dadoed piece.

Tools. Dado blades are specifically made for cutting dadoes and ploughs. Multiple passes with a regular saw blade will also cut a dado. Dado-router bits, dado-chipping tools, handsaws, and chisels can also be used to cut dadoes.

Variations. When cut to the width of a half-lap, the dado is an excellent way of joining leg braces. Housed dado joints provide an extra gluing surface plus more rigidity. The stopped-dado is really a decorative feature when the cabinet has no facings to hide a dado joint.

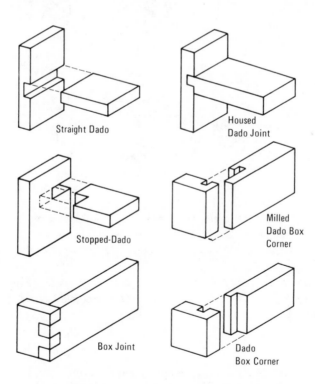

Straight Dado

Housed Dado Joint

Stopped-Dado

Milled Dado Box Corner

Box Joint

Dado Box Corner

Figure 7-10   Dadoes.

Dovetail

Description. The time-honored drawer joint, made by hand for centuries, some dovetails have been around for thousands of years. Each side of a dovetail has a row of evenly spaced, triangular-shaped tenons which fit into corresponding holes in the matching piece.

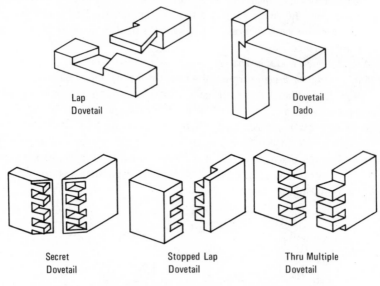

Lap
Dovetail

Dovetail
Dado

Secret
Dovetail

Stopped Lap
Dovetail

Thru Multiple
Dovetail

Figure 7-11   Dovetails.

Uses. Dovetails are primarily used to join the corners of drawers, small boxes, and much larger projects as well.

Assembly. The joints should be glued, but the flared shape of the tenons will allow them to hold without fasteners of any sort. By rounding the edges of the tenons and boring a hole vertically through the tenons for a dowel, you can turn a joint into a decorative hinge.

Tools. Router, drill press, radial-arm saw, flared-router bit, and a dovetail template. The template holds both pieces of wood while the router bit cuts the necessary tenons and mortises simultaneously. You will need 60 seconds to cut an average drawer joint.

Variations. There are numerous variations including the lap dovetail, dovetail dado, through single dovetail, secret dovetail, stopped lap dovetail, through multiple dovetail, and the half-blind dovetail.

Lap

Description. When two pieces of wood overlap each other you have a lap joint. The term *lap* assumes that the overlapping sections have been dadoed so that they are flush and attain the same thickness as the rest of the stock. It is the

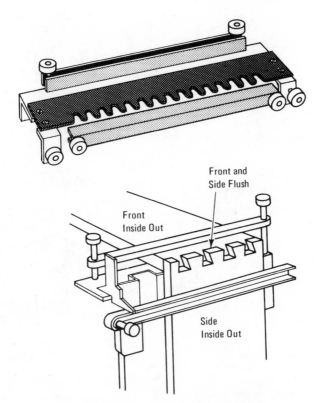

Figure 7-12   Dovetail template.

simplest of all joints to make and is often combined with other joints.

Uses. Excellent for leg supports and strengthening corners.

Assembly. Matching edges of the joint should be smooth and completely covered with glue. Nails or screws can also be used.

Tools. Any saw, dado blade, plane, chisel, or if under duress, sander can make lap joints.

Variations. The lap is so accommodating it will combine with almost all joints. For example, there are middle laps, end laps, middle lap on edge with grooves, dovetail laps, scarf laps, tee laps, and edge-cross laps.

Miter

Description. Strictly speaking, the miter is a butt joint that is any angle other than 90° or 180°, but in common usage the term usually means 45°. The miter is stronger than a butt if only because there is more gluing surface in a slanted cut. Miters are often combined with other joints, to give them more strength.

Uses. The miter is a part of the basic construction in practically all cabinet work. The ends, tops, sides, and fronts of furniture are typically joined by decorative 45° miters; nearly all moldings and decorative work are mitered.

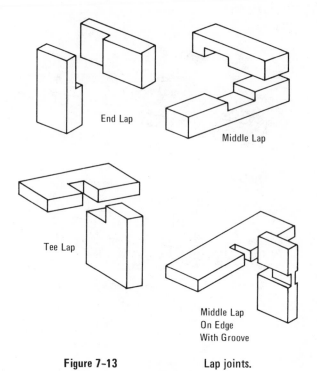

End Lap

Middle Lap

Tee Lap

Middle Lap
On Edge
With Groove

Figure 7-13 Lap joints.

Miters are also used extensively when joining two pieces having the same thickness but different widths.

Assembly. Miters must touch at all points and be fully glued. Nails or screws can be driven into either side of the joint.

Tools. A miter box is a necessary guide when cutting a miter with anything other than a table or radial-arm saw. Some planing or sanding may be needed to achieve complete contact between gluing surfaces.

Variations. Miters can be used with dowels, mortises, splines, half laps, rabbets, and haunches.

Mortise and Tenon

Description. This is the surest of all joints and has been used for years to hold bridges and houses together, as well as furniture. The mortise is a rectangular hole bored in one of the pieces. The tenon is an oblong peg cut out of the matching piece. If the pieces fit snugly, there is no need for glue or fasteners. Using mortise and tenon joints makes any project nearly indestructible.

Uses. Cabinet facings, furniture rungs, door frames, frame and panel construction nearly always use some form of the mortise and tenon. Any joint which requires exceptional strength is a candidate for a mortise and tenon.

Assembly. Be careful that the mortise and its tenon are in precise alignment. Glue and nails or screws are optional, depending on how the joint is used.

Tools. The *mortise* is made with augers, router bits, or drills and a chisel to square off the round corners. The easiest way to drill a mortise is on a mortise machine, but nobody except furniture manufacturers can afford them. Alternatively, a mortise attachment can be purchased for about twenty dollars and used on a drill press or radial-arm saw. The attachment is designed to drill holes and square them off simultaneously.

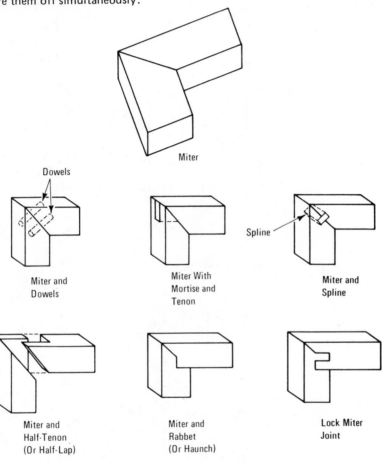

Miter

Dowels

Miter and Dowels

Miter With Mortise and Tenon

Spline

Miter and Spline

Miter and Half-Tenon (Or Half-Lap)

Miter and Rabbet (Or Haunch)

Lock Miter Joint

Figure 7-14   Miter joints.

The *tenon* is cut with a dado blade or multiple passes of a regular blade on a radial-arm or table saw. A handsaw and chisel will also cut tenons.

Variations. If you get tired of thinking up ways to make lap joints, you can always play around with the mortise and tenon. There are many exotic forms such as the bare-faced tenon, haunched tenon, molded and rabbeted joint, mitered tenon, open-mortise tenon, long- and short-shouldered tenon, concealed-haunched tenon and the through-wedged tenon.

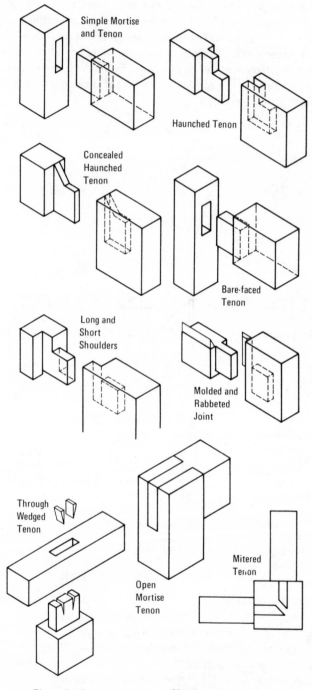

Simple Mortise and Tenon

Haunched Tenon

Concealed Haunched Tenon

Bare-faced Tenon

Long and Short Shoulders

Molded and Rabbeted Joint

Through Wedged Tenon

Open Mortise Tenon

Mitered Tenon

Figure 7-15   Mortise and tenon joints.

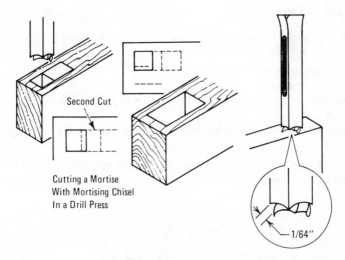

Second Cut

Cutting a Mortise
With Mortising Chisel
In a Drill Press

1/64"

Figure 7-16   Mortising attachment for drill press, radial-arm saw, or hand-power drill.

Rabbet

Description. The rabbet is an L-shaped notch cut out of the edge of one piece which conforms to the thickness (or the notch) of the stock that will fit into it. Rabbets are really a dado that fell off the side of the wood. They are stronger than a butt joint because they provide one extra gluing surface. Nails or screws can be driven into either side of a rabbet.

Uses. The rabbet is a common joint at cabinet corners. It is used in window frames, to recess cabinet backs, and for joining the tops of boxes to their sides.

Assembly. When cutting a rabbet, set the dado blade wide enough to overhang the work. Glue, as well as nails or screws can be used with a rabbet.

Tools. The preferred tool is a dado blade. Rabbets can also be cut with two intersecting passes of a regular saw blade. Jointers, routers, and shapers all make rabbets, as well as radial-arm, table, and hand-power saws.

Variations. Rabbets are sometimes combined with miter and mortise and tenon joints.

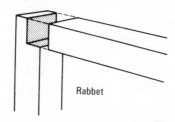

Rabbet

Figure 7-17   Rabbet joints.

Spline (Feather, Tongue)

Description. The spline is a thin strip of wood used to reinforce such joints as the butt and miter. Actually, it is a modified tongue-and-groove, having both sides of the joint grooved to accept it.

Uses. To strengthen other joints.

Assembly. Aligned grooves are cut into both gluing surfaces. The spline is glued into the grooves.

Tools. A dado blade is preferable for cutting the grooves, although multiple passes with standard blades will suffice.

Variations. The feather is a triangle that fits into only part of the joint, usually the corner of a miter.

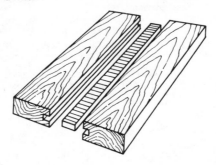

Figure 7-18   Spline joints.

Tongue-and-Groove

Description. The tongue-and-groove is really an open mortise and tenon. One matching edge is grooved. The other edge has a tongue cut out of it that fits into the groove.

Uses. The widest use is in flooring, but it is an excellent way of edge joining two or more boards anywhere.

Assembly. The tongue must fit snugly in its matching groove but be slightly shallower to allow space for excess glue.

Tools. The most accurate tool for cutting is a molder head with tongue-and-groove blades. A dado blade, a router, or a drill press, can all cut tongues-and-grooves.

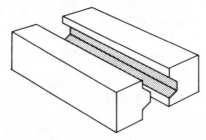

Figure 7-19   Tongue-and-groove joints.

Bending Wood

The oldest known method for bending wood is to apply moisture and heat. But that is not easy, even when you have the right equipment. Since boiling water will weaken the fibers in most wood, you have to have a large steam oven that generates both steam and pressure for long periods of time. You also need a large kiln and some monstrous clamping devices which are hydraulically controlled.

The wood is first dried in the kiln until its moisture content is approximately 15 percent, then it is put in the steam oven where it stays one hour for every inch of board thickness. When the wood is plastic enough to bend, it is clamped in the desired shape and allowed to dry.

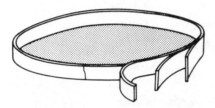

Figure 7-20   Curving wood by bending thin strips together and gluing them in place.

Laminating

For people with less equipment, there is a simpler method called laminating. In this process, several pieces of thin material are bent around the desired curve and glued together. If the curve is not too small and you want to add a lot of extra strength, you can do so by crossbonding, which means every other strip to be glued has its grain running at right angles to the layers above and below it. However, crossbonding makes bending hard to accomplish so you will need some heavy clamps. A smooth layer of glue is put on each laminate as it is bent in place, then all of the strips are clamped until the glue is dry. If the curve is too sharp for the wood to bend easily, the laminates may need to be steamed until they are flexible enough to close around the radius. Since the pieces are necessarily thin, a minimum of steaming should be necessary, but allow the wood to dry thoroughly before applying any glue.

Kerfing

The magic wrought with a saw extends to yet another area: kerfing. A kerf is the width of the saw blade, and therefore is the width of the space that is left behind the saw's path. That space is commonly 1/8". Kerfing means to cut blade-wide slots in a piece of wood. By doing this you can effectively bend any ply or solid wood around practically any radius. And by filling the kerfs with a strong glue you can make the wood almost as strong as it was before you bent it.

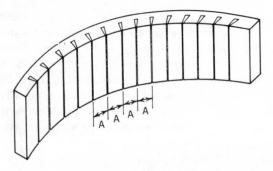

Figure 7-21   Kerfing is cutting numerous slots in a board at regular intervals so that the wood can be bent.

Procedure for Kerfing Wood

1. Measure the radius of the curve that the bent piece will follow.
2. Cut one kerf any place in the stock. The kerf must be deep enough to end between 1/4″ and 1/16″ from the uncut side of the wood.
3. Clamp one end of the stock to your bench. Bend the other end up from the bench until the top edges of the kerf touch. At a point from the kerf equal to the length of the radius, measure the height of the wood from the table top. This distance above the bench top is the space between each kerf.
4. Now cut equally spaced kerfs the full length of the piece.
5. Fill each kerf with glue.
6. Bend the wood *slowly* around its radius.

Kerfing works particularly well with plywood, although it is effective with solid stock as well.

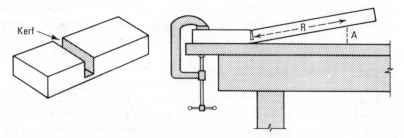

Figure 7-22   Distance between each kerf. Figure it by making one kerf and bending the wood upward until the kerf closes. Distance from wood to table top becomes distance between kerfs.

Review Questions

1. What is a joint?
2. Name four basic principles to remember when making a joint.
3. Name the three ways a joint can be strengthened.
4. What tools are used to cut joints?
5. What is a dovetail template?
6. What is generally accepted as the strongest possible joint? How do you make it?
7. What is the difference between a plough and a dado?
8. Why are grooves sometimes cut in dowels?
9. When is a miter joint most used in cabinetmaking?
10. Where would you be likely to use a rabbet in making a cabinet?
11. Explain how a piece of stock is bent by kerfing.
12. How is wood bent by laminating?

Figure 7–23   Preassemble each joint to make certain the wood surfaces
                                    touch at all points.

Before glueing, preassemble project to ensure that all parts fit properly.

Chapter 8

Putting It All Together

The wood is cut and the joints fit, but how are they held together? Nails, screws, bolts, glue, and wooden pegs all come under the heading of fasteners. Nails are quickest, glue creates stronger joints, but screws are the most reliable. When used with a well-glued joint, screws will make the strongest union of all.

ADHESIVES

In recent years, home craftsmen have developed the habit of using the white glues for practically everything. But as any cabinetmaker knows, a multitude of options are available when it comes to adhesives. Foremost are the cream-colored glues (aliphatic resin), which are stronger and set faster than the whites.

And when it comes to furniture making, remember the *hide glues?* Hide glue comes in liquid form nowadays, as well as in powder and chip form; for jobs like furniture assembly and repair, hide glue remains unsurpassed. Furniture joints undergo tremendous stress and sooner or later they open up. When that happens it is an advantage to be able to clean out the old glue and put new glue in the joint. All hide glues can be dissolved in hot water, so cleaning them is easy. When you are assembling furniture that will not be subjected to the weather, hide glue is an excellent choice, even though it requires three or four hours of clamping time.

But it seems that every day brings new adhesives onto the market. All of them are stronger and easier to use than any glue cabinetmakers ever had in the past. The secret to all of the modern glues is to follow the manufacturer's directions exactly. Beyond that, try to use the right glue for the job you are doing. Some adhesives are waterproof, others are heat resistant. Some need clamping. Others do not. Some are inflammable. Others are toxic. None of them will do anything other than what they were manufactured to do.

Acrylic (3-Ton Adhesive). Used for the extra strong bonding of wood, metal, and glass. It is waterproof and ordinarily sets within five minutes. But it needs twelve hours to cure to develop 6,000 pounds per square inch (psi). It comes in two parts, a liquid and a powder, and is applied with a putty knife or stick. Solvent: acetone (nail polish remover).

Aliphatic (Titebond). A general-purpose cabinetmaking adhesive. It comes in a liquid and must be clamped for about 45 minutes while it sets. It develops 2,000 to 3,000 psi after it has cured overnight. It is rigid and water soluble. Solvent: warm water.

Casein (National Casein Co. No. 30). This comes in a powder which is mixed with water and can be applied with a brush, roller, or piece of wood. This is a standard in the furniture business and is good with such oily woods as teak or lemon. It is a good gap filler but will stain some softwoods such as redwood. It must be clamped for five or six hours and cures overnight to 3,200 psi. It is rigid but not waterproof. Solvent: warm water.

Contact cement (Weldwood Contact Cement). Used especially for bonding plastic laminates and veneers. It comes in a liquid form that is brushed on or applied with a stick to both gluing surfaces. The cement must dry for 15 or 20 minutes before the surfaces are joined, at which point it bonds on contact with high water resistance. Solvent: acetone.

Epoxy (Devcon Clear Epoxy). Epoxy will bond almost anything, particularly dissimilar materials. It comes in two parts that must be mixed and applied with a putty knife or stick. It sets in minutes and cures in about three hours to 3,200 psi. It is rigid and waterproof. Solvent: acetone and elbow grease. Epoxy resists everything.

Hide glue—flake (Usually sold with the retailer's imprint). Used for wood construction, this glue is water soluble and rigid. The flakes are soaked in water heated to $130°F$ until they can be brushed on the wood. They set and cure in about eight hours to 3,200 psi. Solvent: warm water.

Hide glue—liquid (Franklin Liquid Hide Glue). Also used for wood construction, but sold as a liquid and applied with a brush or stick. It sets and cures within eight hours to 3,200 psi, is rigid and water soluble. Solvent: warm water.

Hot melt (Thermogrip Hot Melt). This will work on everything except some plastics. It comes as a two-inch stick which is placed in an electric glue gun and squirted into place. It sets and cures in 60 seconds to over 250 psi, is moderately flexible, and waterproof. Solvent: acetone.

Polyvinyl acetate (Elmer's Glue-All). This is a general household glue which is also good for furniture making. It comes as a liquid and is applied directly from its bottle. It sets in eight hours, cures in 24 to 3,200 psi, is rigid, and water soluble. Solvent: soap and warm water.

Polyvinylchloride (Sheer Magic). Used for wood joinery, as well as china, glass, marble, porcelain, and metal. It comes in liquid form and is applied directly from its tube. It sets in minutes, but its curing time varies and the psi depends on the materials being bonded. It is rigid and water resistant. Solvent: acetone.

Resorcinol (Elmer's Waterproof Glue). Excellent for wood joinery, this adhesive comes in two parts, a liquid and a powder which must be mixed and applied with a brush. It sets and cures in 10 hours to 3,400 psi, is rigid, and waterproof. Solvent: cool water before it hardens. After that, forget it!

Urea formaldehyde (Weldwood Plastic Resin). This may be the glue to use when assembling furniture. It comes in powder form which is mixed with water just prior to application with a brush or spatula. It sets in about 12 hours and cures in 24 hours to 3,000 psi. It is rigid and highly water resistant. Solvent: warm water before hardening.

Preparation of Wood for Gluing

It should go without saying that no matter what glue you are using, it will only perform at its maximum if the gluing surfaces are clean and dry, and the parts fit together as perfectly as possible. Presuming you select the right glue and have the proper clamps on hand, the task of gluing can still go awry unless all of your preparation has been adequate. Gluing is a series of tiny steps performed in one, single motion. As you organize your work for gluing, be sure that every part is within reach and that all of the clamps needed to hold the work together are placed near the area where they will be used.

Clamps and Clamping

There are a variety of different kinds of clamps that are useful when assembling furniture. Sooner or later the cabinetmaker will need all of them. The *bar* or *pipe clamps* are excellent for holding an entire project together. *Hand screw clamps* are good for smaller projects. When setting them, the wooden jaws should almost always be parallel. *C-clamps* are metal and can mar a wood surface. Use scrap blocks under their jaws whenever possible. *Corner clamps* are a godsend when you are assembling a box with beveled or mitered corners. *Spring*

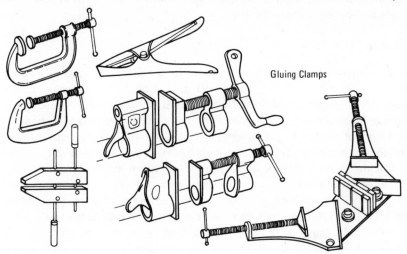

Gluing Clamps

Figure 8-1   Clamps. They hold together practically any shape and size of material.

clamps help with light jobs, and can be applied quickly to hold pieces in place while screws or nails are driven into the wood.

Trial Assembly

Make a trial assembly to be certain that all the parts fit properly and that each joint is tight at all points.

If the glue you are using requires mixing, prepare it just before you are ready to use it. Most glue should be spread over both surfaces; be certain that it penetrates every pore of the wood. When gluing end grains, allow the first coat of glue enough time to set before applying the second coat.

There is a marvelous rumor that the more pressure you put on a glued joint while it dries, the stronger it will be. This is not so. There should only be enough clamp pressure to shut out light coming through the joint. Too much pressure squeezes all the glue out of the joint. Without adequate pressure the wood will not bond. Tighten your clamps enough to make the wood *snug,* but no tighter.

NAILS

A nail can be made of steel, wire, iron, copper, zinc, or brass. Each of the more than 100 different kinds that are manufactured comes in a full assortment of sizes. Railroad and boat spikes are so big you need a sledge hammer to drive them. Wire brads are so thin that a thousand of them weigh less than a pound. From the incredible variety of nails that are available, only about a dozen types are suitable for use in cabinetmaking.

Nail Sizes

Nail sizes are determined by their length, which is known as the *penny.* Penny is written as a number plus the small letter *d.* So a bin full of six penny nails is labeled 6d. Originally, the *d* referred to the cost of the nail per hundred; a long time ago, a 6d nail cost six cents per 100. The *d* came from England, where it is still a symbol for the English penny. In the Colonies, however, the economy changed and so did the system of money, so the *d* now only refers to the length of a nail, no matter what type of nail it is, or how much it costs.

When buying nails, you must designate them, for example, as *10d common* or *8d finish.* This indicates the right length and the kind of head you want. Figure 8–2 shows the various lengths that correspond to each penny size.

The nail's gauge is its diameter and is of no importance when you buy nails. The gauge really only counts, for example, after you have split a piece of wood and want to change to a different diameter of nail, or when you drill pilot holes.

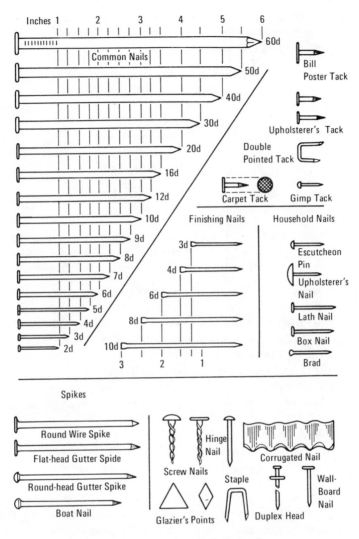

Figure 8-2 Nail sizes and types.

Nails for Plywood

So far as nailing is concerned, the plywood manufacturers recommend specific nail sizes to be used with the different panel thicknesses. They also urge that a plywood joint always be glued as well as nailed.

Nail Types

Common and *box* nails come in about the same lengths. Common nails are the stand-by in rough carpentry. Box nails have thinner shanks and are preferred for toenailing because they are less apt to split the wood. Common and box nails can only be driven until their heads are flush with the wood.

TABLE 8-1 NAIL SIZES USED WITH PLYWOOD

Plywood Thickness	Casing Nail	Finishing Nail
3/4"	6d	8d or 10d
5/8"	6d	8d
1/2"	4d	6d
3/8"	3d	4d
1/4"	3/4–1" brad	3d
	1" blue lathe nails may be used if there is no objection to the heads showing.	

Finishing nails have thinner shanks than commons. They also have considerably smaller heads. A *casing* nail is really a finishing nail with a conical head. Both types are used extensively in cabinetmaking because they can be driven below the surface of the wood with a *nail set* and then hidden under filler. As a rule, the casings hold better than finishing nails.

Annular-thread nails have a wide twist around their shanks that gives them more holding power, provided they are not subject to lateral stress. They are not the kind of nails to use for holding end grains, plywood, hardboard, or particleboard.

Spiral thread nails look like screws. They have superior holding power and work well in end grains. They do not work in plywood or hardboard.

Screw-thread nails are good for anything other than end grains and plywood edges.

Painted-panel nails are relatively new and were originally designed to hold paneling against a furring strip frame. They have screw-type shafts and, as it turns out, they are very tough. Drive one into plywood and then try pulling it out. Chances are you will ruin the wood long before the nail comes free. Panel nails are, therefore, excellent when assembling small projects such as drawers. They are sold in a range of colors, but only one gauge. Their lengths are between 1" and 2-1/2". Don't expect a panel nail to hold a 4' X 4' X 8' plywood chest together.

Knurled-thread nails have almost straight flutes up their shafts and are made to hold in masonry. So if you are hanging cabinets on a brick or cement wall, these are the nails to use.

Cement-coated nails offer both threaded and smooth shanks. They are dipped in a rosin during the manufacturing process. When a nail heats up during hammering the rosin melts and functions as a lubricant. When the nail cools, the rosin bonds it to the wood. When using cement-coated nails never leave one partially in the wood or it will "freeze" there and be difficult to drive home or pull out.

The *corrugated* nail is handy when you want to strengthen a straight or miter joint. But they are difficult to drive home evenly, and even harder to countersink so you can fill them over.

Some Rules for Nailing

There are two rules about nails: select the correct nail for the wood and drive it in properly. Nails can fasten wood because friction is produced from the pressure of the wood against the metal shank. The nail will do its job depending on four things: (1) the condition of the wood; (2) the shape and texture of the nail; (3) the size of the nail in relation to the size of the wood; and (4) the way in which the nail is driven into the wood.

Wood Condition

If you are working with softwood, the nail will go into it easily; it will come out just as easily. The harder the wood, the more difficult it is to hammer a nail into it and the more difficult it is to pull out. If the wood is so hard that it bends your nail, use a thicker nail. But beware: There is a point at which the nail may be thick enough not to bend, but so thick that it also splits the wood. At that point, drill a pilot hole that is no larger than half the diameter of the nail. If you are going to drill pilot holes, however, why not use screws?

The Shape of Nails

The shape and texture of a nail is important because the more nail surface that touches the wood, the better it will hold. *More nail surface* can imply a long, thin nail or a short, fat one. Long, thin, pointed nails will enter wood better than thick, blunt ones. But a thin, pointed nail is also more likely to split the wood, while a blunt nail has less splitting action and actually better holding power. But the biggest, fattest, bluntest nail you can find is not the answer either. The answer is to use nails with diamond-shaped points.

Another way you can put more nail surface against the wood is to choose any of the types that have ridges or spirals along their shanks. These must be driven home slowly because, while they offer excellent holding power, they can also do a lot of splitting.

Nail Size and Wood Size

The size of the nail in relation to the size of the wood is also an important consideration. Pound railroad spikes into louvre slats and you will split the slats every time. There are three guidelines to follow when selecting the correct nail size: (1) pick a nail that is less than three times as long as the thickness of the first piece of wood it will enter; (2) if the wood is dry, use a coated box nail instead of a common nail; and (3) when nailing a thin board to a thick one, hammer the nail only two thirds of the way through the thicker piece of wood. (Make an exception when nailing molding.)

Driving Nails

Carefully consider where and how you drive any nail. If you drive across the grain (through the side of a board) you have more holding power and less chance of splitting. Driving into the end of a board, that is, along the grain, leaves the nail easy to pull out, and any stress on the nail is liable to split the wood. Always set each nail at a different angle, particularly when you are going into the end of the board. This way the nails can support each other and also carry part of the load along their shear lines.

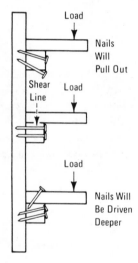

Figure 8-3 Drive nails so that their load is *across* their shear.

Preferably, nails should always be sited so that any strain against them is across the shank, not along their length. You can always pull a nail out; you cannot always shear it off. The approach is to locate the nail so that whatever load it must bear will tend to either drive it in deeper or force it against its shear. Any time you cannot do that, look for another way of fastening; use an angle iron, for example, or straps, bolts, or screws.

SCREWS

Wood screws require a lot more work than driving nails, but are preferable as fasteners in cabinetmaking. A screw will *draw* the sides of a joint tightly together and hold them longer than any nail. You have no choice but to use screws if the work has to be taken apart in the future. They are a definite advantage when greater holding power must be given a joint. And if the project must have an un-marred surface, screws are safer to work with. They should always be used if any load pulling is anticipated along the length of the fastening. In other words, use a screw in any situation where a nail might pull out.

Screw Sizes

Screws are manufactured out of steel, brass, copper, or bronze and are given two dimensions. The ungrooved portion of the shank has a number which refers to its diameter; the overall length of the screw is always given in fractions of an inch.

Shank Numbers

The number applied to the shank has no relationship to any particular diameter, so all you can do is remember that zero is the smallest and the shanks get fatter as the numbers go up to 24. There are some screws that are larger than 24, but

Wood Screws

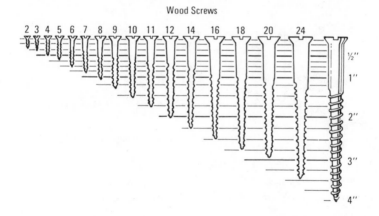

Screw Head Styles   Sheetmetal Screws

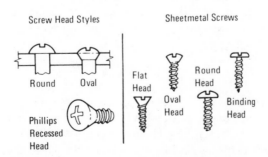

Figure 8-4   Screw sizes and types.

they are too big for any cabinetmaking. Each of the shank numbers has a complete range of screw lengths, so when you buy a screw you must give both the length you need and the shank number.

Screw Lengths

The length of a screw is measured from the point of its tip to a specific part of its head. A *flathead* screw is computed to the *top* of the head. An *oval* head screw is measured to the *rim* of its head. The *roundheaded* type is figured from the point to the *underside* of the head.

Choosing Screws

Deciding which kind of screw is needed begins with the head. Round and oval heads are supposed to be exposed as a decorative part of the cabinet; but if not they should be placed where they are unseen. Flatheads are either countersunk and filled over, or flush with the wood.

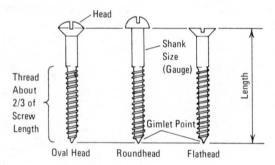

Figure 8-5   Three types of screwheads. Measuring different screw lengths.

The second consideration is the kind of wood involved. Thin screws should be used in the hardwoods while fatter screws are for softwoods. Nevertheless, always use the largest diameter possible because the fatter a screw, the stronger its holding power.

Having chosen the head and considered the wood, then take a length that is less than the combined thickness of woods to be joined. If you are going to countersink your screws, subtract the depth of the countersink when you compute the screw length.

Slots

Most wood screws have one straight slot across their heads to be used with a standard blade screwdriver. But the Phillips head screws have two slots that are crossed and must be driven by a Phillips head screwdriver. The Phillips blade is also crossed and pointed, so it does not overhang the screw. Thus, cabinetmakers tend toward the Phillips head screw because it offers more protection against marring the wooden surfaces. Marring is always a problem, but it is perhaps most critical when dealing with plywood. The edges of the face veneer on a plywood panel are almost delicate and readily splintered, so you need to be particularly careful. The plywood manufacturers recommend that specific screw sizes be used for different plywood thicknesses.

TABLE 8-2 CORRECT SCREW SIZES FOR DIFFERENT PLYWOOD THICKNESS

Plywood Thickness	Screw Length	Screw Size	Drill Size for Shank	Drill Size for Thread
3/4–1″ 5/8″	1-1/2″ 1-1/4″	#8	11/64″ 9/64″	1/8″
1/2″ 3/8″	1-1/4″ 1″	#6	9/64″ 7/64″	3/32″
1/4″	1″	#4	7/64″ 5/64″	1/16″

N.B. If you are drilling near an edge and it splits, one way to solve the problem is to increase the shank drill size by 1/64″.

Of Screws and Drills

The question frequently arises, "How big is a pilot hole?" You can always refer to somebody's chart, but there is another way of selecting the proper sized bit. Hold a bit against the threaded portion of the screw. If screw threads do *not* show above and below the bit, the bit is too big. Try a smaller bit until you can see the threads.

The threads of the screw hold it in the wood, so only the threads need make their way between the wood fibers. No screw is "in tighter" just because you developed blisters driving it in. A hole the diameter of the shaft, minus the threads will make life infinitely easier.

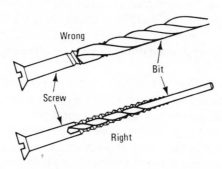

Figure 8-6   Screw threads must be visible above and below the bit shaft, otherwise the bit is too large.

Pilot Holes

Putting screws into softwood usually requires only a small indentation as a pilot. With hardwoods, the pilot hole should be as deep as the length of the screw. Even then you may split hardwood, so enlarge the top third of the hole to the diameter of the unthreaded part of the screw shaft. The smooth part of the shaft has almost no holding power, so there is no reason to force it into the wood and risk splitting it.

BORING MACHINES

Down through the centuries we have bored holes into wood by rotating a twisted piece of metal between the fibers. Some craftsmen still do it that way, but the modern cabinetmaker has two kinds of electric drills that will do more work faster, more neatly, and with considerably less effort than any of the hand-operated borers.

Portable Drill

A portable electric drill is the first power tool most people buy because drilling holes by hand is hard labor. Even the little 1/4″ variety will make holes in wood, metal, or brick. A slightly larger version can be equipped with sanding discs, polishers, abrasives, milling bits, shaping blades, paint mixers, saws, router bits, and water pumps; the accessories you can buy add up to more than the cost of the drill itself. However, a single speed, 1/4″ drill is not beefy enough to handle all the accessories available; buy a more powerful 3/8″ drill with reversibility and variable speed control, so you can use it to drive—and withdraw—screws, along with all those other swell activities.

Power Drill Accessories

The drill bits that can be purchased at almost any hardware store range in size from 1/64″ diameters up to 6″ hole saws. Within these sizes there are high-speed bits for drilling metal, masonry, and practically every other material known to man, as well as standard wood-drilling bits, which should only be used with wood.

The attachments for abrading are almost as numerous as the bits and include such things as perforated discs and drums. Each perforation has sharp cutting edges that will remove old paint and most other materials from wood surfaces. There are also wire wheels that can be used on rust or paint as well, and rotary files that can carve a surface or shape an edge. And there is the standard, flexible sanding disc which converts any drill into a sander-polisher. You can also buy bonded abrasive wheels for cutting steel, brick, tile, or plastics, grinding wheels for sharpening tools, and felt sleeves to use with polishing compounds.

Drill Press

If you only want to drill holes, don't bother buying a drill press; any electric drill will drill equally as well and cost you considerably less money. But if you intend to do any cabinetmaking, then you will have to do a considerable amount of drum sanding, routing, rasping, shaping, mortising, and decorative work, and you can hardly do any of that efficiently without a drill press.

Because the drill press produces speeds from 500 rpm to 4,700 rpm, it has the capability of handling such high-speed cutting tools as router and shaper bits. Moreover, the work table positioned under the drill can be moved, tilted, and enhanced by any number of jigs and homemade devices that will give you precision holes bored at any angle, to any depth.

Screwdrivers

Always pick the longest barreled screwdriver possible and one that has a blade that lodges snugly in the screw slot. The longer the barrel of the screwdriver, the more leverage you will get; the looser the blade is in the slot, the more chance there is of slippage, which will destroy the slot. If the slot becomes damaged, you may be able to smooth or deepen it with a hacksaw or metal file, but that is a lot of work and there is no guarantee you will succeed.

Driving in Screws

There is an old maxim that says that by putting soap on a screw thread it will be easier to drive into hardwood. The old saw is right, but don't do it. In time, soap acts like a kind of glue and cements the screw in its hole; it also rusts steel screws and corrodes brass ones. Trying to draw a soaped screw out of wood becomes "the impossible dream." Don't use oil either, because almost any oil will stain most woods. Instead, coat your screws with graphite or candle wax. They will neither stain the wood, nor rust the screw, and you will be able to remove them even years later.

Removing Screws

Here are two tricks of the trade for removing a tight screw. First, if turning the screw counterclockwise does not loosen it, twist it clockwise, in the opposite direction. Then try to loosen it. Repeat the tightening and loosening action until the screw comes free. Second, if all else fails, hold a hot soldering iron to the screw head for about one minute, then wait one minute longer before attacking the screw again. Heat expands metal; as the screw cools, it should shrink away from whatever binds it.

BOLTS AND ANCHORS

There are three types of bolts and numerous kinds of anchors that, from time to time, have a role in cabinetmaking.

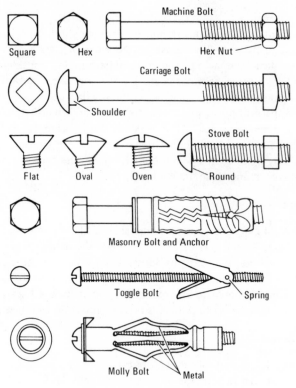

Figure 8-7   Bolts, anchors, and plugs used for hanging shelves and cabinets on walls.

Bolts

Lag bolts are actually heavy-duty wood screws and can be purchased in sizes of up to an inch in diameter and 16″ long. The heads are either square or hexagonal and they are screwed into wood with a wrench. When hanging cabinets on a wall, if you can find a convenient stud to screw into, a lag bolt is about the best hanger you could use.

Carriage bolts have round heads and very coarse threads. The head may be either flat or conical, so that it can be countersunk.

Hanger bolts have endless uses, primarily because they are hybrids: one end is threaded to accept a machine nut; the other half is a wood screw.

Anchors

There are numerous types of anchors that can fasten an object to either solid or hollow walls. Some are lead or plastic plugs that are fitted into holes drilled into masonry walls. When a screw is driven into the center of a lead or plastic plug, it expands against the sides of the hole and locks in place. *Mollies* or *toggle bolts* are also very useful. These fold back on a long bolt so they can be inserted through a small hole in wallboard or plaster. Then they spring open in the space behind the wall and when the bolt is tightened, the wings are pulled tight against the back of the wall.

GETTING IT TOGETHER

The parts are cut and the joinery is made. The glue is ready to be mixed. Assemble the subassemblies first. If a chair or a table is being made, for example, these are usually glued in two stages; the leg assemblies first, then the seat or top.

Figure 8-8 The subassemblies—the drawers and doors—can be glued before the buffet itself is assembled.

Cabinets

With a cabinet, the approach is somewhat different. The subassembly doors and drawers can be put together first, but then the casework must be done in two stages; first the interior work must be completed, then the exterior. Whether the cabinet is a bookshelf, room divider, desk, cupboard, or closet, the way you arrange its interior must take into account every conceivable convenience. The size and positioning of each shelf must be carefully planned. A bookcase that is not deep enough or that has shelves that are less than 10-1/2″ high, is useless. A kitchen cabinet with widely spaced, fixed shelves placed too high on the wall for anyone to reach, is a waste of space. It is the waste of space that the cabinet-maker must specifically address himself to. He must ask himself how the cabinet will function, what kind and size of objects it will hold, then he must design the interior accordingly.

Cabinet Shelves

When designing shelves for inside a cabinet, you have a number of choices so far as material is concerned. A shelf can be solid wood, plywood, glass, or any of the man-made materials, but whatever you select, it should be thick enough so that it will not bend under the weight of whatever is stored on it. As a rule, any shelf over 42″ in length *must* have a center support of some kind. Pine and many of the other softwoods should be supported every 30″ to 36″. Half-inch plywood has approximately the same load-bearing strength as 3/4″ pine, but since it bends much more easily, it must be braced every 24″ to 30″.

How will the shelves be attached in the cabinet? Will they be stationary or adjustable? And what spacing should they have? Standard bookshelves are 7-1/2″ deep and 10-1/2″ high. Kitchen wall cabinets are between 12″ and 14″ deep with adjustable shelves.

Fixed shelves. If you are permanently fixing shelves inside a cabinet, you can set them in dadoes or put them on cleats. If you dado them, the dadoing should be done at the time you are cutting all of your joinery. However, the exposed end of a dado is unattractive to many people, so you might think about using a stopped dado which will give both the cabinet and shelf all the rigidity they need, and still present the appearance of a butt joint. When a shelf is cleated in place, the cleat can be a piece of 3/4″ or 1/2″ wood or a length of quarter-round molding; if a molding strip or a faceplate is attached to the front of the cabinet edges, the cleat will hardly be visible. The cleats are glued and nailed or screwed into the sides of the cabinet, and the shelves are then attached to the cleats or simply placed on them.

Another form of cleat is the metal shelf bracket, which can be dadoed into the underside of the shelf as well as into the sides of the cabinet, or can be screwed flush in place. Also, wooden dowels can be inserted discretely in holes bored into the sides of the cabinet under each shelf.

Adjustable shelving. In recent years, the trend in modern furniture making has been to provide adjustable shelving in cabinets, since the cabinetmaker has no idea how his cabinet will be used once it leaves his hands. Here are some ways of providing adjustable shelving in a cabinet:

1. You can rout out a series of extra-wide dadoes in both sides of the cabinet so the shelves can be slid into any position in the unit.

Figure 8-9 The interior of any casework must be carefully thought out to provide its users with a maximum of storage space.

2. You can bore parallel rows of holes up both sides of the cabinet to accept wooden dowels or metal shelf pins.
3. Screw or nail adjustable shelf standards to the cabinet sides. These must be put up in parallel pairs on each side, and they can be mounted flush or set in dadoes. There are, in fact, numerous types of shelf standards now on the market, any of which will do handsomely for holding adjustable shelves.

Assembly

The general procedure for assembling a cabinet is as follows:

1. Assemble all parts; be sure they are properly cut and that their joints fit as perfectly as possible.
2. Preassemble the unit, holding it together with clamps. Check every part and joint once again.

Figure 8-10   Before gluing, preassamble project to ensure that all parts fit properly.

3. Disassemble the unit and lay each part near the clamps that will hold it. The clamps should all be adjusted to their proper openings. Be certain you have enough cauls to place under the clamps to protect the wood surface. Assemble all of the tools you will need, including hammer, mallet, screwdriver, drill, a straightedge and a square, nails, and screws.

Figure 8-11   After checking the unit, disassemble it and arrange the pieces in their order of use, ready to be permanently put in place.

4. Mix enough glue to complete the assembly and apply it to both surfaces that are to be joined. The glue should evenly cover all of the wood surfaces and should not be so thick that it will cause excessive squeeze out.

5. Now assemble the unit and clamp the joints. If there are to be screws or nails driven into the wood, do it after the pieces are all together.

6. When the unit is completely assembled, make these three checks: (1) using a square, be sure that all of the right angles really are 90°; (2) using a straightedge, be certain that all parts are straight and not warped; and (3) measure the diagonal distance from corner to corner. (The distances should be equal.) If any of these checks reveals an imperfection, correct it immediately, before the glue dries.

7. Allow the glue to dry thoroughly before removing the clamps and preparing the surfaces for finishing.

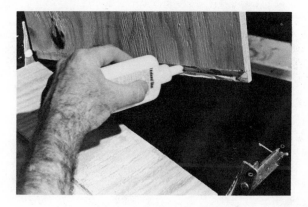

Figure 8-12   After coating the pieces with glue, assemble them. Allow the glue ample time to dry.

Review Questions

1. Name three adhesives that are used in cabinetmaking.
2. Describe five kinds of clamps and compare them.
3. What is the purpose of a trial assembly?
4. What are the best kinds of nails to use in cabinetmaking?
5. Name three types of screwheads and discuss the advantages of each.
6. Name two ways of "unfreezing" a screw.
7. What are two ways of attaching fixed shelves?
8. What do you consider the best system for attaching adjustable shelves in a cabinet? Why?
9. How tightly should a glued joint be clamped?
10. If you assembled a joint and then discovered light showing through it, what would you do?

Finish sanding by hand. Use very fine grit abrasives.

Chapter 9

Preparing to Finish

When the glue is dry and the clamps are taken off truly it is, for many the end of the job. Slap a coat of finish on the thing and get it out of the shop, right? Wrong. Look at the piece very, very closely. See the hammer dents? Notice the minute smears of glue left from your fingers when you were moving fast to get the clamps on? There are chips in the wood around some of the countersinks too. When you *really* take an honest, eyeball level look at the thing, it's a mess.

Before you can begin to finish any project, it must be properly prepared; the wood must be made as perfect, as even, and as smooth as possible. In the beginning, you can do what is called *machine sanding.* Toward the end of the process, however, you will have to roll up your sleeves and "lay hands" on the wood. Like the finishes and the tools, and even the woods we use today, abrasives have improved tremendously over recent years. Now, abrasives and the machines that have evolved with them can actually be used for a modest amount of shaping, cutting, and smoothing raw wood.

ABRASIVES

An abrasive is any substance that can be rubbed against a surface with the object of smoothing that surface. Until recently, cabinetmakers always referred to abrasives as *sandpaper.* Today, none of them have any sand at all. But now, as in the past, each grain of abrasive is, in reality, a separate cutting tool not unlike a chisel or saw.

Modern coated abrasives are comprised of three materials: the abrasive itself, the backing to which it is fastened, and the adhesive that fastens each grain to the backing. The abrasive can be one of four types: flint, garnet, aluminum oxide and silicon carbide. The adhesives used in abrasives are either a hide, or a resin, glue and the backing can be paper, cloth, fiber, or any combination of these.

Abrasives most commonly are manufactured in the form of sheets, rolls, disks, and belts. The sheets used for hand sanding can be any of many sizes, although the most usual dimensions are 9" X 11". The rolls are used on both drum and spindle sanders, while the disks are made for both portable and stationary sanders, and commonly come in sizes between 7″ and 9-1/2″ in diameter. The belts are made for belt-sanding machines and are found in the various widths and lengths necessary to fit the many different models available.

There are also two kinds of abrasive grain coatings, closed and open. The *closed* coat has abrasives which completely cover the backing and are used primarily for semifinishing and finish smoothing. The *open* coats have spaces between large grains of abrasive, making them best for rough sanding or removing soft materials, such as paint or varnish. The advantage of open coat abrasives is that with only about 70 percent of their backings covered with abrasive, they can resist clogging; that is, waste material will not fill in between the grains.

Flint is silicon dioxide, more commonly known as quartz. The flint abrasives are grayish white in color and are normally used for hand sanding in the cabinetmaking industry, since they have neither toughness nor durability.

Garnet is the natural material known as almandite and is used in both hand as well as machine sanding. It is much harder than flint and is generally preferred by cabinetmakers for finished sanding operations.

Aluminum oxide is a man-made product that is harder than garnet. It is created by purifying bauxite (aluminum ore) until it crystallizes, and then adding other tough materials to give it strength. It has sharp grains which make it the preferred abrasive when sanding hardwoods.

Silicon carbide is also a man-made material and has extremely sharp, wedge-shaped grains. It is not only the sharpest, but the hardest of the synthetic abrasives and is ideal for smoothing any of the fibrous woods, plastic, and enamel finishes.

Abrasive Grits

All of the abrasives come with a full range of grits, each of which should be used for specific sanding procedures. The abrasive is always marked on its backing, either with a grit number or a corresponding 0 grade (see Table 9-1).

Always choose the correct abrasive for the work being done. When a series of abrasives are to be used, there is a specific procedure which should be followed closely:

1. Begin with a grit that is just coarse enough to level the surface and eliminate excessive roughness. This step is known as *roughing* and is done with the coarser grits to remove a maximum of material.

2. Proceed to the medium grits for the *blending* stage. Some material will be removed and you should achieve a fairly smooth surface.

3. *Fine finishing* is done with the fine grits to get rid of scratches left over from the two previous sandings.

4. The very fine grits are used in the *final* sanding operation where you will either remove or blend all of the scratches left by the three coarser grits.

If extremely fine grits are required, you may have to go to the wet and dry abrasives which are used with water or oil as a lubricant.

Never start with a very coarse grit and go directly to a very fine grit. You will get nowhere near an acceptable finish.

TABLE 9-1 ABRASIVE GRITS—USES, NUMBERS, AND GRADES

Grit	General Uses	Grit Number	O Grade
Very Coarse	For very rough, un-finished surfaces.	30 24 20 16	2-1/2 3 3-1/2 4
Coarse	For evening after rough texture is removed.	50 40 36	1 1-1/2 2
Medium	To remove final rough texture.	100 80 60	2/0 1/0 1/2
Fine	Finish sanding prior to staining or sealing.	180 150 120	5/0 4/0 3/0
Very Fine	For polishing and finishing after stain, varnish, etc., is applied.	400 360 320 280 240 220	10/0 — 9/0 8/0 7/0 6/0

SANDING MACHINES

There are actually a great many types of sanding machines available to the cabinetmaker and together they will accomplish almost every kind of cutting and smoothing; by using them properly you can bring the surface of almost any wood to a state in which only minimum hand work will be necessary to finish it properly.

Belt-Disk Sanders

These are stationary, motor driven units sold in a variety of sizes. Typically, the belt portion is 6″ X 48″ and can be locked in any position between 180° and 90°. The disk is 9″ or 10″ in diameter and faces a removable, tilting work table with a miter gauge groove. The machine is stable and the work brought to it can be positioned at any conceivable angle. When sanding freehand, apply the work to the abrasive using a light pressure; for more accuracy, use the fence or a miter gauge. The disk is used for sanding both large and small stock with accuracy, while the belt is ideal for end, surface, edge, and bevel smoothing, as well as curves.

Portable Belt Sander

Portable belt sanders are excellent for working on assembled cabinetwork and can be purchased with 2", 3", 4" or 4-1/2" belt widths. Sanding with a portable belt machine is actually done on the *pull* stroke, but the machine must be kept moving over the work all the time or it will cut some pretty deep grooves in the wood surface, particularly if you happen to be smoothing plywood. Cross sanding should be done *first* to level the surface, then finish off by going with the grain. When doing the edge of a piece of wood, it is wise to clamp the material between pieces of scrap so that the sander has a broad, flat surface to ride on, otherwise it is likely to wobble and produce an untrue edge.

The correct method of using a belt sander is to turn on the machine and bring the heel of the belt down on the wood, then push forward as the front end is dropped down on the wood. Sand in short, straight, overlapping strokes.

Rotary Portable Sanders

You can buy circular portable sanders. But you can also get a rubber sanding disk that attaches to your power drill. The rotary hand sanders are good for fast, rough grinding down of work, but that is about all, since they leave circular scratches on the wood that must be smoothed off with other sanding techniques. Don't ever attempt to use the entire face of a sanding disk at one time; the sander will bounce all over the place.

Finishing Sanders

Some finishing sanders operate orbitally, some in a straight line, and others with a multiaction. You can also find some types that convert from orbital to straight line action with the flip of a switch. The orbital action is like the circular disk sanders, best for removing material but it also leaves circular scratches that will show up under a clear finish. The straight-line finishing sanders are like hand sanding and can be used to smooth down finish coats. The multiaction machines sweep back and forth in a half arc and will also leave curved scratches.

The finishing sanders have a lightweight motor that sits on top of a pad which has clips at each end to hold the abrasive paper in place. They are a relatively gentle machine, so using them amounts to turning them on and moving them over the face of the work to be smoothed.

Stationary Tool Sanding

Both the radial-arm and table saws can hold a sanding disk on their arbors. It is easier to use the radial-arm disk if you also have an elevation table which will bring the wood far enough up on the disk to use the bulk of its surface (see Chapter 6). With the table saw, of course, the disk is raised up through the table.

The radial arm can also handle a 1″ to 2-1/2″ sanding drum to do edge-sanding operations. When using a drill press to rotate either sanding disks or drums, use a speed of about 1,800 rpm; when you use the finer grits, lower the speed.

COMING UNGLUED

Once a project is constructed and ready to be prepared for its finish, the first step is to remove all of the excess glue that may have stuck to the wood. Do *not* sand glue stains. Check the entire project carefully, looking for any signs of glue anywhere. If you got any glue on your fingers as you were assembling the piece, chances are you left traces of it on the wood in places other than around the joints.

To remove excess glue, scrape the area with a sharp chisel and make sure that every trace is removed. Stain and most finishing materials will not adhere to glue, so they leave a light spot on the wood. Furthermore, sanding a glue spot only forces it into the wood fibers, where you will never be able to remove it.

HAND SANDING

You can play with the various sanding machines all you want, but sooner or later there will be crevices, carvings, or corners that can only be reached by hand. Even if there are not, ultimately you will have to use your hands, and when you do, here are some rules of the road that should be closely observed.

1. Use the proper grit for the job being done. Hand sanding usually calls for garnet paper.
2. The purpose of sanding is to smooth and finish a surface after it has been properly shaped. So don't bother sanding very much if there is still cutting to be done.
3. You will have a tendency to round off edges and corners if all you do is just fold up the abrasive paper and go to work. Instead, wrap the paper around a block of wood, or use a commercial sanding block. After devoting all that precision to cutting and shaping, it would be a shame to destroy your accuracy with sloppy sanding.
4. Sand with the grain. *Always* sand with the grain. By the time you are hand working the wood there should be no necessity to level off any of its surfaces.
5. Apply only enough pressure to make the abrasive cut into the surface; try to keep the pressure constant throughout.

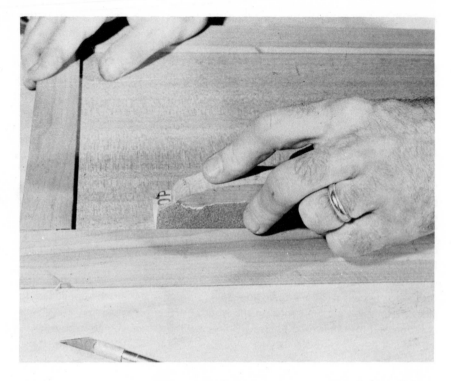

Figure 9-1   Hand sanding with the abrasive wrapped around a block to avoid gouging the wood.

6. Abrasives can be cleaned with a stiff brush. Do it often, so that the grit does not become clogged and cause a lot of wasted energy on your part.

7. Break all edges ever so slightly to keep them from splintering. The corners should be rounded only enough to given them a smooth feel.

8. Much of the intricate hand sanding that might have to be done on an assembled project may be far easier if the pieces are done separately before assembly. You would do, for example, all of the machine sanding and perhaps even more so that when the piece is put together you can go directly to the fine grits.

The standard approach to a frame and panel construction exemplifies this presanding technique. The panels, because they will be recessed in final construction and may also have bevels, chamfers, or what have you in their design, should always be finish-sanded before they are put into their frames. The frame stiles and rails have an inside edge which will be hard to reach after the panels are inserted into their grooves. So finish sand the edges before assembly. But while you are doing this, you might as well do the other sides as well. After the unit is assembled, follow the same procedure in sanding as you would in cutting; that is, do the short sides first. Sand the rails with the grain. Then sand each of the joint lines. Finally, do the stiles.

REPAIRING WOOD SURFACES

While the sanding drags endlessly on, you can break the monotony by pausing to fill or repair every crack, gouge, dent, or hole you come across. While most of this kind of repair work can be done before you begin sanding, there are bound to be places you have missed, so don't put away your repair materials. It is also a good idea to fix a spot the moment you discover it. Otherwise, you might forget about it or never be able to find it again; that is, until it blatantly shows up under several coats of finish.

Four Common Repair Methods

Fillers. Cracks or holes in wood can be filled with a variety of materials. There is wood putty that is purchased as a powder and is mixed with water. Homogenized wallboard compound (premixed) is easier to work with and sands magnificently but cannot withstand much punishment. Plastic wood is the quickest drying and hardest of all and comes in a variety of colors. The most difficult problem when filling cracks or particularly countersinks, is that no matter how much filler is put into the hole, when it dries there is a sag in the middle. Sometimes the sag never appears, but assume it will and be prepared to apply at least two layers of filler. The first application is stuffed into the hole and wiped flush with the surface of the wood. When the filler is completely dry, the second layer is "piled" over it until it is higher than the surrounding surface. When that is dry, sand the area flush. Practically any depression or break in the wood can be eliminated with fillers; and a judicious use of color should make the filler barely noticeable.

Steam. Before you fill any shallow dents (from a hammer, for example), try covering the depression with a damp blotter or cloth and pressing it with a moderately warm iron. Be careful not to soak the wood too much, especially when dealing with plywood. The steam will usually raise the grain sufficiently so that it can be sanded to an even surface.

Wooden pegs. The age-old method of covering nail or screw heads is with wooden pegs or plugs. Plugs can be cut with a *plug cutter* or even purchased at some lumberyards and craft shops. Unless you want the plugs to show as a decorative effect, try to buy ones made of the same wood used in the project. You can also make your own plugs from round stock, but no matter how you get them, plugs are always glued into their holes and then sanded even with the surrounding surface.

Shellac sticks. Small cracks and gouges can be filled with shellac sticks which come in a range of colors such as oak, light and dark walnut, and mahogany. When heated, the sticks become a soft substance that will seep into the crannies of the crack and blend with the surface of the wood. The area to be filled should be cleaned thoroughly. Then heat the blade of a knife or spatula (or use a soldering iron) and rub it against the stick. Rub the material from the knife into the crack. The shellac can be worked into the wood, but always keep the blade moving or it will singe the wood. Continue dropping material into the crack and smoothing it until the space is filled.

SANDING PROCEDURE

You begin with the coarse or medium grits, then go to a fine, and finally a super fine, with several grades in between. In the beginning, you can save your arms by using sanding machines, but there is an order to follow when using them. A circular sander will do some heavy-duty grinding down of rough spots or "highs," but use a medium grit. The circular sander also leaves deep, circular scratches in the wood that paint will barely cover, and varnish will highlight.

Next, use a belt sander. The belts are excellent at covering large areas but be careful that the machine is running before it touches the wood, and keep it moving constantly. Sand with the grain as much as you can. You may be inclined to lean on those circular sander scratches, but don't. You can erase the circular scratches all right, but at the price of "dishing" the wood. Belt sanders can be used with medium and fine grits. But the fine grit that you can buy on the sanding belts is not nearly as fine as you will ultimately need.

After the belt sander, go to the vibrator with fine and super fine grades. When you think everything is nice and smooth, finish the whole project by hand, using a super fine grit wrapped around a block of wood.

Exactly when to stop sanding cannot be learned from a book. Every surface must be smooth to the touch. And *you* must decide whether or not it is smooth enough and if the time has come when more sanding would be a waste of time.

Plywood, by the way, is sanded during its manufacture and rarely requires anything more than a rubbing with fine or super-fine grits. The fir plywood has long, high ridges in its face grain that will forever be long, high ridges. Grind them down and as soon as they are painted or varnished, or just plain get wet, they will rise again. Plywood edges, of course, are another problem. They will smooth with surprisingly little work, especially under a belt sander. But they are inherently porous and must always be filled or covered in some manner.

When the sanding and filling is done, carefully wipe off all the dust from the project. A dry rag will *not* wipe off all the dust particles; a damp rag is no better. Use a *tack* rag. You can purchase one at most hardware or paint stores. Or make your own tack rag with a piece of lint-free cotton or cheese cloth. The cloth is sprinkled (not soaked) with varnish that is 25 percent diluted with turpentine. Fold the cloth tightly, wring it dry, and wipe the wood surface thoroughly.

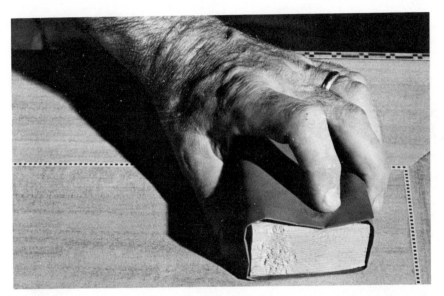

Figure 9-2   Finish sanding by hand. Use very fine grit abrasives.

Review Questions

1. How should you eliminate excess glue on a wood surface?
2. Name four rules to remember when hand sanding.
3. Why should you not proceed from a very coarse grit directly to a very fine grit?
4. What is the disk part of a stationary belt-disk sander primarily used for?
5. What stationary tools other than sanders can be used as sanding machines?
6. What abrasive is preferred for hand sanding cabinetwork?
7. Describe four ways of repairing wood surfaces.
8. In what order should you use abrasive grits when preparing a project for finishing?
9. When should you stop sanding a piece of wood?
10. What are sanding drums used for?

Assemble the drawer using glue and screws.

Chapter 10

Drawers and Doors

DRAWERS

A drawer should not be so high that you need a ladder to reach it. Nor should it be so deep that you cannot find its bottom. If a drawer is too big, when it is pulled all the way out its weight might well tip over the cabinet that holds it. If it is too wide, its handles should still be close enough to be reached simultaneously. There are also countless drawers that are so short they are always being pulled out of their frames.

The Ideal Drawer?

There are no established measurements for the perfect drawer. The only real rule to follow is: Make every drawer big enough to hold whatever it is supposed to hold. There are, however, some guidelines to consider. In general a drawer should be no more than 12″ high or 30″ deep, which is about as long as most arms. Handles should be a maximum of 36″ apart, which is about as wide as most

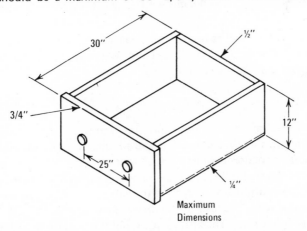

Maximum
Dimensions

Figure 10-1   Recommended drawer dimensions.

people can comfortably reach. Never put a large, heavy drawer at the top of a cabinet. If the drawer is small, give it some sort of stop so it cannot suddenly pop out of its frame.

Essentially, drawers are nothing more than lidless boxes, which make them a quick and easy project to build. But to make a drawer function properly you will probably have to spend a great deal of time.

Drawer Construction

Drawers can be made from any stock; plywood is especially good for the sides, back, and bottom because of its inherent strength. The sides and back of most drawers are between 3/8″ and 3/4″ thick, but usually the stock is 1/2″. Bottoms are normally 1/4″ stock, although they chould be as much as 3/4″. Fronts are anywhere from 3/4″ to 1 1/2″ thick, depending on the decorative detail of the cabinet.

Drawer assembly is either *flush* or *overlapping.* A flush drawer needs more accurate construction so that it can fit inside its frame. Overlapping drawers are designed to hide the spaces between the drawer sides and the frame, so there are more tolerances in their dimensions.

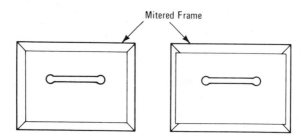

Mitered Frame

Figure 10-2   A flush-assembly frame. An overlapping assembly.

A drawer is supposed to hold considerable weight as well as endure endless wear and tear. Therefore, the joints used in drawers must be carefully chosen to withstand the constant pulling and pushing.

Drawer Joints

The one joint that can support all of the stress and strain put on drawers is the dovetail. If you own a dovetail template and a router or drill press, every drawer you make should have dovetail joinery at all four corners.

When the dovetail is not used, the back and sides of a drawer are usually attached with the butt, dado, or dado with rabbet joint. Either of the dadoes is preferred because when the load in the drawer rams against the back it will not be pushed free of the sides. The butt joint, even if it is made with nails or screws, cannot guarantee as much resistance.

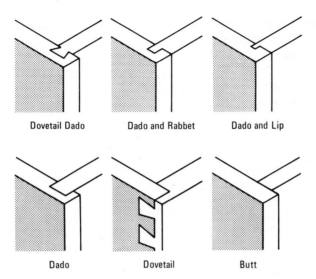

Dovetail Dado   Dado and Rabbet   Dado and Lip

Dado   Dovetail   Butt

Figure 10-3   Joints used to join drawer backs to sides.

Joining drawer sides to their front requires a strong, preferably interlocking joint. The complication is that drawer fronts are usually larger than the side-back-bottom assembly to hide the spaces between the drawer and its frame. Added to this, all of the weight of the drawer, plus the weight of whatever is in it, is literally hauled back and forth by the front piece.

The simplest joinery between the front and sides is a dado or butt joint. But remember all the stress concentrated at these joints, so not only glue them but put screws into them as well. Screws, *not* nails. The load is concentrated along the grain of the sides where a nail will have no holding power. A safer front-sides joint is to rabbet the back edges of the front. This at least lets either nails or screws be placed at right angles to the side grain so that the load against them, when the drawer is pulled, is across their shear.

Rabbeted drawer fronts are not always routed. The front of the drawer can be made flush with the sides. Then a larger lip is attached as a separate face. This paste-on technique works wonders if you want to veneer or mold the drawer front and need to work the face separately. The face is glued to the front and screws are driven into its back from inside the drawer.

Bottoms

The bottom of a drawer serves two functions: It supports the full weight of the drawer's contents; and it establishes the squareness of the entire drawer.

Drawer bottoms can be flush-nailed to the edges of the front, back, and sides. It is better, though, to insert the bottom in a 5/16″ deep rabbet cut out of all four sides. Bottoms can also be fitted into a dado in any two, three, or all four sides. A four-sided dado is best of all because it can be left unglued, allowing the wood to expand or contract without splitting. If the bottom is plywood, you have the option of gluing it.

Remember, if you attach a drawer bottom flush or in a rabbet, it offers almost no holding power. The nails or screws must be positioned in the direction of the load and will have every opportunity to be pushed out of their holes by the load in the drawer.

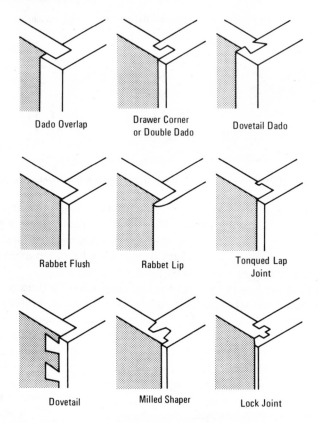

Dado Overlap

Drawer Corner
or Double Dado

Dovetail Dado

Rabbet Flush

Rabbet Lip

Tonqued Lap
Joint

Dovetail

Milled Shaper

Lock Joint

Figure 10-4   Joints used to join the sides and fronts of a drawer.

Drawer Guides

Wooden Guides

Wooden drawer guides are usually hardwood stock and given a coating of wax or soap. They can be attached with both glue and screws. There are three places you can attach drawer guides: to the sides, along the bottom corners, and on the bottom itself.

Side guides consist of square pieces of wood glue-nailed to the drawer

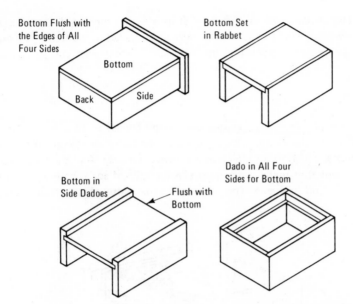

Figure 10-5   Some ways to attach a drawer bottom.

frame on both sides of the drawer. The rails fit into ploughs cut out of the drawer sides, but you can also reverse the arrangement and run ploughs in the frame with the guides attached to the drawer sides. The guides must support the entire weight of the drawer, so glue-screw them in place.

Corner guides have L-shaped strips that hold the drawer up at the bottom edges of its sides. Thus, the weight of the drawer is fully supported by the frame; there is less chance of a rail breaking under weight.

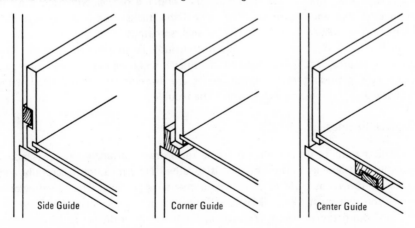

Figure 10-6   Wooden drawer guides can be placed in any of three positions on the drawer.

The *center guide* is a grooved strip of wood running down the center of the drawer bottom. The strip rides over a rail nailed to the frame. If a drawer is unusually large, consider putting two guides under each end to stabilize the drawer action.

Metal Guides

Metal and plastic drawer guides can be purchased in considerable variety at almost any hardware store. They are accompanied by the manufacturer's instruction sheets, which make their installation sound easy. And they are easy to install, except that metal slides need exactly 1/2" of space between each side of the drawer and its frame. The 1/2" equals the width of the metal track and its

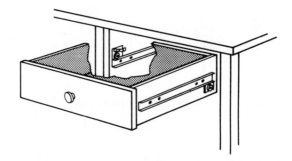

Figure 10-7   Metal drawer guides require a minimum of 1/2" clearance between the drawer and its frame.

slide. Give your drawer less than that 1/2" and the drawer will stick. Give it more than that and the drawer will fall off the tracks. And if the sides of the frame and drawer are not absolutely parallel, something will have to be rebuilt. Even if everything is exact, you may have trouble getting the tracks and slides properly aligned. But if you succeed, the drawer will have more action than you could ever get using wood. Metal guides are difficult to install. Install them properly and they are more than worth the trouble.

Drawer Frames

The smart thing to do is build the frame for a drawer *after* the drawer is made. Assemble a frame and clamp or tack it together. Now measure it carefully and make the drawer as close to your measurements as possible. Once the drawer is built, you will most likely discover some differences somewhere that keep the drawer from fitting perfectly. You can make drawer after drawer and frame after frame, and still not have them come out right. You can make mistakes too if you build a frame around the drawer, but it is easier to fix the unattached pieces of a frame than it is to repair a multijointed box.

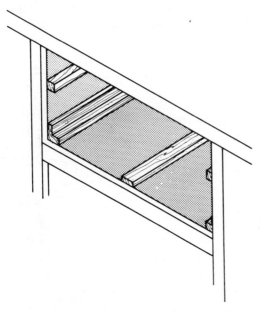

Figure 10-8   Box frame. It permits you to put the drawer guides in any position and still have solid wood to support them.

Box Frames

The simplest drawer frame is a box that measures between 1/16″ and 1/8″ larger in all directions than the drawer it contains. However, box frames consume a lot of wood; if you put six large drawers in a cabinet, with full box frames, the cabinet will end up inordinately heavy and expensive.

Nevertheless, a box frame permits easy installation of the guide rails because they can be attached to solid wood anywhere you decide to put them. If metal drawer slides are used, position both slides on the drawer and attach one of the guides to a side of the frame. Hold the opposite frame side against the drawer and insert the guide over the slide. Align the guide properly and tack it in place with a couple of screws. Test the drawer action. Adjust the guides until the unit works perfectly, and then put the loose frame side in place. This process works pretty quickly with one drawer, but if you are building a tier of drawers, figure on spending a lot of time lining them up properly, even if the drawer fronts overlap the frame.

Dust Panels

The horizontal place that separates drawer cavities is called the dust panel. In the best furniture a dust panel may be of frame and panel construction which has a 1/8″ or 1/4″ panel dadoed into a frame attached to the sides and back of the cabinet. But dust panels can also be single pieces of wood. The front edge

of the panel may be hidden behind the drawer front, or it can be exposed between the drawers above and below it and act as a visible horizontal member of
the cabinet.

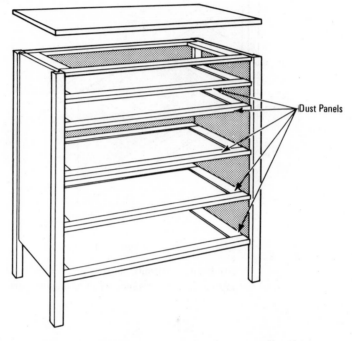

Dust Panels

Figure 10-9   Dust panels—a distinguishing but nonessential feature of fine
furniture.

Open Frames

Another way of making drawer frames is to assemble a series of vertical and horizontal rectangles, which means building a great many right angles going in all
directions. The ladder construction permits any of the guide arrangements to be
used, but it is considerably easier to erect if you have already built the drawers.
Think about how much tinkering you will have to do to make six drawers simultaneously line up in two directions, as well as fit perfectly in their holes. You
can see why it is easier to have the drawers on hand so there is something to
build around.

When the basic drawer frame is complete, the guides should be braced at
the center points so they will not sag. If you are using corner guides, they can sit
on the horizontal members and have full support. Side rails and even metal slides
need a vertical support on center. With center guides, attach a horizontal member under the rail.

Planning a Drawer

There are several things to consider as you plan and design a drawer, beginning with the specific dimensions of each of its parts. Bearing the measurements in mind, each of the following questions must be answered: Will the drawer fit flush into its frame or will it overlap all four edges, or just the sides? What kind of joinery will be used? What kind of guides will be employed? What kind of frame will be around the drawer? If there are to be dust panels, are they to be hidden or exposed?

Figure 10-10   The open drawer frame—a latticework of horizontal and vertical members.

Procedure for Making a Drawer

1. Determine the dimensions of the drawer parts. If the front is to be a flush fit, allow no more than 1/16″ clearance between the frame and its top, bottom, and sides.

2. Rough cut all of the pieces. Drawer fronts are typically between 3/4″ and 1 1/8″ stock. Half-inch material is normally used for the sides, but it can be as thin as 3/8″ for small drawers and as thick as 3/4″ for large drawers, or if grooves are to be cut in them for side guides. Backs are normally 1/2″ stock; the bottom is most often 1/4″ plywood or hardboard, since these will not expand or contract (and therefore split) with humidity changes.

3. If the frame is already built, cut the front so that it fits precisely into or over the frame opening. Bevel the edges of a flush front approximately 1/16″.

4. Cut the joints in the sides, front, and back and plough the grooves for the bottom. The grooves should be at least 1/4″ from the bottom edges of the drawer sides. The bottom may be grooved or cut narrow enough to fit.

5. Assemble the drawer by first joining the sides to the front, then wax the

edges of the bottom and slide it into its grooves. Install the back and position glue blocks under the bottom, against the sides and back. The best professional drawers are assembled with dovetail joints and glue. You can use just glue with any of the other interlocking joints, but otherwise glue and nails or glue and screws are in order. The bottom should never be glued in its grooves but can be nailed or screwed to the drawer back if it is not grooved.

6. Install the guides. If the drawer is flush, it may require stops fastened to the backs of the guides to prevent it from being pushed too far into its cavity. The stops are merely small pieces of wood glued to the guides.

Figure 10-11   Assemble the drawer using glue and screws.

CABINET DOORS

There are only two kinds of cabinet doors, sliding and hinged.

Sliding Doors

Sliding doors can be solid stock, plywood, plastic, glass, hardboard, pressboard, or metal and they are usually installed in pairs. Each door slides on its own track, which is often routed out of the front edges of the top and bottom of the cabinet. Alternatively, the tracks can be made or purchased as separate units. The track under the top of the cabinet is normally 3/8" deep and the bottom track is 3/16" deep. The doors are made 3/8" shorter than the distance between the bottoms of the two tracks. Installation is done by shoving the door upward into the top track and swinging it over the lower track and dropping it into the bottom groove. Track widths are normally 1/4″, and spaced 1/4″ apart. If the doors are thicker than 1/4″ their top and bottom edges are rabbeted to a thickness of 3/8″ so they will slide in the tracks.

Hinged Doors

Hinged doors can be lipped, full overlapped, or flush, and can be hollow-core, solid wood, or a frame and panel construction. They are usually between 3/4″ and 1 1/2″ thick.

Lipped doors are the easiest to hang. They are rabbeted along three sides and hinged on the fourth side so that they close against three sides of the frame. If the frame is too small for the door, the rabbets can simply be made wider and no one will notice.

A *full overlap* door has no rabbets, but is mounted flush against the front of its frame, although it can also overlap only two or three sides. Overlap doors are hung with either a pin or pivot hinge.

Flush doors are fitted inside their frames and must have a back stop. The stop can be the front edge of a shelf behind the door, or strips of wood along the inside edges of the frame. You should allow no more than 1/16″ of space anywhere between the door and its frame.

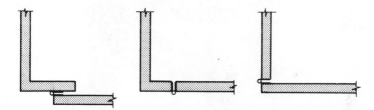

Figure 10-12   Three types of doors—lipped, full overlapping, and flush.

Solid Wood Doors

A small, solid wooden door will last for years without warping. However, having any door made from a single large piece of solid stock, particularly if it is softwood, is asking for trouble. If you must have a large, solid door on your cabinet, attach braces to one side of it. Better still, make the door out of narrow strips that are butted, splined, or rabbeted together. And still put a crosspiece or two, and/or a diagonal brace on at least one side of the assembly.

Frame and Panels

Frame and panel construction has been used by cabinetmakers for centuries as a way of producing light, sturdy, almost split or warp-proof doors for anything from the front of old castles to the lids of jewelry boxes. The frame and panel has not been confined to doors, either. It shows up as dust covers between drawers as well as the sides and fronts of cabinets. A frame and panel requires more time, effort and skill to build, but it is well worth the labor.

Construction frame and panels are made in a variety of ways, but essentially all the construction methods are variations of the butt joint, dado-mortise and tenon, dowel, or rabbet-mortise and tenon-joint assemblies.

The frame is made of one wood thickness, while the panel that fits inside the frame is constructed with a thinner material. The panels can be 1/8" or 1/2" thick, while the frame might be as much as 2-1/2" thick.

To make a frame and panel, first cut the frame pieces to size and cut the corner joints. Assemble the frame to be sure the joints are exact and the frame fits in the cabinet frame. Rout the inside edges of the frame stiles for the panel. Next cut the panel and fit it in the frame: be sure it does not force any of the frame joints apart. Complete all decorative work on the panel, such as chamfering or veneering, before you assemble the panel and frame; if the door is to overlap its frame, also rabbet the inside edges of its stiles before assembling.

If you do not want to dado the frame, the panel can be inserted by using any number of molding arrangements. The panel does not need to be glued in its dado; gluing can prevent the panel from expanding and contracting with changes in the weather and cause it to split.

Figure 10-13   The frame must be preassembled and dadoed before the panel can be accurately cut to fit inside the stiles.

Hanging a Door

It is simpler to construct a door frame around an already existing door than to make the door fit into a frame. Nevertheless, doors are easier to fit in their frames than drawers since they are seldom more than an inch or so thick; they never have to slide into a deep cavity, but simply set between four pieces of wood.

Anytime you can do it, the easiest method of hanging a door is to build the hinge side of the frame, then attach the door. Construct the rest of the frame around the door, beginning with the latch side. Miter joints are in order when assembling the frame. They are more decorative and if precisely cut, they will help square the frame.

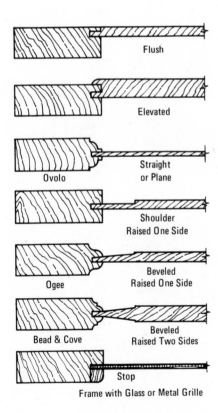

Flush

Elevated

Ovolo   Straight or Plane

Shoulder
Raised One Side

Ogee   Beveled
Raised One Side

Bead & Cove   Beveled
Raised Two Sides

Stop

Frame with Glass or Metal Grille

Figure 10-14   Ways to attach a panel inside its frame.

Review Questions

1. What questions must be answered when designing a drawer?
2. What is the best kind of wood to use for drawer rails?
3. Name and describe three methods of attaching guides to a drawer.
4. What is a lipped door?
5. What is a flush door?
6. Describe the procedure for making a frame and panel door.
7. Describe the steps in assembling a drawer.
8. What is a dust panel and how is it made?
9. What are the two ways you can make sliding doors on a cabinet?
10. What is the easiest method of hanging a door?

Chapter 11

Laminates, Veneers, Carvings, and Inlays

LAMINATES

Into the life of every modern cabinetmaker there must come a plastic laminate at one time or another. If you are a purist, you will turn your back on the whole idea of covering the beauty of natural wood with a man-made material. If you are a modern professional, you will apply plastic laminate to whichever project requires it, and do the best job possible.

The plastic laminates have long been a standard material for both kitchen and bathroom counter tops, but they are also popular for cabinets, furniture, walls, and built-ins because they come in a variety of colors, finishes, and patterns. They resist wear, burns, stains, dirt, and water. The textured and wood-grained patterns actually do look and feel like real veneers, but they also offer the durability and water resistance of their satin-finished brethren.

How Laminates Are Made

Plastic laminates are made up of layers of craft paper impregnated with phenolic resins and covered with a melamine resin. A patterned sheet is saturated with plastic and is topped by a protective "wear" sheet that is additionally coated with melamine resin. The layers are placed between sheets of stainless steel and put in a hydraulic press where they are subjected to both heat and pressure until the assembly develops its hard, brittle surface.

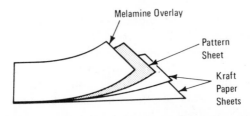

Melamine Overlay

Pattern Sheet

Kraft Paper Sheets

Figure 11-1   Anatomy of plastic laminate

As with any man-made product, there is a total control in the manufacturing process which results in several grades of laminate. All of these grades are commonly available in widths of 24″, 30″, 36″, 48″, and 60″ and lengths of 5′, 6′, 7′, 8′, 10′, and 12′. In most instances, the manufacturers gracefully add 1/4″ to their width dimensions to allow for saw kerfs so that you can cut, say, a 48″ wide sheet into two 24″ widths.

Laminate Grades

Standard grade laminate is 1/16″ thick and used for table and counter tops, vertical surfaces, everything, including edges. It will bend to a 9″ radius without being heated; under 360°F it can be curved to a 2-1/2″ radius.

Postforming grades are 1/20″ thick and made to be heated so they can go around the short radii of curved counter edges.

Vertical grade laminate is 1/32″ thick and can only be used on such vertical surfaces as cabinet sides and doors. When it is cut into narrow strips it is called *edge banding.*

Cores

Since they are so thin and also very brittle, the laminates must be fully supported. This means they must be backed by some kind of solid *core.* The core can be solid wood, plywood at least 3/4″ thick, particleboard, or hardboard, if it is a horizontal surface. Vertical support for a laminate should be no less than 1/2″ plywood. The face veneer of the plywood should *not* be fir. Fir has a high ridged grain that will show through the laminate, or at best create pockets between its ridges where the laminate does not adhere. Particleboard can be only 1/2″ thick and untempered hardboard should be at least 3/16″.

The adhesive used to bond laminate to its core can be a casein, polyvinyl, resin, or really any other glue. The work, however, must be fully clamped and held under a constant pressure until the adhesive has dried. This can be difficult, especially with the curved lip of an on-site counter top. So use contact cement, like practically everyone else. But no matter what adhesive you choose, follow the manufacturer's instructions.

Cutting Laminates

Remember that laminate is hard, brittle, and thin, so it must be fully backed during any cutting operation. It also comes in large sheets which must be reduced to manageable pieces, so rough cut the material first. In this case, rough cutting means leaving at least 1/2″ of waste outside every guideline. The guides can be marked on the face of the laminate with a grease pencil since it will neither scratch the surface nor be difficult to rub off. Because of the resins in the material, your cutting tools should be carbide tipped.

When cutting with a stationary circular saw, keep the face of the laminate *up,* and make sure the sheet is fully supported. Band saws must also have the decorative side up and the blade should have a buttress-type tooth. However, you will be more successful cutting with a band saw if the laminate is already bonded to its core.

A portable circular saw or sabre saw must have the good side of the laminate *down* so that chipping will be held to a minimum. The material should be clamped to the bench top with a piece of wood held in place as a guide. A portable router will also cut plastic laminate. The face should be kept *up* and the material well supported.

When there are no power tools available, or the piece to be cut is too intricate, there are some hand methods of getting plastic laminate down to size. A metal hacksaw will work if it has at least 32 teeth per inch. A crosscut saw with 12 or more points can be used if the angle of cut is kept almost flat against the sheet. You can also score the face veneer of the laminate with an ice pick or an awl, digging at least halfway through the sheet. Then bend the material upward and break it off.

Drilling

Use either a brace and bit and go slowly, or carbide-tipped bits in a power drill. And still go slowly. Always drill from the decorative face side and keep the work supported so there will be a minimum of chipping.

Bonding Laminate

The tools needed to bond laminate are: a hammer, 2″ bristle brush, hand roller, block plane, flat mill file, some heavy wrapping or waxed paper, and contact cement. The procedure for applying laminate to a table top is equally as uncomplicated as the tools used.

1. Cut the laminate 1/8″ to 1/4″ longer than the top in each direction.
2. Smooth the core material, filling in any dents, splits, or gouges, and then sand them even with the surface.
3. Apply the edges to the work (see page 184, edge treatment discussion in this chapter).
4. Apply contact cement to both the back of the laminate and the top of the table and allow it to dry. If a piece of the wrapping paper does not stick to the glue surfaces, the cement is ready for bonding.
5. Place the wrapping paper on the top and align the edge of the laminate with an edge of the top, then press it into place. Now slide the paper out from under the laminate and press the laminate down on the top.
6. Roll the surface of the laminate with the roller, working from the center out toward the edges in all directions. You can also use a small piece of softwood which is placed on the surface and tapped with a hammer. In either case, be sure to cover every square inch of the surface.

7. Remove any excess laminate along the edges with a hand plane or a router fitted with a straight router bit and a laminate trimmer attachment, which will trim and bevel the edge at the same time.

8. Clean any excess adhesive from the laminate surfaces by scraping them with a scrap piece of laminate. Soap and water or alcohol will polish the surfaces to their original luster.

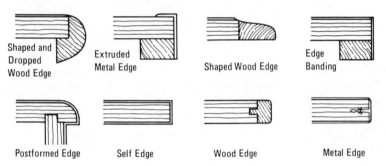

Shaped and Dropped Wood Edge   Extruded Metal Edge   Shaped Wood Edge   Edge Banding

Postformed Edge   Self Edge   Wood Edge   Metal Edge

Figure 11-2   The edges of a laminated piece can be covered with strips of laminate, metal strips, or wood.

Edge Treatments

There are numerous ways of dealing with the edges of a laminated project. The edge can be given a shaped wooden, or one of the many metal, edgings sold at lumberyards. These are always added *after* the top surface of the panel is laminated.

If you elect to edge band, apply the edge to the project first. Cut the edge band to slightly wider than the edge and apply glue to both the laminate and the edges. When the adhesive is dry, align the strip with the edge and press it in place, then roller it.

With rounded corners that have a small radius, bond one side of the corner and then mark the area of the radius with a crayon and hold a heat lamp near the face of the laminate. When the crayon melts, the laminate has heated to about 300°F and can be bent. Wear an asbestos glove when pushing the laminate around the curve and pressing it into place. Roller the entire edge band.

When jointing the ends of an edge band, trim off the excess edging with a hacksaw, then roller the joint until it is tightly bonded. Once the edge is properly bonded, trim off any excess above the surface with a straight router bit. You want the top of the edge exactly level with the core surface; this edge should be well covered with glue when the top laminate is laid down. The bevel around the top joint will be made with a bevel router bit and is actually made in the top piece of laminate.

VENEERS

Wood veneers rarely arrive at a cabinetmaker's shop in a condition to be simply cut and glued. The wood veneers are fragile, often brittle pieces of wood. If they have endured considerable handling, long storage, a few humidity changes, and bumpy transportation, they will require immediate repair work.

Repairing Veneer

Often, the veneer splits along the grain at its ends. Butts, burls, and crotches may also crack around their eyes and pinholes. The edges of a split can be repaired by carefully butting them together and holding them in place with a strip of veneer tape. The tape is stuck to the *good* side of the sheet, that is, the side that will *not* be glued. Once the veneer is glued to its core, the tape is peeled off and at that point not even you will be able to locate where the split occurred.

Figure 11-3   To repair splits in veneer butt the edges together and hold them with veneer or clear tape.

Veneers also tend to curl up in ripples which make them impossible to glue. Sprinkle water on the wood by slapping your hand against the dampened bristles of a whisk broom. *Do not completely dampen the wood.* Now place the veneer between two pieces of plywood. Clamp the sandwich or put it under heavy weights (bricks, iron bars, for example).

If you are flattening more than one veneer, sandwich each sheet between brown paper and stack them under the weights. The brown paper can be a gro-

Figure 11-4   To flatten warped veneer sprinkle water on the wood and clamp or weight the veneer for at least 24 hours.

cery bag, provided you cut out the seams. Do not use newspaper because the ink will stain the wood. Stack the veneer sheets and brown paper on a flat surface and put a plywood panel on top of them. Now pile about half a ton of bricks on the panel; the more weight, the better. Allow the veneer to stand for at least 24 hours, then change the paper padding and keep the veneers under weight until you are ready to use them. Drying time should be at least one day, and three days are ideal. Anything after that is a plus because veneer must be completely dry when it is glued, or it will split as the adhesive dries. Moreover, the glue will not hold particularly well. To summarize, the smart approach is to put the veneer under weight as soon as you get it in your shop and let it stay there until you need it.

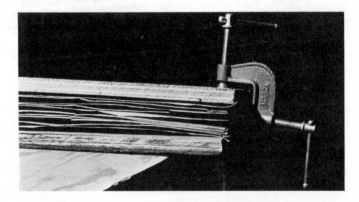

Figure 11-5   Flattening more than one veneer

Storing Veneer

Some simple rules for storing veneer that should always be observed are as follows:

1. Never store veneer on end.
2. Keep veneers on a flat surface with a light weight (such as a plywood panel) on top of them.
3. Keep the edges of the veneer as even as possible so they can support each other.
4. A cool, even slightly damp basement is a better place to store veneers than a hot attic or furnace room.

Backing

One out of 100 times you will encounter a piece of warped burl or crotch that refuses to straighten out. The answer is to glue it to another piece of veneer before you do any work with it. Certain veneers, such as aspen crotch and thuya burl are so delicate they require backing no matter what their condition, because they will develop cracks with any weather change. The one other time backing is mandatory occurs when you are gluing veneer to fir or fir plywood. Fir has a high, uneven grain and any veneer glued to it is so thin that it will follow all the peaks and valleys of the fir. So, fir must always have a sheet of poplar or sycamore crossbanded between it and the face veneer.

Professionals have argued for years over whether veneer and its backing should have their grains running with, or at right angles to each other. If you opt to have the grains going in the same direction, use plain mahogany for the backing. If you prefer to crossband, the usual choice is poplar or sycamore. Both are slightly less stable than mahogany so they should never run in the same direction as the grain of the face veneer.

Veneering Tools

The few tools needed to veneer include: an old hacksaw blade, a craft knife, razor blades and emery boards, gummed veneer tape (one dollar a roll) and a veneer saw (about three dollars), a T-square, ruler, glue spreader, assorted rollers (normally used for baking or hanging wallpaper), an awl, a hand plane, a few more clamps than you already have, and a glue injector.

The veneer saw is terrific. Its teeth leave a narrow kerf and are rarely sidetracked by the pull of a tough grain. Nor will the saw chip the veneer edges the way a craft knife sometimes does. The craft knife is especially important when you cut across a regular grain or make a curve. But with a craft knife always use a sharp, pointed, tapering blade. Always cut from an edge toward the center. Always use a straight edge as a cutting guide. Always put clear tape on the underside of a cut to minimize chipping.

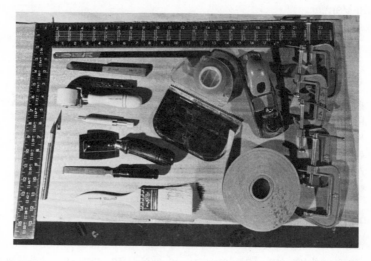

Figure 11-6   Besides a veneering saw and glue injector, veneering requires only basic tools.

Butt Joints

The big headache when matching and joining veneers is to make the joint. It must be an absolutely straight line, which is not easy to accomplish. To achieve a straight line, cut both edges at the same time. Line the two pieces up and hold them under a cutting guide such as a steel square. Then, saw through both sheets and you should have a reasonably well matched cut—except it will not be good enough. Clamp the two sheets together in a jointing jig and plane the edges with a block plane. The blade set should barely bite the wood.

Figure 11-7   To cut a matching butt joint place the two pieces on top of each other and cut them together.

Figure 11-8   Planing veneer edges in a joining jig

The jointing jig is constructed from two pieces of hardwood such as maple or oak, measuring approximately 1 1/2″ X 3″ X 24″ and bored at each end for carriage bolts and wing nuts. Both sides of a veneer joint are clamped between the hardwood and held in place by tightening wing nuts to the bolts. The jig can be planed, or sanded, or run over the blades of a joiner-planer, since planing the hardwood down evenly will not hurt the efficiency of the jig.

Figure 11-9   Once the edges of the butt joint are taped, bend the joint open and run a bead of glue down the seam. Lay the pieces flat and allow the glue to dry.

After the edges are smooth, they should match when the sheets are butted to each other on a flat surface. Try to bring the figure in the veneer together at all points before you cover the joint with veneer tape. When the tape is in place, turn the sheets over and bend open the joint. Run a bead of cream glue along the joint and lay the work flat to dry. Once the glue is dry you can handle the joined pieces as if they were a single veneer.

The Good and Bad Sides of Veneer

Which is the "good" side of a 1/42" thick piece of veneer? The *tight* side, naturally. Glue is always put on the *soft* side. The way to find which side is which, is to "thumb" the edge of the end grain. One side of the veneer will produce more chipping than the other; this is the soft side.

There are two exceptions to putting glue on the soft side of veneer. If you match consecutive sheets from the same tree to create a match design, every other sheet must be glued with its tight side down. Then there is bird's-eye maple. The eyes on the tight side of bird's-eye maple feel like bumpy peaks. This is the side that must be glued, because if you lay the bird's eye maple down with its peaks up, the tiny eyes will pop out of the wood.

How to Measure Veneer

The safest way to measure veneer is to place it under the piece it will cover and make a tracing on the wood. Now cut the veneer a fraction wider than your pencil lines. Or, cut any two adjacent edges precisely on the guidelines, but give the other two sides a little extra. Whichever approach you use, it is best to have an overhang of veneer that you can trim off, or you might end up with a short edge somewhere.

Glues Used in Veneering

There are three modern glues used in veneering, white (polyvinyl resin), cream (aliphatic emulsion), and contact cement. As a rule, white glues are applied to small projects or when numerous small pieces are being assembled and you need time to get them in place. The cream glues develop tack faster than the whites and are somewhat stronger. The creams are good for larger, less complicated assemblies. The contacts are preferred with large projects. They require time to set, but then bond on contact and do not need clamping. Because there is no clamping time, contact cement is the first choice for almost any project.

Some Tips on Gluing Veneer

When gluing veneer it is mandatory that you cover every square inch of surface, least the veneer develop blisters. By definition, veneer is porous; it provides all kinds of nooks and crannies for glue to seep into and grip the wood. But veneer is also thin, so it is essential that its gluing surfaces be free of dust or any foreign

TABLE 11-1 CHARACTERISTICS OF GLUES USED IN VENEERING

Glue	Size of Project	Temp.	Appli-cation	Clamp Time	When to Trim Edge	Glue Line
1 White (polyvinyl resin)	Small	70°	Heavy, even	1 to 12 hrs.	12 hrs.	Thin
2 Cream (aliphatic emulsion)	Medium	75°	Heavy, even	1 to 12 hrs.	12 hrs.	None
3 Contact	Large	70°- 90°	2 coats 1 hr. apart	none 1/2 hr. recom-mended	immediately	None

TABLE 11-1 (Cont'd.)

Blister Repair	Setting Time	Spreader	Clamps Weights	Clean Up	Comments
1 Use	Delayed	Comb, brush	A must	Use warm water at once	Wait 3–10 min. after applica-tion before assembly
2 Occasional uses	Stiffens faster than white	Comb, brush	A must	Use warm water at once	Preferable for nonporous woods and hardboard
3 None	After 2nd coat, bond within 2 hrs.	Comb, brush	Optional	Warm water lacquer thinner	Can be used on any project

matter. Minute as they are, dust particles can prevent any glue from adhering properly. The nature of glue is to harden by losing its moisture. Much of that moisture soaks into the veneer causing it to warp. Therefore, when using the white or cream glues, apply the glue to the *panel, not* the veneer. With contact cement you have no choice but to put glue on both the panel and the veneer. Above all, any glue coverage must be total, it must be even, and it should be a little heavy. Actually, contact cement should be applied in two coats with the

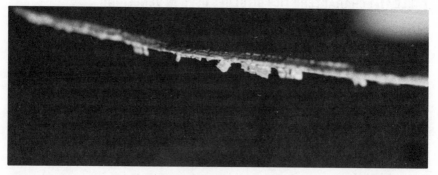

Figure 11–10   The splintered, or soft side of veneer is the side which should
be glued.

second application coming about an hour after the first. One way to determine
whether you have applied enough white or cream glue is by *squeeze out.* If there
is no squeeze out at the edges, when the veneer is pressed in place, you did not
put on enough glue. Peel the veneer off and add more glue; it is better to clean
glue off the edges than not to have enough of it at the very place veneer is most
vulnerable to moisture and lift-up.

　　With contact cement, both gluing surfaces are covered and then given a
second coat. The surfaces are ready to be bonded when a piece of brown or wax
paper can be slid over them without sticking.

Figure 11–11   When the contact cement is dry place a piece of wax or
brown paper on the core and line the veneer with one edge of
the project. Now slide the paper out from under the veneer.

Bonding With Contact Cement

Place a sheet of brown or wax paper on the panel and leave about a one-inch strip of glue exposed along one edge. Align the veneer with the exposed edge of the panel and press the wood into place. It will bond immediately. Now slide the paper back an inch or two at a time and press down on the veneer, bonding it in position. As soon as the paper is completely out from under the veneer, roller the entire surface. It is not usually necessary, but if it makes you feel better, you can also weight or clamp the veneer for half an hour or so after it is rollered.

Rollering

Rollering is the most important step in veneering. The objective is to get every millimeter of both gluing surfaces to join and bond. So lean hard on your roller and work in zig-zag directions down the center of the veneer. Then roll along each side, pushing your roller out toward the edges. Keep rollering until your arms ache. When you are exhausted, put a plywood panel over the veneer and either clamp it tightly or weigh it evenly. With contact glue, the clamping need only be for a few minutes if at all. Wait at least 12 hours for the white or cream glues to harden.

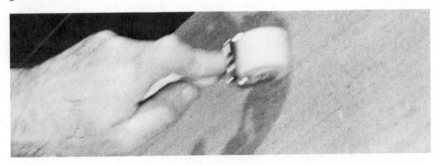

Figure 11-12   Roller in a zig-zag pattern down the center of the veneer, then out to all the edges.

Clamps

When veneering, clamps operate the same way they always do, but there should be more of them. You must put pressure on *every part* of the veneer, so put a clamp every few inches along the edges.

The Order for Applying Veneer

The order in which veneer is attached to a cabinet or any project is very important. Put the veneer you will see last, on first. Thus, you veneer the back of a cabinet first, then its ends, the front, and finally, the top. By following this reverse procedure you are sure of covering as many veneer end grains as possible.

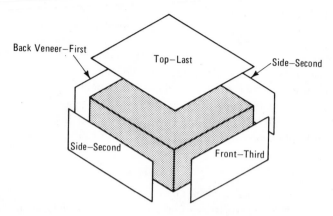

Figure 11-13   Apply veneer to less visible areas first.

Repairs

However, each veneer laid down will demand some sort of repair work, and this should always be completed before you continue gluing. The reason is that you will have to clamp or weight the repair for a day or so. The actual repairs include trimming edges, peeling off tape, repairing dents, blisters, edge lifting, and cracks. Other than trimming the edges, all of this work must go back under pressure after it is completed. If there is a minimum of such repairs, you possibly can make all of them at once and then clamp the entire work only one time. Most likely that will be inconvenient, or at best awkward, so plan on clamping separately after each surface is repaired. From this point on, all the work you do is aimed at protecting the veneer for posterity and there is no advantage to saving an extra day of clamping time.

Trimming Edges

When the glue is dry, stick clear tape to the face of the veneer, along the overhanging edges. Turn the project over so that the veneer is face down. It should rest on a flat, hard surface. Now trim off the excess edges using a veneer saw or craft knife; the clear tape will reduce the chance of any splintering or chipping. Cut very lightly along the edges at first. Then make deeper and deeper cuts until the excess veneer is free. Never hack off thin veneer in one whack, or it will splinter even with a tape backing.

The trimmed edges must be sanded lightly; always use a sanding block, so the edges of the sandpaper cannot catch under a sliver of wood and rip the whole veneer. Again, veneer chips very easily. Always sand by pushing, *never pulling* the sandpaper away from the edges. As for power sanding, if you are so impatient, or so lazy, as to risk ruining all of the long, hard labor put into building and veneering a project, then at least follow this procedure. Buy the finest grit

Figure 11-14   Trimming veneer edges. Stick clear tape to the good side of
the edge, and cut through it from the underside. The tape
helps reduce and often eliminate splintering.

abrasive you can find and sand something with it. When the grit is worn smooth,
put the paper on a vibrating sander. Administer the vibrator very briefly and
very lightly to the veneer. Pray a lot. With luck you may not gouge the surface
too much.

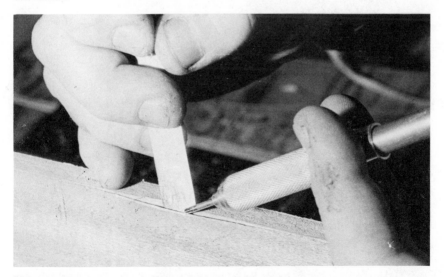

Figure 11-15   To repair loose edges pull the veneer away from its core and
inject white glue into the slit, then clamp the veneer back
into place.

Repair of Loose Edges

During the course of hand sanding, you will find areas where the edges have not adhered properly. Use the tip of a spatula to pry the edge back, insert white glue with a glue injector, and immediately clamp the edge. White glue is preferred over cream glue because it is thin enough to settle into the crack. Contact does not run at all, which makes it too hard to apply to both sides of the split.

Peeling Tape

While the edges are drying you may be able to work on the face of the veneer. By this time, the face has veneer tape over the joints and splits, and clear tape along the trimmed edges. This tape must all be removed. Use a wet cellulose sponge to *very carefully* dampen the tapes. Allow only the tapes to get wet. Water is a natural enemy of wood and when that wood is thinner than paper it is particularly vulnerable. After the tape is thoroughly wet, slide the blade of a thin-edged spatula or dull kitchen knife under its edges. Work carefully and deliberately; sooner or later you will be able to peel the tape. Actually, the tape will split apart and leave a layer of fuzz on the wood. Moisten the fuzz too, but not too much. Hold a very sharp chisel or cabinet scraper vertically against the veneer and pull it toward you under pressure, and you should be able to clean off most of the fur.

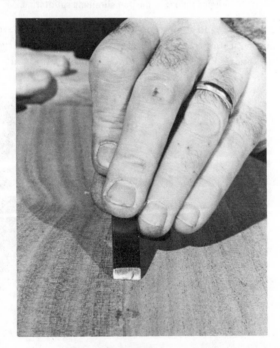

Figure 11-16   To peel tape from veneer, dampen only the tape, then scrape it with a sharp chisel.

Fixing Dents

After the tape is completely removed, go over the veneer looking for any dents or nicks in the surface. With an eyedropper, dampen each depression with a drop or two of hot water. As soon as the dents have been soaked, clamp or weight the veneer for 24 hours; at the *least,* let all that wet wood dry overnight.

Blisters

Blisters occur because not enough glue got under the area, or there was a change in humidity, or there was too little rollering. Notice that only one of those three causes can be attributed to nature. Start out by just rollering the blister. If it is a big area, first test around the edges and see if the wood is willing to go down. Do not pounce on the middle of a big blister or you will split the wood. If you can depress the edges, roller toward the center. When the veneer is flat, put a weight on it for 24 hours. When rollering fails, try heat—if you are certain there is enough glue under the blister. Lay a sheet of aluminum foil over the blister and iron it with a moderately warm electric iron. Caress the bulge a little with the iron, then roller it. Repeat the procedure until the blister is flat, then clamp it in place for a few hours.

   If there is not enough glue under the blister or if everything else fails, slit the veneer with a craft knife on both sides of the bump along the grain. Lift one edge of the slice with your knife and squirt a little white glue under the veneer. Press the blister down to spread the glue. Now do the same thing along the other slit. Then place a piece of softwood over the blister and pile weights on top of it for at least 12 hours. After that, if the blister rises again, go back to the warm iron technique, since now you know for sure there is glue under the veneer.

Cracks

Cracks may appear in the veneer, and the butt joints may be more obvious than you like. The easiest way to fill any kind of minor split is with a shellac stick. The sticks come in a range of shades, such as mahogany, walnut, cherry, ebony, holly, and maple. Given two shades that are close to the right color but not exact, pick the lighter shade. Or try mixing colors as you put them on the wood.

   Heat the blade of a spatula and rub it against the shellac stick, then push the warm wax into the crack. Continue adding warm shellac until it is built up over the top of the crack. Allow the shellac to harden overnight; use a chisel to scrape off the excess shellac, then sand it lightly.

   If you cannot match the color of the veneer with any of the shellac on hand, you can always make your own filler. With a veneer saw, scrape sawdust from an extra piece of the veneer. Pile the sawdust on a sheet of wax paper, and make a puddle of white glue next to it. Put a little glue on your spatula along with a slightly smaller amount of sawdust. Push the mixture into the crack or joint. As you begin filling the split, use less glue and more sawdust to "top off" the work. Allow the glue and sawdust to dry for at least 24 hours, then scrape

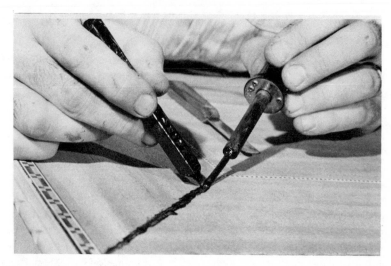

Figure 11-17   Use a shellac stick to repair minor splits and damages.

away any excess with a chisel. Sand the split lightly. There is only one trick to use when filling cracks: Always work *with* the grain and try to be as irregular as possible. You want the filler to seem like it is part of the figure, so your craftsmanship is measured here by how little of what you do can be seen.

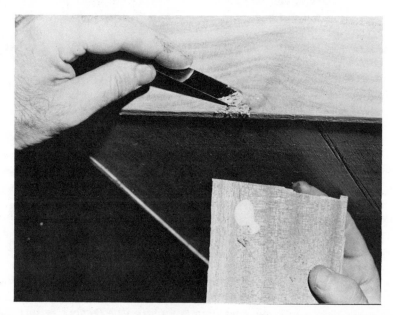

Figure 11-18   Another repair method. Use a veneer saw to make sawdust from a scrap piece of veneer. Mix the sawdust with white glue and fill the crack. Allow the mixture to dry before sanding smooth.

Finishing Veneer

Once the veneer is glued and repaired, clamp or weight it until you give it a final finish. The sooner you put some kind of finish over that raw wood, the less chance that changes in the weather will make it expand or contract, and develop new cracks.

There are countless ways of finishing veneer. You may want to stain it, for example. Woods such as mahogany, walnut, oak, lacewood, or any of the burls, are open-pored and need a wood filler to bring out their grains. Filler will also enrich a stain, if you choose to use one first.

Lemon, linseed, or tung oil can be hand rubbed into veneer and then covered with shellac, varnish, or both. If you choose a urethane varnish, it is available in high gloss, satin, or dull finishes, each of which can either be applied with a brush or spray gun. The advantage to the urethanes is that they are easy to apply and do a superb job of sealing a delicate veneer under a relatively indestructible finish (after all, polyurethane varnishes are normally used on floors).

Figure 11-19   Decorative carvings used in cabinetmaking and furniture design

CARVINGS

There may come a project, such as a cabinet or bureau, that demands not only veneer, but decorative carvings as well. Assuming you choose not to become an old-time whittler for the glory of one piece of furniture, there are a great many different carvings now available on the market. They cost between fifty cents and four dollars apiece, depending on their intricacies. Having gone out and bought some, you could rush home and just paste them on the veneer. But the purists will wag their heads at you for trying to make life easy for yourself. The purists presume you will cut a hole in the veneer and fit the carving in place.

There are two ways you can cut holes in veneer. You can lay the carving on the veneer and trace it with a pencil. Then chop out the hole with a craft knife. That sounds easy, but you are in grave danger of splintering the veneer. You will also end up with an uneven cut because the grain will be pulling at your knife every inch of the way.

Your second option is to make a balsa wood sandwich. Place the veneer between two sheets of balsa wood and tape all three pieces together. If possible, use balsa that is the same size as the veneer. This will allow you to be exacting about where you mark the hole, plus it will protect the edges of the veneer. Mark the hole on the top balsa sheet and bore through the three sheets. Insert a fret saw in the hole and saw away. When the hole is cut, sand the edges of the sandwich *before* you remove the balsa sheets. If the hole has any imperfections between it and the carving, they should be small enough so you can fill in the spaces after the veneer and carving are glued to the project.

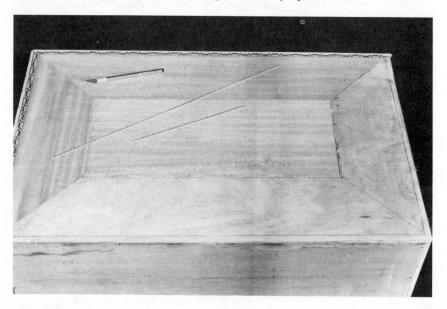

Figure 11-20   Before you cut inlay, mark off exactly where it will be placed.

INLAYS

Even if carvings do not interest you, inaly borders should. The wide selection of ready-made borders on the market offers something for everybody, whether they are doing antique restoration or creating modern furniture. The inlays range from 1/16″ to 2″ wide, are sold in 3′ lengths, and are usually 1/28″ thick although rosewood is more likely to be 1/32″ (see Chapter 4). That means they are thicker than the veneer you will be putting around them, so they have to be *inlayed* in some kind of a rout and then sanded down.

Using Inlays

The general procedure for applying an inlay border requires that you first rout, or saw out a groove that is slightly shallower than the thickness of the inlay. The border is then glued in place and sanded down to the level of the surrounding surfaces. That's all there is to using inlays except, of course, applying them is a little more complicated than it appears at first glance.

Inlaying Inlays

The buffet has simple veneer panels on its drawer fronts and doors. The sides and top are also veneered, but the top is designed to have a 1/2″ border around its outside edges and a 3/16″ band 4″ inside the outside edges. The procedure for accomplishing both an inside and outside inlay is as follows:

1. Mark off exactly where the band and border will fall on the buffet top.
2. Measure and cut veneer for the rectangle in the center of the top. Two sides of the rectangle are cut exactly on their lines. The other two edges are given 1/4″ of excess.
3. Measure and cut the four 1/2″ band strips. An inch is added to each end so the strips will overlap at the corners and can be mitered.
4. Measure and cut the four 4″ wide veneer strips between the band and the edging. They are each cut full length. They will therefore overlap at the corners to allow for mitering. The strips are also slightly wider than the band and edge lines so that one side can be trimmed.
5. Measure and cut the 3/16″ edge strips, leaving enough length for overlapping so they can be mitered.
6. Preassemble all of the veneer and inlays to make certain everything fits properly.
7. Lay narrow masking tape on the outside 1/2″ of the top. The tape is placed exactly along the edging guidelines. Also put tape over the two sides of the 3/16″ band that will be covered by excess veneer on the center rectangle.
8. Spread contact cement on the center piece and the middle of the top.

After the second coat of glue is applied, remove the masking tape that covers the 3/16″ banding lines.

9. Line the *exact* edges of the center rectangle along the two banding lines. Roller the center rectangle.

10. Carefully trim the excess veneer along the banding lines.

11. Apply glue to the 3/16″ banding strips and the banding rout around the center rectangle. When the second coat of contact cement is dry, place a strip of wax paper at each corner where the bands will meet.

12. Glue the 3/16″ bands against the center rectangle. Their ends will overlap at the corners, on top of the wax paper. Care must be taken that the bands are placed tightly against the edges of the center veneer.

13. Cut a miter joint through both bands at each corner with a craft knife. When the bands are cut, remove the wax paper and roller the joints.

14. Glue the four veneer strips around the 3/16″ band. They must be butted as tightly against the band as possible. These strips should overlap on top of the wax paper at each corner. Cut the miter angle at each corner, remove the wax paper, and roller.

15. Trim the outside edges of the strips along the 1/2″ border guideline. When the excess veneer is completely sawed through, remove it by peeling off the masking tape around the edge of the buffet top.

16. Glue the 1/2″ border in place, again allowing for overhang at the ends so they can be mitered.

17. Clamp and weight the entire top for 30 minutes. Repair any dents, blisters, or raised edges.

18. When all repairs are complete, sand the border and banding until they are flush with the veneer.

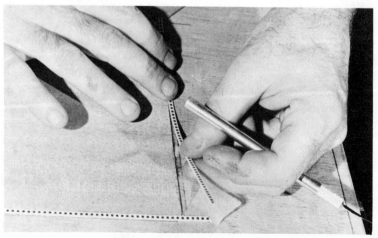

Figure 11-21   Allow bands to overlap at corners with a piece of wax paper between them.

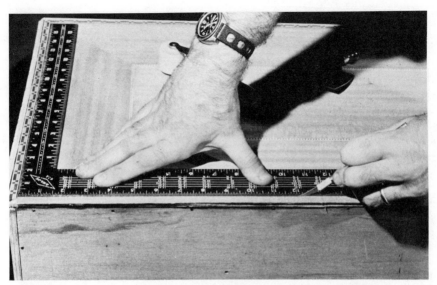

Figure 11-22   Trim outside strips along the border after they are glued in place.

Review Questions

1. Where are plastic laminates used in cabinetmaking?
2. Describe the procedure for applying plastic laminates to a counter top.
3. Describe four ways of edging a laminated table top.
4. What is the difference between plastic laminate and veneer?
5. Name three rules to follow when storing veneer.
6. How do you flatten warped veneer?
7. What are the advantages and disadvantages of the three glues used in veneering? When is each used?
8. In what order should you apply veneer to the top, bottom, sides, back, and front of a box?
9. How are inlay strips applied to a veneered cabinet?
10. What is the single most important step in veneering?
11. Describe the steps in laying a warped sheet of bird's-eye maple veneer.
12. When are mahogany, sycamore, and poplar used in veneering?
13. How do you repair a split in veneer?
14. How do you make a butt joint in veneering?
15. What is the purpose of backing?

The buffet with its molding and trim attached.

Chapter 12

Millwork and Fancy Cuts

Finishing a cabinet is not all a matter of abrasives and varnish, for some decorative touch, some final creative flourish can be added to lift each piece away from its basic arrangement of straight, vertical, and horizontal lines.

If you elect to apply a decorative effect to the furniture you build, you have available not only a variety of milled moldings (see Chapter 4), but a great many designs that can be wrought in your shop by using molder heads, shapers, the stationary saws and/or a portable router. What you specifically select to enhance a particular piece is strictly a matter of personal judgment, but whatever you do will radically change the appearance of your project.

SOME SIMPLE DECORATING IDEAS

Consider the changes that can occur with a simple, rectangular bookcase which begins with nothing more than a few shelves between verticals. A simple decorative effect is achieved by attaching a straight rail that crosses under the front of the case top. Or you could add a parallel rail under the bottom shelf. Now extend this basic concept of *framing* to both of the vertical sides of the case, and perhaps to its partitions. If the bookcase is made from 3/4″ stock, this face framing could simply be 1″ × 2″ stock which is either left square along its edges or rounded off. But such a face frame will look quite different if instead you use any of the many moldings available at most lumberyards. Now, however, more decisions are necessary, for will a cove, a half-round, or some more complex combination of curves look best? One thing is for sure, each kind of molding will give the piece a uniquely different look. Depending on the molding you choose, you may also find that the horizontal edges should be treated in a manner that is in keeping with the verticals. Molding, by the way, is almost always joined with mitered corners.

The top of a bookcase is another area that can easily be decorated. You could build the top so that it is flush with the sides or it could be extended beyond the sides by 1/2″ or 3/4″. This overhang could be over just the sides, or just the front, or all three. The top might be left as a simple overhang; its edges might also be trimmed with a cove or quarter-round molding fitted under its edges.

Figure 12-1   A simple, undercorated bookcase.

Bookcases tend to be built from 3/4″ stock, which presents a thick, solid looking project, if only because the wood is all 3/4″ thick. Bookcases, therefore, often appear heavy, sometimes ponderous, particularly if their edges are all square. This overbearing appearance is increased by the solidity, the very size, of the case itself. All of a sudden, a project that seemed delicate when you were in the designing stage turns out to look cumbersome because of the necessary thickness of the wood and the squareness of the cabinet. Your eye is startled by this thick, square look and immediately searches for some kind of visual relief. Molding and trim provide that relief because of their curves, even a 1/4″ beading glued down the center of a 3/4″ edge of a board, that only barely breaks the monotony of squareness.

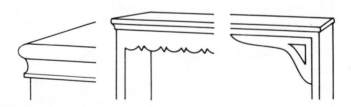

Figure 12-2   Top overhang, with a variety of decorative moldings.

Figure 12-3   Decorative molding and trim assembled on the baseboard.

The bottom of a cabinet or bookshelf can also be decorated by using a baseboard that surrounds the front and sides of the unit. Cabinet baseboards can be as simple as a $1'' \times 4''$ plate attached around the bottom of the project. But the plate can also have molding along its top edge or on its face. Or it can be made from a combination of boards, plates, trims, and moldings. The base itself can be a straight piece of wood, but it might also be curved or scrolled and have feet.

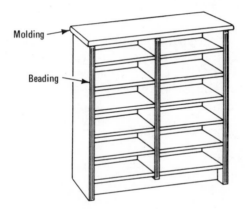

Molding

Beading

Figure 12-4   The bookcase decorated with molding instead of straight rails.

The feet on the sides of the case are cut out of the bottom edge of each side, then the baseboard is scrolled with a jigsaw or band saw. Boards for both the front and the sides are then mitered and glue-screwed in place. Made in this manner, the base serves only the purpose of enhancing the bottom of the project.

Alternatively, the base can be made to support the entire unit; a heavy cleat is glue-screwed around the underside of the sides and front of the cabinet. The cleat must be at least $1'' \times 1''$; and it will support the unit better if it is cut from hardwood stock. The base is glue-screwed to the cleat and extends below it to the floor. Bases assembled in this manner are often shaped pieces of wood with flutings, coves, curves, or carvings. You may be able to find exactly the right configuration you need in your local lumberyard. You can also create the curves you want with a table saw, although a shaper would make the job somewhat quicker to perform.

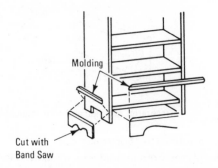

Molding

Cut with
Band Saw

Figure 12-5   Feet on the casework may be cut out of the baseboard with a
sabre or band saw.

DISHING WITH A TABLE SAW

The procedure for "dishing out," or cutting a curve in the center of a board is
always the same. For the sake of illustration, suppose you have a piece of hardwood stock which is 1 1/8" thick and 3 1/4" wide and you want to cut a dish
2 1/8" wide and 3/8" deep along its center.

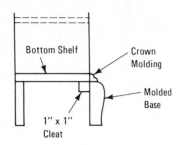

Bottom Shelf   Crown
Molding

Molded
Base

1" x 1"
Cleat

Figure 12-6   Baseboards may be attached to a cleat and trimmed with
molding.

1. Set the saw blade so that it is 3/8" above the table. The blade will be too
   wide at table level to cut the 2 1/8" dish.
2. Set a diagonal fence so that by cutting the wood at an angle the blade will
   remove only 2 1/8" of wood inside the dish. When you have worked out
   the proper fence angle, clamp the fence tightly to the saw table. Keep the
   clamps well out of your way.
3. Lower the saw blade to 1/16" and make the first pass, holding the wood
   firmly on the table. Feed the stock *very* slowly through the saw.

4. After the first pass, raise the blade about 1/8″ and make sure the channel is in the right location. Continue raising the blade no more than 1/8″ at a time for each pass until the channel reaches the correct depth (3/8″) and width (2 1/8″).

To complete the milling of the piece, you must proceed through three additional steps:

5. Round off the top corner of the piece to a 3/8″ radius, using a router or a block plane.

6. Round off the opposite side of the curve with a block plane.

7. The bottom corner is beveled either with a jack plane, table saw, or jointer.

MOLDING AND SHAPING MACHINES AND MACHINE/ATTACHMENTS

The majority of moldings and trim that you will find on the market are milled from softwood, which is an acceptable addition to perhaps 90 percent of all woodworking projects from trimming windows and doors to decorating built-ins. But if you are building a piece of fine furniture that is going to be veneered with, say, rosewood, you would hardly want to trim the piece with pine millwork. So the chances are you will have to find an appropriate piece of hardwood and shape it yourself. And that requires the services of some special machinery and/or accessories, that you can attach to your stationary tools.

Shapers

The shaper is a simple, yet versatile machine, used primarily for cutting edges on straight or curved pieces, making decorative moldings, and producing flutes, reeds, grooves, and joints. The versatility of shaper operations comes not from the machine, but from the kinds of cutters you put on it.

The shaper itself is a heavy base that supports a table top with a miter-gauge groove and a fence. There is a spindle located behind the fence which rotates the cutters at speeds of between 5,000 rpm and 10,000 rpm. The shapes of the cutters are identical to those used with a molder head.

Cutters

While they may vary somewhat, there are four types of shaper cutters: three-lip cutters, grooving saws, three-knife cutter heads, and clamp-type cutter heads.

Three-lip cutters are the safest kind to use. They consist of three blades honed into a given shape and can be purchased with carbide tips.

Grooving saws can be used for making many kinds of joints such as the tongue-and-groove.

Three-knife safety cutter heads are very much like the molder head accessory used on stationary saws. They are designed to accept a variety of shaped knives.

Clamp-type cutter heads have two knives and must be properly adjusted or they will come loose and cause all kinds of damage.

Shaping Methods

There are four basic methods of working with a shaper:

1. You can shape with a guide or fence, particularly when you are working on straight edges.
2. You can use depth collars, which will control the depth of cut. The collar is assembled on the spindle with the blades, which is a help when working with irregularly shaped surfaces.
3. Patterns can be used, particularly when you are producing a number of identical pieces.
4. Forms can also be used if you are doing large production jobs that make it worth the time and effort to devise special jigs and clamping devices.

Shaping Procedure

1. Select the cutter for the shape needed. In many cases, you will need meshing cutters, such as when making a rule joint for a table leaf or a tongue and groove.
2. Mount the cutter on its spindle so that the majority of the cutting will be done at the bottom edge of the stock. Be sure the rotation and feed are correct. Cutters must rotate so that the flat side of the blade (not the beveled side) cuts the work first. This usually means the work must be fed into the machine from right to left.
3. Adjust the fence faces. The fences should be in line with each other and parallel to the miter gauge groove. Whenever possible, cover the spindle with a safety shield.
4. Run a scrap piece of wood past the cutters to make certain you are getting the cut you want. If the cut is a deep one, you may want to make it with several passes, chipping away a little more wood each time.
5. Cut the wood by moving it steadily, and not too quickly, past the cutters.

Molder Heads

Molder heads can be purchased for use on both table and radial-arm saws, and on a drill press, if the spindle speed is at least 5,000 rpm. The molder head is attached to the arbor, on either a table or radial-arm saw. With the radial arm, the motor is then adjusted to its vertical position. You have to set the infeed fence back by the amount of wood being removed so that the work will be fully supported on its cut side. You must also work more slowly than you would with a shaper, but the end results are the same.

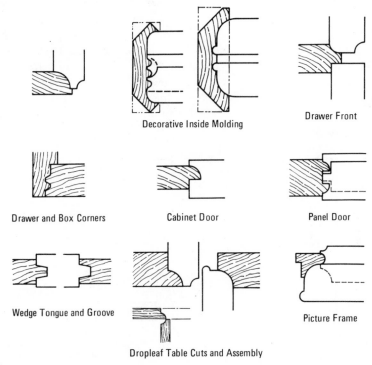

Decorative Inside Molding

Drawer Front

Drawer and Box Corners

Cabinet Door

Panel Door

Wedge Tongue and Groove

Picture Frame

Dropleaf Table Cuts and Assembly

Figure 12-7. Molder-head attachment for a radial arm, table saw, or drill press.

Shaping on a Drill Press

The standard drill press chuck must be replaced with a shaper adapter. Never use the chuck that holds your drills. The drill press can handle either the molder head or the standard cutters used on a shaper.

Shaping on a Table Saw

A little tricky, but it can be done. Instead of turning cutters into a vertical position, the wood must be held on edge and handled accordingly; that is, the wide surface of the wood must be held against a saw fence, rather than the table top. For making some cuts, this is quite acceptable, but for most shaping you will find it is more convenient to use a radial arm or drill press.

Shaper Blades

There are more than 50 shaper blades, each with a different pattern. But the 50 becomes hundreds once you learn to use only part of a curved blade, or to combine the blades, as well as use them at different angles.

There is no special procedure for shaping a piece, other than to try and make your cuts in such a manner that you will always have a maximum amount of wood left on the stock to hang on to. A sample of shaping a piece with several different cuts is offered here as a general approach to shaping:

Molding a cabinet door frame. Suppose you are making a frame and panel construction and wish to shape the frame rails from a piece of 1 1/8″ X 1 5/8″ stock. When it is shaped, the rail will have one large curve, one small beading, and a dado along its inside edge to accept the panel.

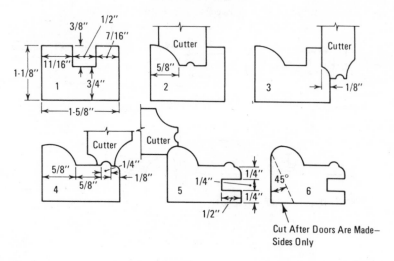

Cut After Doors Are Made—
Sides Only

Figure 12-8.   Six steps to shaping a cabinet door frame in a frame and panel construction.

1. Plough a groove in the top of the piece that is 3/8″ deep and 1/2″ wide, positioned 7/16″ in from the inside edge of the rail.
2. Using a 3/16″ to 3/8″ quarter-round cutter, shape the front curve of the large curve.
3. Using the same cutter, shape the 1/8″ curve along the inside edge of the rail.
4. Using the beading part of the cutter, shape the bead at the top front of the rail.
5. Round off the back of the large curve, still using the same cutter.
6. Groove the center of the front edge of the rail 1/2″ X 1/4″ for the panel. Use a dado blade. If the front edge of the rail is to be beveled, cut the bevel when all of the shaping and routing is completed.

Shaping With a Router

The portable router is a motor sitting on an adjustable base. The motor operates at speeds up to 28,000 rpm. There are over 35 different router bits that can be purchased and combined to make a whole series of curved edges. A brief survey of some of the various types of router bits and their uses follows.

Straight bits will cut grooves, dadoes, inlays, and rabbets and are available in diameters from 1/8″ to 3/4″. *Core-box bits* are like veining bits but larger. *Chamfer bits* cut 45° bevels on wood edges. *Rabbeting bits* cut rabbets. *Beading bits* are able to leave a sharp break or decorative bead at each end of the round. *Roman ogee bits* cut decorative edges on the inside of panels. *Cove bits* cut a concave radius and are used for making drop-leaf table rule joints. *V-grooving bits* make V-shaped cuts that imitate plank construction on plywood panels. *Dovetail bits* are used to cut dovetail dadoes or straight dovetails to form a right-angle joint in drawer construction.

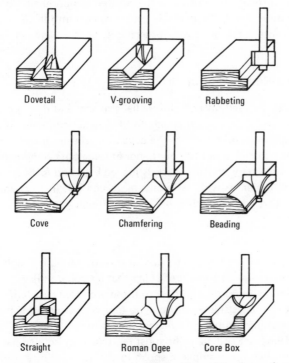

Dovetail	V-grooving	Rabbeting
Cove	Chamfering	Beading
Straight	Roman Ogee	Core Box

Figure 12-9. Router bits and the shapes they cut.

Cutting Control

You have four options when it comes to keeping a portable router from flying out the window any time it feels so inclined.

1. Use a straightedge or edges, clamped to the work. Or build a T-square that can be used for cutting rabbets and grooves.

2. Use an edge guide (purchased as an accessory) anytime you are not cutting more than about 12″ inside the edge of the work.

3. A bit with a pilot end attached to its bottom allows you to pull against the edge of the wood and keep control of the machine.

4. Templates or patterns can be cut out of 1/4″ stock and clamped or nailed to the stock.

Freehand routing is bravely done with no devices or guides of any kind and is perfectly okay if you don't want to make any straight lines. So how good the cutting is depends on how good you are—or how strong. Usually, when you are freehanding, you use a veining bit and your purpose is to clean out material in the background, to make raised letters, for example. If you really want to make your life difficult, try freehanding a cut that is more than 3/8″ deep.

On the other hand, the portable router can get into the middle of a board to shape the center of door panels, for example, or make any number of decorative routings.

Routing on a Radial Arm or Drill Press

Router bits can be used on both the radial-arm saw and drill presses. The drill press needs a special conversion chuck and the radial arm needs a chuck accessory for the rear of its motor shaft. The advantage of using either machine is that the bit will not go flying out of your hands at some critical moment. The bit, in fact, remains stationary and the work is moved back and forth along a fence, or even freehand, under it, with infinitely more control. In fact, you can almost relax when you are routing with either of the stationary units.

Turning

For turning, you need a lathe. You can turn wood on both a table and a radial-arm saw, but that requires some special jigs that let you do the work. Even these, however, will produce no results equal to those produced by a lathe.

A lathe combines the skill of a hand-tool worker with the power of a machine. Wood turning is a pleasant recreation for many people and has particular value to modelmakers and men who must reproduce an isolated part identical to one that is missing, for example, a spoke in antique furniture. In industry, the original patterns must be turned by hand, but then they are set up by automatic lathes which mass produce the particular product.

Types of Turning

There are two kinds of turning: cutting and scraping. Cutting tools include the *gouge, skew,* and *parting tool,* while the scraping tools are the *flat nose, round nose,* and *spear point.* When cutting, the outer edge of the wood is pierced and peeled off. In scraping, the tool is driven into the wood, and a gouge is used to pull away large pieces of waste material.

With the lathe you can cut tapers, coves, Vs, and all kinds of complicated designs which consist of straight turnings, tapers, Vs, coves, and concave or convex surfaces.

Legs and Posts

Primarily, the lathe is used to shape such essential structural parts as the legs and posts found on chairs, tables, desks, beds, and chests. Legs are an important identifying feature of furniture styles and can be produced in a variety of ways other than on a lathe, not only from solid lumber, but by laminating as well. Perhaps more importantly, legs can be purchased at most well-established lumberyards. The trend today, even among furniture-making concerns, is to purchase the needed legs and posts from those manufacturers who have specialized in making them. On the market today, you can find curved legs and turned ones, long ones and short ones. You can select from Roman, Colonial, Greek, Spanish, European, and plain-tapered designs.

Leg Shapes

There are several types of legs used in furniture construction:

Straight legs (square). These are the simplest to make because they consist only of a square piece of laminated, or more commonly, solid, lumber.

Square legs (tapered). There are a couple of different kinds of tapered legs.

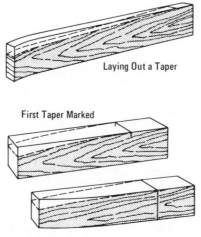

Laying Out a Taper

First Taper Marked

First Taper Cut, Second Taper Marked

Figure 12-10.   Plans for making a tapered leg.

Many contemporary pieces have legs tapered on only two sides. The inside taper offers a look of lightness to the entire design of the furniture, while there is a delicate gracefulness to the fully tapered leg, particularly if it is fluted or reeded.

To make a tapered leg, begin by making certain that the stock for all four legs is absolutely square. Then the procedure is as follows:

1. Lay the four legs next to each other and mark the place where the taper is to begin. Square the line completely around all four sides of each leg.
2. Determine the amount of wood to be removed at the bottom of the taper. Set a gauge to this amount and mark the amount of waste on the foot of the leg.
3. Cut the taper on each side using a taper jig and plane the taper surfaces until they are true.

Round legs (tapered). These are widely distributed in lumberyards and are made of plastic, wood, or metal. Normally, they have a ferrule and metal brackets for attaching them. If you are making them, cut square tapered legs and round them off using a plane and abrasives or a lathe.

Turned legs and posts. The legs and posts that you can turn on a lathe—or that you can buy—may have almost any combination of concave (cove) and convex (bead) shapes. Short, straight lines called *fillet* separate the various parts of the turned leg, and tapered surfaces may be either long or short. And all of these elements can be combined with short, square sections.

Figure 12-11.   Turned legs and posts are best done on a lathe.

The turned leg is characteristic of Early American and Colonial furniture as well as Traditional pieces. In modern furniture manufacturing processes, the turned leg is often joined with what is known as a *compression joint.*

Compression Joint

To make a compression joint, the end of the spindle is turned a thousandth of an inch larger than its socket hole. The dowels or the end of the spindle are then squeezed by rolling the wood between rollers which compress the wood fibers. The wood remains compressed as long as it does not take on any moisture. But after the glue is applied and the dowel inserted in its hole, moisture on the glue causes the wood to swell back to its original size, creating an unusually strong bond.

Cabriole Legs

The major characteristic of 18th century traditional furniture was the cabriole leg. In the beginning, it was designed by the French as an S-shaped leg, although it has varied considerably over the centuries. The English have always emphasized the knee; the French stress the foot and ankle. The cabriole is typically made with a square top if it is to be attached to a square or rectangular top. Sometimes is has a cat-faced top if it is to be attached to a circular or oval top. (The cat face is a large rabbet cut from the top of the leg which fits against the rail above the leg.) Because of its double curves, the cabriole would appear to be a difficult design to make, but actually it is relatively simple.

Figure 12-12.   The cabriole leg can have a square top or a cat-faced notch which allows it to overlap the frame to which it is attached.

Procedure for making a cabriole leg

1. Draw an accurate pattern for the leg on heavy cardboard.
2. Select a piece of stock that is thick enough to make the leg. If the leg has a rather full S-shape, you may need to glue up extra pieces wherever they are needed to fill out the curves. Be sure to match the grains of the glued pieces carefully.
3. With a large enough piece of stock in hand, trace the pattern on any two *adjoining* surfaces.

4. Make the two cuts needed to form one side of the leg on a band saw. Do not cut off all of the waste, but stop the saw about 1/4″ from the end of the curves so that the waste remains attached to the leg and can be used to support the leg when it is cut on the adjacent side.

5. Now turn the leg over and cut the two curves on the second pattern, and remove *all* the waste on both sides.

6. After rough cutting the leg, smooth and sand to its final shape.

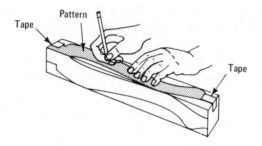

Figure 12-13.   Plans for cutting a cabriole leg.

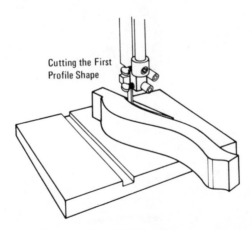

Figure 12-14.   The leg pattern must be cut out from two adjacent sides.

Reeding and Fluting

Both reeding and fluting are decorative cuts on posts and legs. Reeding is a series of equally spaced convex (beaded) divisions; fluting is a series of concave (coved) divisions. Both cuts are done in the same manner, but with different cutting tools.

Both fluting and reeding can be done on a lathe, a shaper, a drill press, a radial-arm saw, or with a portable router, but you will need to make a fluting jig to hold the work in rigid position as it is being cut.

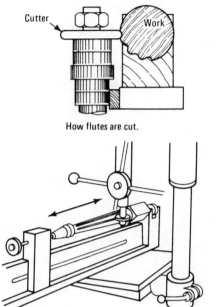

How flutes are cut.

Figure 12–15.   Reeds and flutes are often used as a decorative feature in furniture.

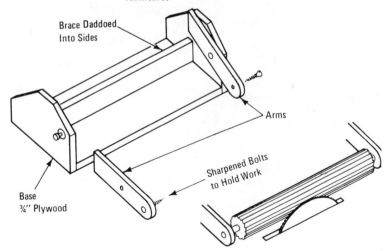

Brace Daddoed Into Sides

Arms

Base ¾" Plywood

Sharpened Bolts to Hold Work

Figure 12–16.   Reeding and fluting is best done on a lathe, but this simple jig will allow you to do the same work with either a radial arm or a table saw.

Figure 12-17.   Molding head cutters and the shapes you can mold with them.

Review Questions

1. Describe some original ways of decorating the front edges of a simple bookcase.

2. Suggest some ways of decorating the top of a cabinet with a 3/4″ overhang.

3. Name two ways of making baseboards for a cabinet.

4. What is the procedure for dishing out the center of a board with a table saw?

5. What is a shaper used for?

6. Using the cutter shapes shown in this chapter, design your own shape for a piece of molding to be used on a buffet.

7. What is the difference between a molder head and a shaper?

8. How is a portable router used for making decorative cuts?

9. What is a turning jig for?

10. What is the procedure for making a cabriole leg?

To apply varnish, use long brush strokes *with* the grain.

Chapter 13

Finishing Touches

It is very human to build a cabinet and keep telling yourself that each little error will surely be covered at some later stage. If you wish to be a very human cabinetmaker then you can even look at your finished work and not see a single one of the flaws in its surfaces. But if you choose to be professional in your approach to building furniture, then you will always have, in the very front of your mind, that no mistake can ever be hidden by the next stage, or the one after that, or least of all, by the finish.

Paint hides very little of anything; the clear finishes exaggerate practically every flaw, including a depressing number of things that you did not even notice before it was applied. A finish protects, enhances, glorifies, immortalizes. But no finish can be any better than the surfaces it covers. Moreover, there are countless mistakes that occur as the finish is applied, even when that finish is going down on a perfect surface.

A perfect finish is even and smooth. It has no dents, gouges, scratches, or imperfections; the filler hides its cracks and holes; it blends into the grain of the wood and is exactly level with the surrounding surface. Arriving at so flawless a finish is no picnic. A cabinetmaker can spend weeks filling and smoothing a piece of wood, and when he is finished it will *look* no different than when he began.

But fill and sand you must, or you will not achieve a decent finish. You must sand until the thought of abrasives or wood putty leaves you exhausted. And only then can you begin to consider applying the finish.

FINISHING EQUIPMENT

The essential equipment used in finishing furniture is a spray gun, brushes, and on rare occasions, a paint roller.

Spray Guns

The basic spraying unit includes a small compressor, an air hose, and a suction spray gun. Essentially, the compressor draws air through an intake valve, compresses it, and blasts it out an exhaust valve into the air hose. The spray gun on portable spray units is usually of the bleeder type, which means that you can only control the amount of paint entering and leaving the gun. Nonbleeder spray guns give the operator control over both the paint *and* the air. Spray guns can be used in a spray booth set up in a corner of your shop or out of doors on a dry, windless day. Wherever you use a spray gun, wear a respirator.

Spraying

The only way to learn how to handle a spray gun is to use one, but here are some tips to remember:

1. Keep the nozzle of the gun about 6″ or 8″ from the surface being sprayed. If the gun is too close, the paint will be applied too heavily and tend to sag. If it is too far away, there will be excessive dusting, which produces a sandy finish.
2. Keep the gun at right angles to the surface at all times as you move it back and forth across the surface. Move your arm, not your wrist. Wrists get tired faster than arms, and besides, they tend to arc the gun nozzle off its perpendicular line with the surface.
3. Begin each stroke before pulling the trigger, then bring the paint onto the surface and release the trigger before the stroke is finished.
4. When spraying a corner, hold the gun far enough away so that the paint covers both sides at the same time.
5. Overlap each stroke about 50 percent.
6. When spraying a curved surface, keep the gun at the same distance from the surface at all times; that is, follow the curve.

Some Problems With Spraying

Streaks come from tipping the gun up or down. Or dirt may be in the nozzle.

Orange peel is when the paint looks like the skin of an orange; this condition occurs primarily with lacquer. Its cause may be related to several factors; the air pressure is too high or too low; the gun is being held too far from the surface; the paint is poorly mixed; the painting surface improperly prepared; the paint is improperly thinned. *Runs* and *sags* occur if the gun is tilted too much, if an excess of material is applied, or if the material is too thin. *Misting* occurs while you are spraying. It means the material is too thin or the air pressure is too high. *Starving* means the nozzle is not receiving enough paint, at which point it is probably sputtering. This results from dirt in the air hose, a clogged nozzle, or not enough paint in the spray can.

Brushes

Brushes come in all sizes and qualities. The best and most expensive are *sport bristles* made of boar hair. But there are also *nylon bristles* which are commonly used for enamel and varnish. If the bristles of a brush are bent back, they should spring into place without any loose ends flying all over the room.

Varnish or enamel brushes. These are used for heavy paints and are usually 4″ or 5″ wide with a straight cut edge that is good for long strokes on large, flat surfaces.

Wall brushes. These are identical to the varnish brushes, but with longer bristles.

Utility brushes. Between 1″ and 1-1/2″ wide, these are used for painting trim.

Sash brushes. These are used when the work to be painted is intricate. They have long handles and oval or round bristle heads; the bristles can be straight or chisel-cut.

Breaking in a Brush

Before using a new brush hold it under a faucet and pull at the bristles. Having the loose bristles come out in your hand is better than having them spread all over your project. Then wrap the bristles in heavy paper and store the brush flat, or hang it up. Never stand a brush on its bristles.

Cleaning a Brush

The process for cleaning brushes is always the same; only the solvent changes.

1. Soak the brush in the proper solvent. Brushes used with varnish or enamel require a solution of 50 percent varnish and 50 percent turpentine. Paint and stain brushes need a solution of two parts linseed oil and one part turpentine. Use alcohol for shellac brushes. Lacquer brushes must be cleaned with lacquer thinner.
2. Squeeze all excess solution from the bristles.
3. Use a comb to pull out any material imbedded between the bristles.
4. Wipe the bristles against your hand or the side of a can.
5. Wash the brush thoroughly with a good detergent and warm water. Wipe it dry and again comb the bristles.
6. Wrap the bristles in heavy paper and either store it flat or hang it up.

Tips on Using Brushes

When painting with enamel or varnish, dip no more than the bottom third of the bristles in the material and flow the material on liberally, with a minimum of strokes. Do not bend the bristles any more than is necessary. Immediately cross-stroke, that is, paint at right angles to the original direction. Use a light touch and very little material on the tip of the bristles to fill in the ridges left by the brush and provide a smooth finish.

Always hold the brush at right angles to the painting surface, and never paint with the side of the brush; this causes *fingering*.

Dip the brush into the finishing material and tap the bristles against the side of the can. Never scrape the bristles or they will loosen.

Never let a brush stand on its bristles. This will curl them.

Rollers

Unless you are painting huge, flat surfaces (like walls) a roller has little value in finishing cabinet work. The roller is dipped into the paint (or varnish) and then rolled across the surface. It is then rolled back across the first stroke at a 45° angle. Various roller pads can be purchased to help you achieve different textures to the painted surface.

FINISHING SUPPLIES

Various finishing supplies are needed to complete different finishes:

Turpentine. A solvent for paint and enamel, made from the resin of pine trees.

Linseed oil. Made from flaxseed, linseed oil is used in paints and stains.

Alcohol. Used as a thinner and solvent for shellac.

Benzene. A cleaning fluid made from tar, also an excellent general-purpose solvent.

Mineral spirits. An alternative to turpentine and can be used as a thinner or solvent. It is pure, distilled petroleum.

Waxes. These may be in liquid or paste form, but they all consist of beeswax, paraffin, carnauba wax, and turpentine. They provide water resistance to a finished surface.

Pumice. Made from lava, this is available in several grades of white powder which is combined with water or oil to rub down a finish. The usual grades employed in furniture finishing are FF and FFF.

Rottenstone. This comes from shale and is a reddish brown to greyish black powder which is considerably finer than pumice. It is mixed with oil or water to produce a smoother finish than pumice.

Tack rags. You can buy them. Otherwise you can make one by dipping a clean, lint-free cloth in a solution of varnish that has been diluted about 25 percent with turpentine.

THE STAGES OF FINISHING

Whenever possible, avoid a deadline for putting the finish on any project. Having gone through all the labor of building it, you can destroy its final appearance with one errant flop of a brush wielded in haste. This is the phase that should not be hurried. The wood must be meticulously prepared. Each coat of the finishing material must be given its proper drying time. Each coat must be totally prepared for the next application.

Now is not the time to save money on materials, either. Use the highest grade silicon carbide or open-coat aluminum oxide abrasives. Select the highest quality paints or varnishes, and use the best brushes or rollers.

Adopt a state of mind which presumes there will be a minimum of two coats of finish and perhaps more, even if you also apply a sealer and a primer coat first. Cabinetmakers are fortunate to have at their disposal modern finishing materials which are better today than ever before. The drudgery of finishing has been reduced by modern technology to less than a third of what our forebearers endured. But there are still no honest-to-goodness one coat finishes.

There are several basic steps to finishing fine woods, although not every project will require each of them.

Bleaching

Bleaching takes the color out of wood and is necessary when you want to achieve a light or honey-colored finish. It will also change the natural color of a wood; reduce, for example, the amount of red in mahogany.

If the color of a wood is too dark, or if there are undesirable stains in it, you can bleach the wood to a lighter shade by applying any readily available household chlorine bleach. First, heat the wood, either by putting it in sunlight, or under a spotlight. Then soak the wood with undiluted bleach; keep the project wet until all of the discoloration disappears. Never allow the bleach to dry before the next application. When the stain is gone, wash the bleach off the wood with a 50–50 solution of water and white vinegar, then wipe dry. Allow the surface to dry for 12 hours or more at 70°F with good air circulation. When it is dry, sand the wood lightly, making sure not to sand any deeper than the bleach has penetrated.

One problem to be aware of, especially if you are bleaching a solid, glued-up stock, is that all that water applied to the wood surface can make it *cup.* As a precaution, when you are washing off the bleach, dampen the undersides on the surfaces with water to equalize the moisture content on the wood.

Prestaining

When you are faced with a wood that has considerable variation in its color (like walnut), and you want a consistent hue, you can stain the light parts to darken them in keeping with the deeper shades. Use either a water-soluble or an alcohol-based sap stain and continue applying it to the light areas until they darken to the proper shade. There are several reasons that a water-soluble stain is used at this stage: they are inexpensive, primarily because they come in powder form and must be mixed with water; they can be applied with a brush, they dry quickly, and they can be darkened simply by adding more coats to the wood.

They do, of course, swell the wood fibers and raise the grain, so they may distort glued joints.

Staining

The objective of any stain is to soak into the fibers of the wood, thereby accentuating the grain and also coloring it. Conversely, paint or varnish sit on the wood surface and more or less cover the grain. A whole rainbow of stains are sold today and each of these can be mixed to create an endless number of shades. But use a standard can of mahogany stain on a piece of pine and the wood will not look like mahogany. You can lighten a stain that is too dark by thinning it with turpentine or mineral spirits, but most of the popular stains are too thin and must be darkened. Your options are to either add color or apply several coats to the wood you want to stain.

You can also buy stains with wax, varnish, and/or wood sealer in them. These are not much good at staining, waxing, varnishing, or even sealing. When the manufacturer combines functions in his product, he is trying to market a one-coat finishing product. The result is usually nothing more than a colored wash.

You have one alternative to commercial stains; one option that not only costs less but is also a more precise way of achieving the color *you* want the wood to have. The alternative is to make your own stain.

Obtain a can of *penetrating oil stain* (sold at large paint stores) and two tubes of artist's oil, a burnt umber, and burnt sienna. Burnt umber is dark brown; burnt sienna is reddish. When mixed in different proportions, they will produce almost any shade of brown, to which can be added any other oil color you wish. When staining, first pour enough of the penetrating oil stain to cover your project into a nonplastic dish and then stir in the artist's oils.

When you have the color you want, dip a clean, lint-free rag into the stain and rub it *into* the wood. Let it stand for an hour or two before rubbing off any excess oil that remains on the surface. If you do not wipe the excess, the wood will continue getting darker. Watch the wood changing color until it attains the tone you want and then arrest the staining action by wiping it. If the color becomes too dark, lighten it by wiping turpentine on the wood. If the stain is too light, give the project a second coat. Allow 24 hours for the stain to dry before applying any of the finishing materials.

Stain sometimes creates blotches because of imperfections in the wood. The best way to minimize this unevenness is to put a sealer into the wood first, providing it is not a straight-grained hardwood. Then stain it. It is also wise to test-stain a scrap of the wood you are covering. Usually, the color is a different shade in its mixing dish than when it is on the wood.

Wash Coating

Sometimes a thin coat of shellac or lacquer thinner is wiped over a stain to keep it from *bleeding.* A recommended wash that will seal most stains is made of 7 parts alcohol and 1 part 4-lb. cut shellac.

Fillers

Rubbing a filler into the wood fibers is optional, depending on the wood you are working with, and the ultimate color of the project. White zinc, white lead, or a clear paste with some light color added is used if your aim is a blond finish. Which of these you use depends on the wood. Pine, cherry, bass wood, poplar, fir, and cedar are small-pored, close-grained woods and do not need any filler at all. Birch, beech, gum, and maple are moderately open-pored and may, or may not, require a liquid filler. Such open-grained woods as oak, mahogany and walnut take a paste filler.

The application of filler varies according to whether it is liquid or a paste. A paste filler is mixed with turpentine, benzene, or naptha until it is the consistency of heavy cream. Whatever coloring you intend to add is then mixed with a little turpentine until you attain the proper shade. Then it is added to the filler. Apply the mixture with a stiff brush, rubbing it into the pores of the wood and occasionally working *across* the grain. Also add an extra heavy coating to any end grains. Now rub the filler into the wood with a piece of burlap, heavy cloth, or the palms of your hands. Wait about half an hour, and then use a coarse cloth to wipe off any excess filler that shows on the surface of the wood. Finish cleaning by wiping with a soft cloth. Your objective is to pack the filler into the pores of the wood; but if you rub any filler too hard, it will come loose, if not on the spot, after the top coat has been applied. So work carefully. If, when you are finished and the filler has dried, you find a residue, a rag soaked in turpentine will soften it enough to be scraped off.

Sealers

Many professional wood finishers prefer to put a clear sealer on every wood, no matter what the finish is to be. Wood is never a perfect material. Even a hard, close-grained piece of teak or ebony has soft spots that soak up the finishing material and produce a flat or sometimes rough area. Wood sealer is made to fill up the wood fibers in those soft spots and also prevent the stain from bleeding. Any sealer will do the job; lacquer sanding sealers are unusually effective. The sealer is a clear liquid that covers easily with a brush or rag and dries in minutes. It is, however, wiser to allow a day for drying before sanding. A light sanding normally produces a satiny touch to the surface.

There is nothing better than a coat of something wet to show up all the imperfections in the wood that you missed, as well as all those dents and gouges you forgot to fill. When the something wet is a sealer, you still have time to complete repairs to the wood after it is dry. Admittedly, going back to your wood putty and sandpaper is a bore, but best you repair any imperfections now, than stare at them once the finish has locked them into the surface forever.

Glazing, Distressing, and Special Effects

It is at this point in finishing that the wood is ready to receive its final finishing coats. If the finish is to have any overtones, they should be applied now.

Glazing is done to give the wood a shaded, highlighted, or antiqued appearance. The typical method of glazing is to use a light tint in the stain or filler. Then rub a darker shade of glaze over the surface and wipe most of it off, except in corners and along edges or other areas where you want the piece to look worn. Several glazes are sold on the market that come already tinted or require you to add the appropriate pigment. You can also make your own glaze by mixing a tablespoon of, say, burnt sienna with a half-pint of turpentine and then adding a tablespoon of lamp black.

Distressing is a common treatment used on both French and Italian provincial furniture to give it the appearance of old age. It is done by banging away at the wood with an old mace, pieces of chain, chunks of coral, or anything that will create gouges and scratches. These imperfections are then filled with black glaze or a dark stain, crayon, paint, or anything that will *age* the surface of the wood.

Shading can be done simply by applying a darker stain or glaze to the edges and corners of the project. *Splattering* will get you a speckled texture. You achieve it by flicking a glaze or stain over the surface with the bristles of a stiff brush. Be careful you do not overload the brush or you will have blobs instead of splatters. You can get good enough at splattering (with some practice) so that each splatter is a little dot that looks just like a worm hole. The trick is not to put too much material on the bristles, then to bend them back with a stick, and let go. If the bristles are nice and stiff they will spring into place and spray tiny old worm holes all over the wood.

Top Coats

The final coats of a finish can be varnish, shellac, lacquer, enamel, or an oil; all of them require some amount of hand rubbing and polishing after they are dry.

Varnish

Varnishes are available in high and medium glosses, satin finish and flat, are resistant to liquids, and have always been easy to apply. They consist of resins, linseed oil, drying agents, and enough turpentine to make them flow. Varnishes have been used for centuries. Although they have always been slow driers, they produce a finish that is harder than anything else. Nevertheless, heat can blister varnish and many liquids will stain it.

But in the twentieth century there came polyurethane. The urethanes are varnish. They are as easy to apply as regular varnish, dry faster, resist water, alcohol, dirt, and the violence of small children. They are also so clear they hardly darken any wood they cover. They cannot, however, be put on top of shellac, lacquer, or most sander-fillers.

Figure 13-1   Before any finish coat is applied, carefully clean the surface with a tack rag.

All varnishes will gather specks of dust while they are drying, so only use them in the most dust-free environment possible. Even then, use the fastest drying varnish you can find; there is no advantage to a slow dryer. In fact, the longer a varnish is wet, the more dust it will collect.

The wood must be totally free of any foreign matter before it is varnished. Wipe the surface thoroughly with a tack rag and then flow varnish over the wood with either a high-grade brush, a rag, or a foam rubber pad. The foam rubber pads are a boon. They hold a good amount of material, leave no brush strokes, and are disposable. In other words, most of the delicacy of applying varnish with a brush can be forgotten.

When using a brush, apply the varnish with a minimum of strokes, then finish off by going lightly over it with the tip of the bristles, using almost no varnish. Once you learn how to just "kiss" the varnish, you will be able to erase any sign of brush strokes and produce a uniform finish. Remove excess varnish from the brush by tapping its bristles lightly against the container. Do *not* drag the bristles over the rim of the can; dragging makes the varnish bubble and the bubbles will prevent a smooth finish. Bubbles are the big enemy of varnish, so always stir it, *never* shake.

Figure 13-2   To apply varnish, use long brush strokes *with* the grain.

If you are going to wipe the varnish on a cloth, fold the material and soak it in the varnish. Now spread the varnish with long strokes running with the grain. Do not rub, or in any way try to force, the varnish into the wood. Wipe away any runs immediately; varnish does not level itself and a goober will dry into a nice, hard goober.

Most projects require at least two coats of varnish. Each coat should be sanded lightly until its sheen is dulled, but do not scrub the finish, only sand it to a uniform texture that shows no shiny areas. Then dust the surface with a tack rag and apply the next coat. Some experts prefer that a very fine-grade aluminum oxide abrasive be used on the first coat, and a #400 (super-fine) wet and dry paper on the second. You can also use a fine grade of steel wool on varnish.

If the wood has been stained, varnish may streak the color unless you apply a sealer first. A thin coat of shellac will seal most stains and will also act as a base to reduce the amount of varnish needed to no more than two coats.

No matter how careful you are, the wood will collect specks of dust. Or there will be tiny bumps or the final coat will have too much gloss. So you could go on sanding your varnish and applying a new "final coat" forever and still not get a perfect finish. This is why the last coat of varnish is always hand rubbed.

Shellac

Shellac comes in two colors, orange and white. It is an excellent primer-sealer on any plywood destined to be painted and also works under varnish. But it will darken any wood it is put on. Shellac consists of the resinous secretions from the Asian insect, lac, which is mixed with denatured alcohol. The amount of lac used is indicated by the *cut* of the shellac. A two-pound cut, for example, means that two pounds of lac is mixed with one gallon of alcohol. A three-pound cut would be three pounds of lac per gallon of alcohol.

Because of its alcohol content, shellac evaporates quickly; buy only as much as you can use in a relatively short time. Whatever cut you buy is diluted to a 3-cut ratio by adding whatever amount of denatured alcohol is necessary. To do this properly, follow the thinning chart printed on the shellac can.

Only stir shellac because shaking it causes bubbles that will stay on the wood and cause an uneven finish. If possible, use a new brush for each coat applied; used brushes are cleaned with alcohol, followed by a mild solution of household ammonia and warm water. Obviously the wood should be thoroughly wiped with a tack rag before any shellac gets near it.

Brush the shellac into the wood with long, even strokes that overlap slightly. It is possible to brush shellac in any direction because the brush marks will fade as the shellac dries. If the shellac is a 3-lb. cut, the first coat will be dry enough after two hours to rub down with a fine-grade steel wool pad. It is then wiped with a tack rag and the next coat is applied. If the final coat is too glossy, a light rubbing with fine steel wool will dull it to a satiny sheen. Two coats are sufficient to provide a solid base for a varnish top coat. If you are not varnishing, as many coats as you wish may be added, but each should be rubbed down with steel wool and dusted.

Lacquer

Some lacquers are made to cover metals, others are for woods; some are meant for brushing, others can only be sprayed. The wood lacquers are available in pigmented as well as clear gloss, semi-gloss, and flat finishes. So when you are buying a lacquer, be specific about what it is going to cover and the kind of finish you want. There is also a special sealer which must be put on most wood before it is lacquered. And take note of the particular brand of lacquer you buy. Lacquers are made from a variety of formulas and often the only way you can thin a given brand is to use the special thinner made by its manufacturer.

Lacquer is probably the most widely used top coat in the furniture industry and for some pretty good reasons. It dries almost on contact, producing a thin, clear coating that can be covered with a second application within minutes. A lacquer finish is hard, resistant to most liquids and temperatures, and is easy to rub down or spot repair. There are also some disadvantages, including the fact that lacquers dry so quickly it is difficult to apply them with a brush. They are also not as hard a finish as the urethanes, and excessive moisture (such as in a bathroom) has been known to peel lacquer right off the wood it was so painstakingly put on.

When you are spraying lacquer, unless your equipment has a large capacity, the lacquer must be thinned about 50 percent. Remember that lacquer dries quickly, so be prepared to keep spraying until the gun is empty or stop and clean the nozzle from time to time. You will have to spray on four or five coats, and each one should be lightly sanded and cleaned with a tack rag before the succeeding coat is applied. When you are finished, the final coat will require hand rubbing. But before you do anything else, clean your painting equipment with lacquer thinner. If you wait too long (even five minutes) cleaning can be quite a chore.

If you intend to brush on a lacquer, use a soft-bristled brush and work quickly. Apply the lacquer in long, overlapping strokes and don't worry about going back over your work the way you would varnish. You will have to wait two hours between coats before sanding with a fine grit abrasive, but after the third coat is dry, it can be hand rubbed and polished.

Enamel

When you decide to paint a cabinet, in almost every case you should use an oil-based enamel. Enamel is, in reality, varnish with a pigment in it. Your choice of paint over a clear finish is naturally dictated by the project and how it will be used, as well as the wood you made it from. If the wood figure and grain do not have much character (such as pine or poplar), you might as well cover it with paint.

The procedure for painting is in itself uncomplicated, but do not omit any of the steps or you will lessen the ultimate finish. Sand the surfaces to be painted and wipe them with a tack rag. Apply a coat of filler, particularly if the wood is a softwood or an open-grained species, such as oak, walnut, mahogany, or chestnut. Hand sand the filler when it is dry, and apply a primer coat. Don't strain yourself to do a perfect job, but don't leave any goobers or take any holidays either. When the primer is dry, sand it and wipe it *clean* with a tack rag. Each of the finishing coats must have a light sanding which is boring, but necessary. Fortunately, two or three coats of a high-grade furniture enamel is usually enough, although only you can decide just how many coats you need. After the final coat has dried for about a month, give it a coating of furniture wax.

Rubbing a Finish

The procedure of rubbing begins after the last coat has had at least seven days to dry and harden. Mix a paste of FFF pumice and motor oil (never linseed or any of the drying oils). Dip a heavy, folded pad of cloth (preferably felt) into the mixture and "sand" the surface with long, straight strokes with the grain. Use moderate pressure. By the time the finish has a smooth texture, you will have also dulled its luster considerably. To restore the luster, mix a modicum of powder rottenstone and rubbing (or motor) oil into a paste (or slurry) and rub it into the surface. Rottenstone is a finer mixture than pumice. Wipe the excess paste off the surface when you have attained the desired luster. Continue wiping paste off the wood using successively clean cloths until the surface squeaks. All this sounds easy enough, but don't expect to accomplish everything in an odd half-hour of spare time.

Some Hand-Rub Finishes

Unquestionably, the most important ingredient in any of the best varnishes is tung oil. Tung oil is one of the oldest of all wood preservatives and was used to weatherproof clothing, shoes, boats, and houses in China for centuries before Marco Polo brought it to Europe in the Middle Ages. Most of the world's tung oil is still produced in China, although the United States currently produces over 50 million pounds of it each year. Eighty percent of the American tung oil is used in the manufacture of both exterior and interior paints and varnishes. Nautical paints and varnishes must have tung oil to give them water and weather resistance. Heat will not "draw" it out of the wood it is applied to, and it is a superb sealer for wood, metal, concrete, and brick. Many professionals believe that tung oil produces a more durable finish than linseed oil, lacquer, varnish, or shellac; it does not darken with age, mildew, or bleed excessively.

You can rub the oil into wood with a cotton pad or with your bare hands. Rub until the oil completely saturates the wood. When the tung oil has dried overnight, it will present a low luster finish. If you want a satin sheen (medium luster), rub in a second coat; keep applying coats until the oil achieves the degree of gloss you want. Wait until each coat is completely dry before putting on the next one. Always apply tung oil on a dry, warm day or in a heated room.

Tung oil solidifies into a jelly when it is exposed to air. No matter how tight the can is sealed, enough air will get into it to make it congeal. If the tung oil on hand is less than three-quarters of a can, put it in a smaller container. Or fill the can with stones so there is no space in it for air.

Linseed Oil

If you have a year or so to spend on finishing a project, use boiled linseed oil;

not raw linseed oil. The label must read "boiled," which is an inaccurate statement. Boiled actually means that the manufacturer has added drying agents. Raw linseed oil hardly ever dries, which makes it excellent for anything outdoors, but is unsuitable for living room furniture.

There are various methods of applying linseed oil; everybody who uses linseed oil has his own system. In general terms, the procedure is to mix two parts linseed oil with one part turpentine or mineral spirits and place it in an open container over a fire. If you are using a stove, put the can in boiling water. When hot, dip a rag in it and rub it into the wood. Work about 15 or 20 minutes on only one small area at a time. Using both hands, rub the oil into the wood until it becomes saturated, then wipe away any excess oil with a clean rag. Reheat the linseed oil and go on to the next section, then the next, until the wood is totally saturated and wiped clean. Be sure to scrape any excess oil out of the corners and crevices lest it harden or even worse, become sticky.

If you rub boiled linseed oil into the wood long enough and hard enough, you might be able to put on a new coat every 24 hours, although it is more usual to allow a week's drying time for each coat. The more coats you put on, the more lustrous your finish will become, but apply at least three coats. Linseed oil gives a beautiful, mellow luster, although it is not very water resistant. It can withstand mild heat and probably will not show scratches as much as varnish. Naturally, the project ought to be given another coat or two every six months or once a year during its lifetime.

Beware of the rags you use with linseed oil: Burn them; throw them in water; anything, but do not leave them lying around. They are highly combustible. Never heat linseed oil in a closed can, either—it will most likely explode.

French Polish

There is a variation on the linseed oil finish called French polish. French Polish is a technique that produces that high gloss that everyone is always trying to duplicate by slobbering wax all over their best furniture. Make a ball of lint-free rags about the size of an apple and soak it in hot boiled linseed oil. Then squeeze the ball dry and dip it into one-pound cut shellac. Rub the mixture into the wood.

You cannot slap your cloth on the wood in any old way. Treat it like a belt sander; get it moving before you touch the wood and then keep it moving. Wipe the wood in a circular motion, with enough pressure to force the shellac and linseed oil into the pores of the wood, but not so much pressure that the pad sticks. When the pad starts to dry out, work your way over the nearest edge without ever stopping until the pad is clear of the surface.

When the entire project is covered, allow it to dry for 24 hours. Then put on the next coat. With the French polish technique, each coat adds to the sheen; you only stop putting on coats when the finish is as glossy as you want it. If it becomes too glossy, you can always tone it down by rubbing in a pumice-oil paste.

Lemon Oil

No wax should ever be put on any finish, but you can preserve a furniture finish with *pure* lemon oil. *Pure,* not lemon oil that has beeswax or linseed oil or any of the silicones added to it. Once a month, dampen a rag with pure lemon oil and rub it into the finish. Pure lemon oil is not greasy. However, all excess must be wiped off, since it will not evaporate, nor will the wood absorb any more than is rubbed into it—which, by the way, is a very small amount. The lemon oil will pick up any dirt on the furniture and leave it on the cloth, so it also acts as a cleaning agent.

Lemon oil *cannot* be applied on top of wax, so your furniture has to be thoroughly cleaned of all wax. A clean finish will last four or five times longer than one that is choked with layers of wax; lemon oil fills between the fibers of the wood and prevents it from absorbing moisture. Your furniture will last even longer if you rub lemon oil into its undersides once or twice a year to protect the wood.

Review Questions

1. How do you remove excess glue from wood?
2. What are three ways of filling holes or cracks in wood?
3. What are circular sanders used for in prefinishing? Belt sanders? Vibrating sanders?
4. How do you use a spray gun?
5. How do you break in a new brush?
6. How should brushes be cleaned and stored?
7. What are the advantages of the urethanes over regular varnish?
8. How do you brush varnish on a surface so that no brush strokes are visible?
9. Why is lacquer the most common finish used in the furniture industry?
10. What is the procedure for hand rubbing a varnish finish?
11. Compare and contrast a wax polish with pure lemon oil.
12. How do you apply French polish?

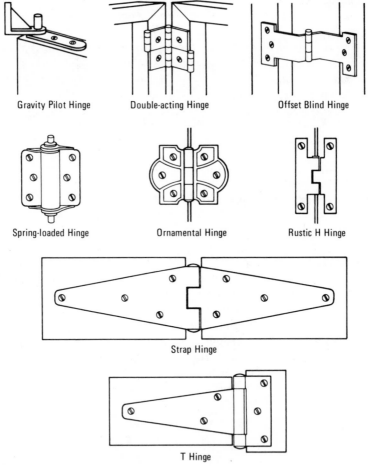

Gravity Pilot Hinge   Double-acting Hinge   Offset Blind Hinge

Spring-loaded Hinge   Ornamental Hinge   Rustic H Hinge

Strap Hinge

T Hinge

Figure 14-1   Door hinges.

Chapter 14

Hardware

There are too many types and styles of cabinet hardware to illustrate here, or in any book other than a catalog. But there are some basic and important facts to learn about hardware and its use in different woodworking projects.

To begin with, you can find a compatible hardware design for practically any furniture you build. Hinges and pulls, for example, can be purchased in Contemporary, Italian provincial, Spanish, French provincial, Traditional, and Early American styles; there is a plethora of hinges, drawer guides, pulls, knobs, casters, leg braces, and shelf supports to suit nearly any construction. You will notice all these just by glancing through any hardware catalog you happen to run across in stores or lumberyards. Allow yourself some research time whenever you are in a store that has catalogs and spend five or ten minutes just thumbing through the pages; it will give you an awareness of how various pieces look.

The reason for knowing what is available on the market should be obvious. You must have the hardware in hand before you begin building any project. It is the hardware that gives any piece its ultimate look; besides, how can you determine the exact location of a unit in a cabinet, or provide the proper clearances, if you do not know what metal work you are going to use?

HARDWARE REQUIREMENTS

In general, hardware is most often needed around the doors and drawers in cabinets, under chairs and tables, and in cabinet interiors. But it is for doors that most of the different types and kinds of hardware are intended.

Door Hardware

You will need catches, pulls, locks, and hinges for doors; in general, a *hinged door* requires some kind of surface hinge. *Lip doors* need a concealed or semi-concealed hinge. *Overlapping doors* work best with pivot hinges. *Sliding doors* require a groove to slide in. This groove can be routed out of the wood above and below the doors or can be purchased in metal, wood, or plastic styles. *Rolling doors* require handles, wheels, a metal or plastic track, and base guides.

Folding doors demand a special set of bi-fold hardware that includes a track, rollers, and pivot, as well as flush hinges. *Drop doors* often use a continuous or piano hinge for added strength, plus some type of lid support which can be either a special folding hinge or something as simple as a chain. *Open-frame doors,* in addition to their hinges and pulls, have a metal, plastic, or wooden grill rather than a solid panel inside their frames.

Hinges

Perhaps the largest single collection of utility hardware is hinges. They range from 8-foot long piano hinges on down to 1/2" or less. You can buy special cabinet hinges that are completely hidden; pivot hinges, double-action hinges for folding doors, no-mortise hinges, and just plain butts. All are primarily used to open and close doors, but be very aware that the style and design you choose can make your hinges a desirable—or unfortunate—design feature.

Hinge installation—flush doors. The most common hinges used on cabinets are the butt, pivot, or decorative surface-mounted hinges. As a rule, you will need only two hinges for doors up to 2' X 3', and the hinge size should range between 1" and 2-1/2". Doors larger than 3' in height, normally must have at least three hinges, usually 2-1/2" or 3" in length.

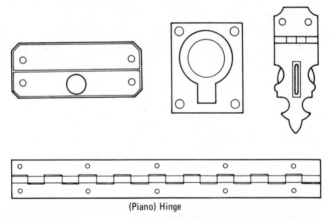

(Piano) Hinge

Figure 14–2   Hinges used in cabinetmaking.

Decorative surface hinges. To install decorative surface hinges, first fit them to the door, making certain the barrels are in line with the edge of the wood. Now place the door in its frame. The door should have 1/16" clearance on all sides if it is to be painted. With a fine piece of furniture, about one millimeter of clearance is normal. Place one screw in the frame side of each hinge and work the door. If it opens and closes properly, put the rest of the screws in place. If the door does not work, make the appropriate adjustments in the door before completely butting the hinges in position.

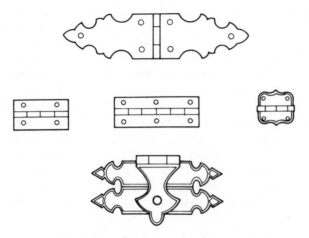

Figure 14-3   Face-mounted hinges.

Butt hinges. The procedure for installing but hinges is always the same:

1. Wedge the door in its frame.

2. Measure an equal distance up from the bottom and down from the top of the door. Mark the top and bottom of each hinge on *both* the frame and the door. Make your mark carefully with a T-square.

3. Remove the door and place a hinge between each of the marks. The barrel of the hinge should line up against the front edge of the door when one leaf of the hinge is flat against the door edge. Draw an outline of the hinge leaf. Repeat outlining the hinges on both the door edge and the frame.

4. With a router or chisel, rout out a dado inside the hinge outlines, making it *exactly* the depth of the hinge leaf thickness (usually about 1/8"). The dadoes must not only be the precise depth, but also even.

5. Attach the hinges to the door, drilling small pilot holes for each of the FH screws.

6. Hold the door in place against the frame with the free hinge leaves inserted in their frame dadoes. Drill pilot holes for one screw in each hinge.

7. Insert one screw in each hinge and test the door. If the door stands too far away from the frame, you may have to plane it down on the *latch* side. If the door binds on the hinge side, the dadoes are too deep. You can either shave the hinge side of the door down or *shim* the hinges. Shimming is done by removing screws from the hinge leaf and sliding a piece of cardboard or thin wood under the hinge to bring it up flush with the door edge. When the door works properly, put all of the screws in the hinges.

There are two ways of simplifying the process of installing butt hinges. One of them is to use a hinge template which is merely a rectangular piece of metal with sharp, turned down edges. The template is hammered into the edge of the wood until it is flush with the wood and is then pried loose, leaving cut marks around the hinge that need only be chiseled out to produce the hinge dado. The second method is to dado only the frame side of the hinge, but make the dado as deep as the combined thicknesses of both hinge leaves. The hinge is then installed in the dado and surface mounted to the door edge.

Concealed loose-pin hinges. These hinges are used on plywood doors and look like a butt hinge except that one leaf is L-shaped so that it can be screwed into the inside back face and edge of the plywood. When installing them, either cut a recess into the door that is equal to the thickness of the barrel, or cut the recess in the frame slightly deeper than twice the thickness of the two leaves together.

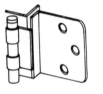 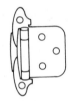

Figure 14-4
Semiconcealed hinge. Lipped doors normally require semi-concealed hinges with a rabbet bent in the leaves attached to the door.

Hinge installation—lip doors. Lip doors are easier to hang than flush doors because they overlap the frame, with the advantage that no cracks show. There is also much more tolerance during installation, because the rabbet cut around the inside edge of the door can be any width you need to fit inside the frame. Lip doors are usually fitted with semiconcealed hinges, which come in a wide variety of styles and finishes. But buy the hinges *before* you rabbet the door because the rabbet on the hinge will dictate the depth of the rabbet in the door. The hinges can be purchased with different rabbet depths.

When the lip door covers all four edges of the frame, follow this procedure:

1. Measure the width of the opening.
2. Add twice the amount of the lip (overhang) to the width.
3. Measure the height of the opening.
4. Add twice the amount of the lip.
5. Cut a rabbet equal to half the amount of the lip around all four sides.
6. Round off the edges of the lip.
7. Install the hinges on the door.
8. Hang the door and attach the hinges to the frame.

Hinge installation—doors without frames. When the edges of a door are flush against two, three, or all four front edges of the cabinet, it is necessary to use pin and pivot hinges. The pivot hinges are particularly good with plywood doors since they are screwed into the veneer face, rather than the edges. They come in pairs for small doors and in threes (called a pair and a half) for larger doors. When installing them, a small angular cut must be made at the top and bottom edge of the door to receive the hinge.

Hinge installation—drop doors. Drop doors can serve as desk tops and can be lipped or flush mounted. The hardware needed for them includes a set of butts or a piano hinge, some kind of support to hold the door in its 90° position when it is open, catches, and pulls or handles. The most usual support mechanism is a folding stay, which amounts to nothing more than a long hinge, or a chain.

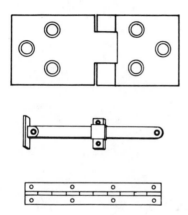

Figure 14-5   Hardware used in drop doors.

Catches, Latches, and Locks

There are all kinds of locks, latches, and catches for use on doors. Cabinets with light, 3/4" thick doors need only a magnetic catch, from which there are a variety to choose; there are just as many mechanical catches, however. If you prefer a lock, there is a selection of untold hundreds. Locks can be either hidden, or out in plain view, where their design often adds to the appearance of the cabinet. Most locks come with installation instructions which should be followed carefully.

Drawer Hardware

The hardware used on drawers includes pulls, locks, and guides. Drawer guides vary slightly in cost depending on their construction. Essentially, they all have a pair of slides screwed to the sides of the drawer which roll inside guides mounted on the cabinet walls. The more expensive guide units have ball bearings, while others incorporate extensions that permit the drawer to be pulled almost entirely out of the cabinet. Once the guides are installed, which can be a time-consuming process, they offer a truly comfortable drawer action that is worth the effort. The effort itself would appear to be minimal; just screw the slides to the sides of the drawer, position the guides on the sides of the cabinet, and then attach them. But metal drawer glides are unforgiving animals. They require exactly 1/2″ of space between the drawer and the sides, no more and no less. So if your construction has been in the least bit off, you will have to shim the track or rout the sides of the drawer, or do something to make them absolutely parallel and 1/2″ apart at all points. There are no time-saving tricks to attaching drawer guides; you just have to sit there and keep fooling around endlessly until they are perfectly aligned.

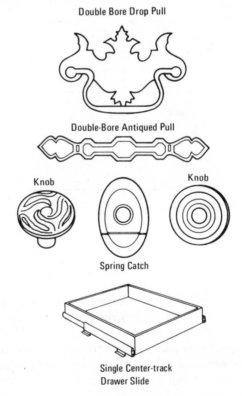

Double Bore Drop Pull

Double-Bore Antiqued Pull

Knob   Knob

Spring Catch

Single Center-track
Drawer Slide

Figure 14-6   **Hardware used with cabinet drawers.**

Handles, Knobs, and Pulls

The hardware used to open cabinet drawers and doors has so many variations that you can imagine any design you wish and then go out and buy it. You can have traditional furniture pulls, recessed handles, Early American decorative knobs, modern creations made of wood, metal, glass, rhinestones, seashells, and every other material ever used by mankind. Installing them usually amounts to drilling holes for screws or bolts and then tightening the hardware in place.

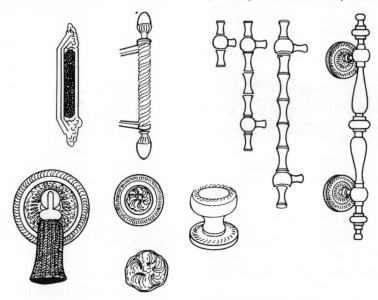

Figure 14-7   Handles, knobs, and pulls.

Chairs and Tables

The hardware necessary to complete a chair or table includes table top supports, drop-leaf supports, corner braces for legs, casters and glides.

Casters and Glides

Modern manufacturers have devised an astounding number of ways to design the simple wheel (or caster as it is called if it goes under a piece of furniture). *Casters* are rarely over 6″ in diameter, but they can be extremely fat, or even ball shaped; they can have stems or base plates, swivels and often ball bearings, and are manufactured out of plastic, wood, rubberized compounds, or metal. The round casters that have an angled rubber tread are unique under heavy furniture because they will spin as well as rotate, so they can follow an arc more easily than straight-swiveled wheels.

There are no special advantages to stemmed casters as opposed to those with base plates. The stem requires a hole drilled into the bottom of the cabinet; the base plate is screwed or bolted in place. Either way, a caster can be hidden from view by attaching it to a brace recessed inside the base of the project or by adding a skirt around the bottom that reaches to within 1/4″ of the floor.

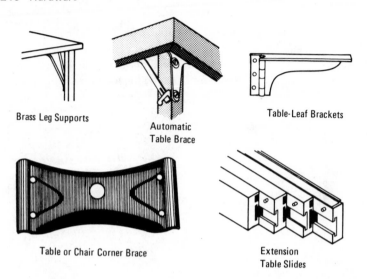

Brass Leg Supports

Automatic
Table Brace

Table-Leaf Brackets

Table or Chair Corner Brace

Extension
Table Slides

Figure 14-8　　　　　　Hardware used in making chairs and tables.

If casters are not appropriate, use furniture glides. Glides may be plastic, rubber, metal, or wood and usually have a nail in their center which is driven into the bottom of the project. Glides do not move, but merely raise the piece 1/4" or so off the floor. Some glides are attached to a threaded bolt so that they can be raised or lowered to level the piece wherever it is standing.

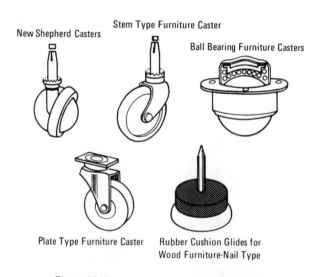

New Shepherd Casters

Stem Type Furniture Caster

Ball Bearing Furniture Casters

Plate Type Furniture Caster

Rubber Cushion Glides for
Wood Furniture-Nail Type

Figure 14-9　　　　　　Casters and glides.

Leg Braces and Shelf Supports

Within the broad category of hidden hardware that has no decorative function, you will find such things as braces and supports. Some of the table legs that you can buy come with a threaded bolt in their base which screws into a metal plate attached to the bottom of the table. The plate may have only one bolt hole; it may also have two holes, one perpendicular, and the other slightly angled. However, table legs take a heavy beating from all directions, so whenever possible, use something more than a 1/4" bolt to attach it. The leg should be forced into its corner and held there by one of the many corner braces on the market, or with a brace made of wood.

A folding leg arrangement under a hidden table or drop leaf, can be achieved with any of several folding leg brackets. Some of these are accompanied by a locking brace mechanism similar to the kind used on card tables. These braces are also similar to the drop-leaf support hardware which allows a shelf or leaf to be folded downward, but which then locks when opened to hold the shelf horizontal.

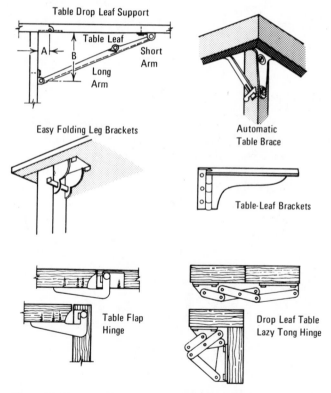

Figure 14–10 Leg braces and shelf support hardware.

Finally, there are the lid supports. These usually consist of a slotted, thin metal strip. The support slides up and down on a knob inserted in the slot and is held in any position simply by tightening the knob.

Decorative Hardware

The hardware market also has some purely decorative items such as L- and T-shaped brass or steel which you can fasten across joints on the face of a cabinet. In keeping with these, there are also metal corners to be tacked around the corners of a chest. All of these are attractive but add no real strength to a well-made project.

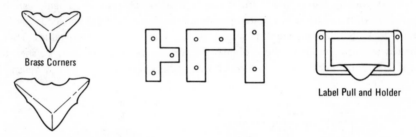

Brass Corners

Label Pull and Holder

Figure 14-11   Decorative hardware adds little additional strength.

Specialty Hardware

Manufacturers have also turned their attention to creating a variety of weird and wonderful items that can be used as part of some rather unique projects. There are sliding pot racks, disappearing wastebasket holders, and clothing carriers for deep, narrow closets. To find these specialty items look through the assortment offered by your local stores. They keep appearing in stores and mail-order catalogs, but because they are so specialized, sometimes they vanish as suddenly as they arrive. If one catches your fancy, buy it on the spot, on the premise it may not be around three months from now when you need it.

Review Questions

1. What kinds of hardware are needed for doors?
2. What is the procedure for installing a butt hinge?
3. When is a concealed loose-pin hinge used?
4. Why is it important to purchase the hinges for a lip door before the door is made?
5. What is the difference between a caster and a glide?
6. What are the advantages of a caster with an angled tread?
7. Compare and contrast stemmed casters and casters with base plates.
8. What are metal L- and T-straps used for?

Figure 14-12   The finished buffet.

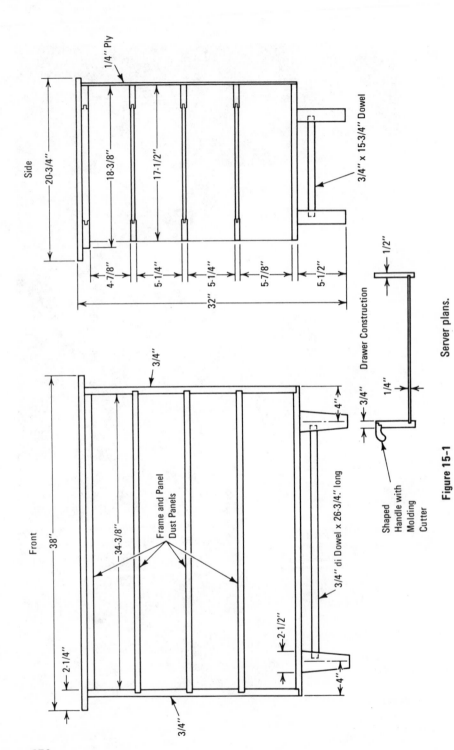

Side

1/4" Ply

20-3/4"

18-3/8"

17-1/2"

4-7/8"   5-1/4"   5-1/4"   5-7/8"   5-1/2"

32"

3/4" x 15-3/4" Dowel

Front

3/4"

38"

34-3/8"

Frame and Panel
Dust Panels

2-1/4"

2-1/2"

4"

3/4"

3/4" di Dowel x 26-3/4" long

4"

Drawer Construction

1/2"

3/4"   1/4"

1/4"

Shaped
Handle with
Molding
Cutter

Server plans.

Figure 15-1

250

Chapter 15

Variations on the Theme

While there will be variations in the specific projects so far as their construction and design are concerned, the general procedures for assembling furniture whether it's a table, chair, or any casework, are always the same. But no matter how carefully a piece is constructed, sooner or later it will need some kind of repair.

CASEWORK

Casework is a box in all its forms. You can stand a piece of casework on end, turn it on edge, put shelves and dividers inside it, attach doors to its open end, insert drawers in it, or practically anything else that strikes your fancy.

Casework finds its way into kitchens as cabinets, counters, and enclosures for appliances. But it also appears in such living space furniture as desks, bookshelves, and all kinds of end tables, cabinets, and bureaus. In short, casework is the essence of a considerable portion of the art of cabinetmaking.

The majority of modern casework is made with both hardwood- and softwood-veneered plywood, although solid stock is often used. A double example of casework is the server shown in Figure 15-1 which has a china cabinet on top of it. The server part could be a bureau, and the china cabinet is really nothing more than a shelf case that might hold books as easily as dishes.

Server

While it is possible to make an attractive, stable server from plywood and solid softwood stock, this kind of piece will be infinitely more durable if some of the framing is made of hardwood. The plywood used ought to at least be a hardwood veneer so that a clear finish can be applied with good results.

Should the server be made with cherry, mahogany or any of the cabinet woods, it would call for a different styling on the drawer fronts and the use of more traditional hardware. The legs, too, might become cabrioles rather than tapered. Decorative molding might also be applied on the drawer fronts, or the entire cabinet could be veneered with any of the more exotic woods.

Building Procedure

1. Cut the top, back, side panels, and all frame members to size.

2. Cut tongue and groove joints in frame members and dado their edges for the dust bottoms.

3. Set dado for 3/8" X 3/8" cut and stop-dado sides for top and bottom frames; rabbet frame ends.

4. Set dado for 3/4" X 3/8" and cut stop dadoes in side pieces for drawer frames.

5. Rabbet back the edge of both sides for back panel and inside surfaces for 1/8" X 1 9/16" facings.

6. Glue and assemble all frames. Glue facings into place and trim them for top and bottom stop-dadoes.

7. Drill and countersink screw holes in top frame. Bore 3/4" dowel holes in bottom frame for legs.

8. Glue and assemble sides to the frame.

9. Cut legs to size. Bore 3/4" holes for rungs and dowels. Cut tapers (with taper jig) and round all corners. Cut rungs and dowels to length and glue them into the legs. Attach the leg assembly with glue and dowels.

10. Measure all drawer dimensions and cut all pieces to size.

11. Using a dado head, cut tongue and rabbets on the ends of all drawer fronts. Dado both ends of the drawer sides and groove all members for the bottoms. Groove drawer fronts for the drawer pulls; notch drawer backs for drawer guides.

12. Assemble all drawers with glue and wire brads. On the three bottom drawers, trim off the tongue on the drawer fronts of the three bottom drawers. The top drawer is not trimmed.

13. Cut four pieces of stock 3/4" X 1" X 37" for drawer pulls. Rabbet the top edge of each piece and shape the front contour with a shaper attachment. Shape the bottom contour with a molding head. Cut the pulls to length and glue into place.

14. Make and install the center drawer guides and drawer stops.

15. Fit and glue-nail the back panel in its rabbets.

16. Cut the top end cleats to size and cut stop grooves in them for blind tenons.

17. Cut tenons on the ends of the top and trim them to fit in the cleat grooves.

18. Glue all cleats in place. Cut and glue the top supports in place.

19. Cut all edge facings to size and glue in place.

20. Attach the top with F.H. wood screws.

21. Finish sand the entire server.

22. Apply finish.

TABLE 15-1 BILL OF MATERIALS—SERVER

Number of Pieces	Part Name	Size	Material
1	Top	3/4″ × 20-3/4″ × 34-1/4″	Plywood
2	Ends	3/4″ × 19-3/8″ × 25″	Plywood S1S
1	Drawer front	3/4″ × 5″ × 33-1/2″	Plywood S1S
2	Drawer fronts	3/4″ × 6″ × 33-1/2″	Plywood S1S
1	Drawer front	3/4″ × 6-1/2″ × 33-1/2″	Plywood S1S
2	Top/bottom frames—front	3/4″ × 2-7/8″ × 34-3/8″	Hardwood
2	Top/bottom frames—backs	3/4″ × 2-7/8″ × 34-3/8″	Hardwood
4	Top/bottom frames—ends	3/4″ × 2″ × 14-1/8″	Hardwood
6	Drawer frames	3/4″ × 2″ × 34-3/8″	Hardwood
6	Drawer frames	3/4″ × 2″ × 15″	Hardwood
2	Drawer sides	3/8″ × 4-13/16″ × 17-1/4″	Hardwood
4	Drawer sides	3/8″ × 5-3/16″ × 17-1/4″	Hardwood
2	Drawer sides	3/8″ × 5-13/16″ × 17-1/4″	Hardwood
1	Drawer back	3/8″ × 4-11/16″ × 32-7/8″	Hardwood
2	Drawer backs	3/8″ × 5-1/16″ × 32-7/8″	Hardwood
1	Drawer back	3/8″ × 5-11/16″ × 32-7/8″	Hardwood
4	Drawer bottoms	1/4″ × 16-1/2″ × 32-7/8″	Plywood S1S
1	Dust bottom	1/4″ × 13-3/8″ × 31-1/8″	Plywood S1S
3	Dust bottoms	1/4″ × 14-1/4″ × 31-1/8″	Plywood S1S
2	Top end cleats	1″ × 2-1/4″ × 21″	Hardwood
4	Legs	1-1/4″ × 2-1/2″ × 6″	Hardwood
2	Rungs	3/4″ dia. × 26-3/4″	Dowel
2	Rungs	3/4″ dia. × 15-3/4″	Dowel
4	Dowels	3/4″ dia. × 1-3/4″	Hardwood
4	Drawer pulls	3/4″ × 1″ × 33-1/2″	Hardwood
2	Top facings	1/8″ × 1″ × 33-1/2″	Hardwood
2	Side facings	1/8″ × 3/4″ × 25″	Hardwood
2	Side surface facings	1/8″ × 1-9/16″ × 25″	Hardwood
2	Top supports	1/4″ × 3″ × 33-1/2″	Plywood
2	Top supports	1/4″ × 3″ × 13-3/4″	Plywood
1	Back panel	1/4″ × 25″ × 34-3/8″	Plywood
4	Drawer guides	1/2″ × 3/4″ × 15-7/8″	Hardwood
4	Drawer slides	3/8″ × 1-1/2″ × 15-7/8″	Hardwood
4	Wedges	0″-1/8″ × 3/4″ × 3/4″	Hardwood
4	Drawer stops	3/8″ × 3/4″ × 33-1/2″	Hardwood
10	F. H. wood screws	No. 10 × 1-1/2″	
	Wire Brads	No. 16 × 1-1/4″	
6	F. H. wood screws	No. 6 × 3/4″	

China Cabinet

The china cabinet could have paneled wooden drawer fronts or hinged frame and panel doors that were perhaps veneered. Or it could be completely open with no drawers and used as a shelf case. No matter what changes are made in the basic design, the cabinet remains an example of essential casework.

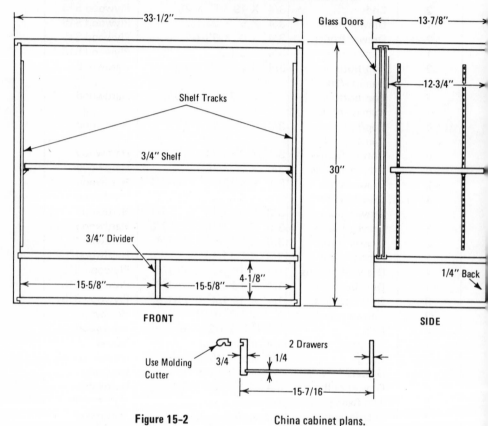

Figure 15-2   China cabinet plans.

Building Procedure

1. Cut all members to size.
2. Set dado to 3/8″ and cut stop dadoes in sides to receive the bottom and bottom shelf. Dado both ends of the top. Cut dadoes in case bottom and bottom shelf for drawer separator. Cut rabbets on top edges of sides, ends of case bottom, bottom shelf and drawer separator.
3. Set dado for 7/32″ and groove top and bottom shelf for glass doors.
4. Cut rabbets on back edge of top and sides for back panel. Drill 1/4″ holes 1/2″ deep in sides for shelf support pins.
5. Assemble case with glue.

6. Cut adjustable shelf to size.

7. Cut facings and glue in place.

8. Check drawer dimensions and cut all pieces to size.

9. Cut all necessary dadoes and grooves in drawer parts.

10. Assemble drawers with glue and wire brads.

11. Cut one piece of stock 3/4″ X 1″ X 36″ for drawer pulls. Rabbet top edge; shape front contour with shaper attachment and bottom contour with molding cutter. Cut pulls to length.

12. Glue drawer pulls in place.

13. Install back panel with #18 X 1″ nails.

14. Finish sand entire project.

15. Apply finish.

16. Make four shelf support pins from 1″ dowel.

17. Cement felt to entire bottom of cabinet.

18. Have sliding glass doors made at your local glass dealer and install.

TABLE 15-2 BILL OF MATERIALS—CHINA CABINET

Number of Pieces	Part Name	Size	Material
2	Sides	3/4″ X 13-3/4″ X 29-5/8″	Plywood S2S
1	Top	3/4″ X 13-3/4″ X 33-1/4″	Plywood S2S
1	Adjustable shelf	3/4″ X 11-3/8″ X 31-7/8″	Plywood S2S
1	Bottom shelf	3/4″ X 12-7/8″ X 32-3/4″	Plywood S1S
1	Bottom	3/4″ X 12-7/8″ X 32-3/4″	Plywood S2S
1	Back panel	1/4″ X 32-3/4″ X 29-5/8″	Plywood S1S
2	Drawer fronts	3/4″ X 4-1/16″ X 15-15/16″	Plywood S1S
4	Drawer sides	3/8″ X 4-1/16″ X 11-3/4″	Hardwood
2	Drawer backs	3/8″ X 4″ X 15-1/16″	Hardwood
3	Drawer dividers	1/4″ X 2″ X 11″	Hardwood
2	Drawer pulls	1/4″ X 1″ X 15-15/16″	Hardwood
1	Facing—top	1/8″ X 3/4″ X 33-1/2″	Hardwood
2	Facings—top	1/8″ X 3/4″ X 13-7/8″	Hardwood
2	Facings—sides	1/8″ X 3/4″ X 29-1/4″	Hardwood
2	Facings—bottom	1/8″ X 3/4″ X 32″	Hardwood
1	Facing—shelf	1/8″ X 3/4″ X 31-7/8″	Hardwood
2	Drawer bottoms	1/4″ X 11″ X 15-1/16″	Plywood S1S
4	Drawer stops	3/8″ X 7/8″ X 2″	Hardwood
1	Drawer separator	3/4″ X 12-1/2″ X 4-7/8″	Plywood S2S
4	Shelf sup. pegs	1/4″ dia. X 7/8″	Dowel
2	Sliding doors	3/16″ X 16-1/2″ X 24″	Crystal Plate Glass
1	Felt	13-7/8″ X 33-1/2″	
	Wire nails	No. 16 X 1-1/4″	

Chairs

Probably the most difficult construction in cabinet-making is the chair, and for a great many reasons beginning with the fact that very rarely will you find any right angles in a chair. The front of the seat is wider than the back. The back legs are at an angle from the back rest and are likely to be closer together at the seat than they are at the floor. The seat is contoured. The rungs in the back support are often set in an arc. When you get down to it, anyone who tries to make a chair on his own has to be a little bit off his rocker. Furniture factories make them by the thousands, of course, but they have all those big machines (like shapers and bending equipment) and besides there are lots of people in furniture factories and they can keep each other from talking to themselves.

If your macho demands that you take on a chair at least do a simple one, which has design features that do not demand a factory full of heavy-gauge hardware. The plans included here can be followed with a normal assortment of equipment, but before you leap to your bench saw consider: These plans are for a dining room chair. But who do you know who needs only *one* dining room chair?

Procedure

1. Lay out back posts and cut. Dress front edges.
2. Cut all other pieces to size.
3. Taper front legs and side rails.
4. Cut all angles on ends of front legs and rails.
5. Cut end lap joints on front legs.
6. Cut angle on top and bottom edge of front rail.
7. Bore all dowel holes.
8. Shape all pieces with 3/16″ radius.
9. Sand all pieces smooth.
10. Assemble chair in this order: Join front legs and side rails with glue and F.H. wood screws. Attach side rungs and back posts. Assemble back spindles, back rail and top rail. Join back assembly, front and back rungs and front rail to side assemblies.
11. Cut and drill corner blocks; glue blocks in place.
12. Finish shaping corners and sand entire project.
13. Apply finish.
14. Cut out plywood seat and bore 1/2″ vent holes.
15. Upholster seat and install.

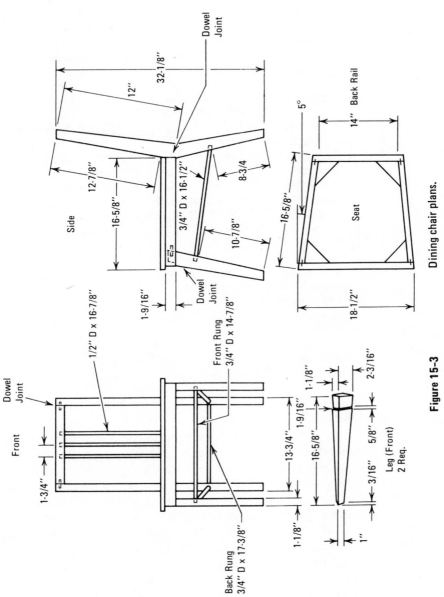

Figure 15-3 Dining chair plans.

TABLE 15-3 BILL OF MATERIALS—CHAIR

Number of Pieces	Part Name	Size	Material
2	Back posts	1-1/8" X 3-9/16" X 32-1/8"	Hardwood
2	Front legs	1-1/8" X 2-3/16" X 16-3/8"	White Oak
2	Side rails	3/4" X 2-3/8" X 18"	White Oak
1	Front rail	3/4" X 1-9/16" X 18-1/2"	White Oak
1	Back rail	1" X 2-5/16" X 14"	White Oak
1	Top rail	1" X 1-3/16" X 13-1/8"	White Oak
1	Front rung	3/4" dia. X 17-3/8"	White Oak Dowel
2	Side rungs	3/4" dia. X 16-1/2"	White Oak Dowel
1	Back rung	3/4" dia. X 14-7/8"	White Oak Dowel
4	Back spindles	1/2" dia. X 16-7/8"	White Oak Dowel
2	Corner blocks	1" X 2-1/4" X 5-7/16"	Hardwood
2	Corner blocks	1" X 2-3/4" X 5-7/8"	Hardwood
1	Seat panel	1/2" X 16-5/8" X 18-3/8"	Fir Plywood
14	Dowels	3/8" dia. X 1-1/2"	Hardwood
6	F. H. wood screws	No. 10 X 1-1/4"	
4	F. H. wood screws	No. 10 X 1-1/2"	
4	F. H. wood screws	No. 8 X 3/4"	
	Foam rubber Upholstery material		

Tables

The tops of many tables, cabinets, and desks are actually removable parts assembled after the rest of the piece is finished. They do not have to be that way in every instance, but tradition dictates that they be. Forget tradition. Do what you want to do about your tabletops.

When you decide to make a drop-leaf table, the first decision you must make so far as the top is concerned is what kind of joint you will use between the leaves and the top. You can use simple butt hinges or a piano hinge, but these require some sort of support under the leaf when it is open. An alternative is a flap or drop-leaf hinge, which locks into the form of a brace for the leaf when it is up. So far as the joints between the table and its leaves are concerned, you can use a simple butt joint, but the traditional configuration is the *rule joint*. The rule joint consists of a cove molding on the leaf side that fits over a thumbnail molding on the tabletop edge. Both sides of the joint can be cut with a shaper head or router.

There are several ways of attaching a tabletop to its frame. You can use angle irons, glue blocks, rabbeted blocks, fasteners, or angled screws. In what is considered quality construction, a web or skeleton frame, or a false top, is often installed at the top of the casework. The top is then fastened from below with some kind of fastener.

Drop-Leaf Table

Many of the procedures needed to build a table are incorporated in the construction of a drop-leaf table, and a study of the plans here will suggest to you how these basic steps can be applied to any kind of table.

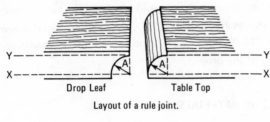

Drop Leaf   Table Top

Layout of a rule joint.

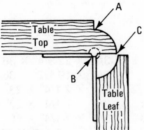

The distance from A to B and from B to C must be equal. B is the center of the hinge barrel.

Figure 15-4   The rule joint is made by using two compatible molding blades.

Construction Procedure

1. Cut all center frame members to size.
2. Cut and taper the legs.
3. Cut angles on one end of the bottom gate rails.
4. Drill screw holes in the top rail of the center frame.
5. Bore all dowel holes in all members.
6. Glue up the center frame.
7. Round the corners on all frame members and sand smooth.
8. Install all hinges.
9. Layout and install brackets.
10. Cut the top and leaves to size.
11. Cut tenons on ends of top and three sides of the leaves. Trim tenons for blind tongue and groove joints.

12. Groove all cleats, stopping them 1/2" from the ends for blind joints.
13. Miter leaf cleats and bore dowel holes.
14. Glue cleats to the top and leaves; glue facing strip in place.
15. Bore 5/8"-diameter holes 1/2" deep and glue stops to the underside of the leaves.
16. Drill screw anchor holes in the top; glue battens with #8 X 1 1/4" F.H. wood screws.
17. Rabbet for hinges in the top and leaves and install the hinges.
18. Fasten top to frame with #10 X 2 1/4" F.H. wood screws through top rail and #10 X 1 1/4" F.H. wood screws through the brackets.
19. Finish sand the project.
20. Apply finish.

TABLE 15-4 BILL OF MATERIALS—TABLE

Number of Pieces	Part Name	Size	Material
1	Top	3/4" X 22-3/4" X 36-1/4"	Plywood S1S
2	Leaves	3/4" X 19-1/2" X 36-1/4"	Plywood S1S
2	Top cleats	3/4" X 2-1/4" X 23"	Hardwood
4	Leaf-end cleats	3/4" X 2-1/4" X 22"	Hardwood
2	Leaf-side cleats	3/4" X 2-1/4" X 40"	Hardwood
4	Legs	1-1/4" X 2-1/2" X 29"	Hardwood
4	Gate top rails	1-1/4" X 2" X 10"	Hardwood
4	Gate bottom rails	1-1/4" X 2" X 13-3/4"	Hardwood
4	Gate side rails	1-1/4" X 1-1/2" X 16-5/8"	Hardwood
2	Center frame side rails	1-1/4" X 2-1/4" X 28-1/4"	Hardwood
1	Center frame bottom rail	1-1/4" X 3-1/2" X 17-3/4"	Hardwood
1	Center frame top rail	1-1/4" X 3-1/2" X 17-3/4"	Hardwood
4	Edge facings	1/8" X 3/4" X 35-1/2"	Hardwood
4	Brackets	1-1/4" X 3-1/2" X 3-1/2"	Hardwood
2	Top battens	3/4" X 2-1/2" X 19-3/4"	Hardwood
40	Dowels	1/2" dia. X 1-1/2"	Hardwood
12	Dowels	1/2" dia. X 13-3/4"	Hardwood
8	Dowels	3/8" dia. X 1-1/2"	Hardwood
4	Gate Stops	5/8" dia. X 3/4"	Dowel
7	Brass butt hinges with screws	Pr. 2"	
4	F. H. wood screws	No. 10 X 2-1/4"	
8	F. H. wood screws	No. 10 X 1-1/4"	
8	F. H. wood screws	No. 8 X 1-1/4"	
6	Glides		

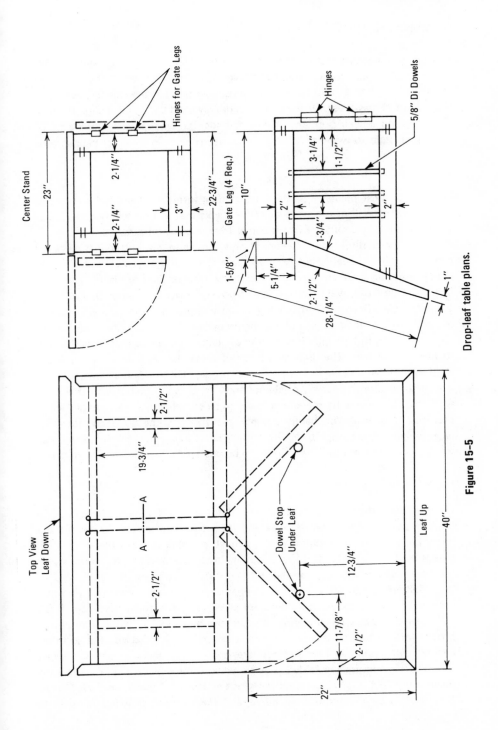

Drop-leaf table plans.

Figure 15-5

COMMON REPAIRS

The weather changes from humid to dry, from cold to hot. The wood in your furniture swells and contracts and swells again, in an endless cycle of change that can go on as often as four times an hour. Sooner or later, the glue begins to give and a joint comes loose. Or the glue does not give and the wood around it splits. The rungs on a chair pop loose from their sockets. Or the back support splits. Table legs begin to wobble. Cabinet tops warp. Hinges work free of their screws.

Regluing

Glue is the most reliable fastener for mending furniture. Nails and screws will often weaken small or old parts or cause cracks that in time will become major splits. So think "glue first" when it comes to repairing furniture.

Until recently, cabinetmakers always turned to the hot animal glues for making furniture repairs, but now we have the white polyvinyl resin and aliphatic resin glues which are made especially for mending furniture. They are, like the hide glues, water soluble and they also offer better bonding qualities than the hides. Better still, they come in plastic squeeze bottles and are ready to use with none of the mixing and heating processes that the old hides required. In its defense, liquid hide glue is also now available and can be used directly from its plastic container. The drawback to all of these glues is that you must clamp the furniture for as long as the glue needs to dry. Given a home workshop that is well stocked with a variety of clamps and a repairman who has the patience to wait several hours for his mending project to be completed, there is no particular problem. If time and/or clamps are not available, try the 60-second hot-melt glues which are applied with an electrically heated glue gun. But whatever glue you choose, there are still some rituals to be observed when mending furniture.

Procedure for Regluing

Old glue has a shiny, hard surface that will not let any new glue adhere to it. So the old glue must be scraped away and the wood then sanded. You can use a putty knife, screwdriver, chisel, knife, almost anything to clean the glue. If the glue is really stubborn, you can try soaking it with warm water, but water swells the wood and it will have to be allowed to dry before the new glue is applied.

Sanding. After the old glue is chipped away from the joint, sand the wood with a fine-grit abrasive. But there are some rules for doing that, too. First, whenever possible, wrap the abrasive paper around a block of wood to provide a broad working surface that will minimize rounding off otherwise flat surfaces. Second, when sanding hard-to-reach crevices, fold a sheet of abrasive paper several times and use the folded edge to get into the crevice. Do not *crease* the paper, only fold it, since creasing weakens the backing. Finally, on curved areas, first sand in the direction of the curve, and *always* finish off with the grain to smooth out the scratches left by the abrasive. When sanding round parts, wrap the abrasive around the part and slide back and forth, with the grain. To get into dowel holes, wrap a piece of abrasive tightly around a dowel stick or pencil and rotate it inside the hole.

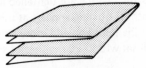

Several folds turn a large sheet of abrasive into a hand-sized pad with multiple sanding surfaces.

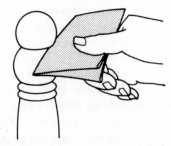

For hard-to-reach edges and crevices, use the fold of a sheet of sandpaper.

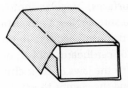

A sanding block is always used to smooth flat surfaces.

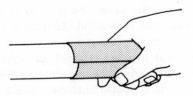

To sand rounded elements, wrap sandpaper around the element and move along the grain.

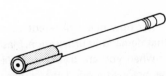

Dowel sockets can be cleaned by using a strip of sandpaper wound around a pencil or dowel.

Figure 15-6.   Use abrasive paper to sand crevices, corners, and dowel holes.

Dry run. When all of the old glue is removed, assemble the parts to make sure they fit properly. Clamp the pieces together and then remove the clamps and place them near the area where you will be doing your final assembly, with their jaws properly set. The dry run should give you an idea of the order you must follow.

If you find that a joint is only slightly enlarged, you can mix sawdust with the glue to help fill the gap, or use one of the gap-filling glues such as the hot melts, epoxy, or acrylics.

Regluing. Apply more glue than is needed to both surfaces of the joint. The excess will ooze out of the joint as the clamps are tightened and should be wiped off immediately with a damp cloth. If no glue appears at the edges of the joint, you did not put enough on. Open the joint and add more glue. While such adhesives as the white or cream glues will set within 20 minutes or so, the clamps should be left in place at least overnight.

Clamping hints. While all of the clamps—C, bar, spring, strap, and pipe—are useful for holding different kinds of furniture together while the glue dries, perhaps the most versatile clamp of all is the wood or *hand-screw* clamp. The jaws of the hand-screw clamp can be set in four basic configurations, allowing you to clamp parallel surfaces, parallel but off-set surfaces, irregular contours, and to pinch small areas together with a powerful pressure applied to their tips. Bear in mind, however, that the jaws of any clamp are being applied to a finished surface which can be scratched, so always use a piece of cardboard, rubber, or cloth as a buffer. Some professionals glue pieces of felt to the jaws of their clamps so that they never have to worry about marring anything the clamps touch.

The pressure exerted by clamps should always be as close to a right angle with the surface being glued as possible. If it is not at right angles, there can be slippage that causes the joint to be out of line. And do *not* overtighten any clamp. The purpose of clamping is to hold the parts together while the glue dries, not to make the glue work better. Most glues, in fact, will have trouble drying if they are clamped too tightly. Too much pressure can also cause the wood to warp or the repair to simply break open. While the primary objective of clamping is to distribute the pressure evenly along the length of the joint, when using more than one clamp, be careful that each of them exerts no more, and no less, pressure than all the other clamps.

Improvised clamping. Somehow, no matter how many different types of clamps you have, there are always situations that demand improvisation. Masking tape is one of the first materials to reach for when you are trying to replace a chipped corner, for example. The tape can be wrapped around the corner over the glued chip, or be used to hold it in place until a configuration of clamps can be placed against it. Tape can also be an effective clamp when there is a split in a dowel or round rung that your clamps cannot get a good hold on.

Another useful binding material is string or cord. A double strand of cord can be wrapped tightly around the legs of a chair near the rungs, for example. The string should have a cloth padding under it wherever it touches the wood. After it is tied as tightly as you can get it, use a screwdriver as a lever to twist the cord until it is bowstring tight. If your problem is to distribute pressure evenly across, say, the top of a table, place boards on either side of the gluing area and tie them together with cord, then twist the cords with a lever. The boards act as the jaws of a clamp, and the rope as if it were the screws that tighten them.

Dowels

Dowels can break and need to be replaced, but they are always preferable to nails or screws which might further damage the wood. Remember that a pair of dowels inserted in a joint will provide a strength equal to that of the mighty mortise and tenon, and even one dowel will lend tremendous strength to a broken part.

Removing Dowels

There are two prescribed ways of removing a broken dowel. The first is to pull it out with a pair of pliers, providing you can get a good grip on it. If it is really stubborn, or too deep in its socket to get hold of, drill it out. Use a drill bit that is slightly smaller than the diameter of the dowel and drill into its center. Be careful not to drill beyond the dowel itself; check the hole often, and watch for a change in the color of wood shavings. Sometimes (but not always), that will indicate that you have penetrated the furniture itself. With most of the dowel drilled away, clean the hole with a thin file or abrasive wrapped around the end of a pencil.

Replacing a Dowel

Most lumber yards and hardware stores stock furniture dowels in 36" lengths and 1/4", 5/16", 3/8", and 1/2" diameters. Try to get hardwood, but don't be surprised if all you can find is fir or pine.

Test the new dowel in its socket. It should fit snugly, but also slide in and out of the hole smoothly. When cutting the dowel, make it a fraction shorter than the combined depth of the two holes in which it will reside.

Adding New Dowels

In general, do not just put dowels into a piece of furniture anywhere you feel like it. You can assume that the original cabinetmaker or furniture factory knew what they were doing when they placed the dowels in the construction.

There are, however, instances when adding dowels can strengthen a piece of furniture. A broken leg, for example, will be stronger if you insert a dowel through the break. A chair or table rung can be strengthened by drilling a socket through the outside of the member and inserting a dowel. (Select a repair area where appearance is not important.) Then sand the dowel end flush and finish it to match the rest of the furniture. In particular, whenever a piece has broken off at a dowel joint, consider adding a new dowel at right angles to the first one.

When adding dowels, position them so there is as much solid wood as possible around the hole. And do not drill the socket holes any deeper than is necessary, or you will weaken the wood.

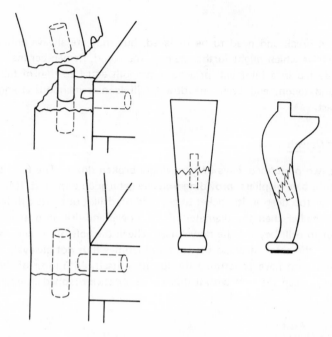

Figure 15-7.   Positioning new dowels to give added strength to a broken furniture part.

Sticking Drawers

The best-made drawers in the world can develop sticking problems for any number of reasons including dampness (and therefore swollen members), rough runners, loose joints, or just too heavy a load in the drawer.

If you suspect that dampness has swollen some of the drawer parts, remove the drawer and examine it for signs of wetness or parts that have become rough as the humidity raised the wood grain. Any rough parts should be sanded smooth, if that does not work, plane them. You can also rub hard wax or soap on the runners to make the drawer slide more smoothly. When you examine a drawer, take a close look at its joints. If any of them are loose, reglue them.

Reinforcing Shelves

When bookshelves begin to sag or come loose, the easiest repair may simply be to drive a pair of nails in the form of a "V" through the upright and into the shelf end. A better repair is to position a pair of small-angled irons under the shelf and screw them to the vertical. If the angle irons are likely to be seen, rout out a groove in both the vertical and the shelf to recess them; then fill over the iron with wood putty or plastic wood.

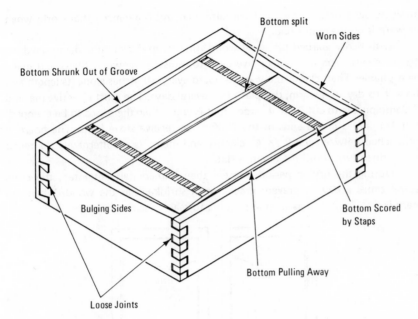

Bottom split

Worn Sides

Bottom Shrunk Out of Groove

Bulging Sides

Bottom Scored
by Staps

Bottom Pulling Away

Loose Joints

Figure 15-8. Some reasons for nonfunctioning drawers.

Sticking Doors

Cabinet doors usually stick because the wood or the frame has swelled, a condition that may also have caused warping.

First, look at the door to determine where it is sticking. If it hangs at an angle, you can probably repair it by shimming one of the hinges. If the top of the door is sticking, shim the bottom hinge. If the bottom of the door sticks, shim the top hinge.

If the door is not warped, remove its hinges and plane down the high spots. If the planing must be done on the hinge side, you will have to deepen the recesses for the hinges after the door fits properly; before resetting the hinges, consider plugging the screw holes with wooden match sticks dipped in glue. When the glue is dry, drill pilot holes for the screws and reposition the hinge in its recess.

Sliding doors that stick may have swelled too much at their top and/or bottom edges. Sand or plane the face of the edges until they fit loosely in their tracks, then give them a coating of soap or hard wax so they will slide easily.

Warped Wood

Doors, tables, counters, and desk tops can all warp from the ravages of time and humidity changes. The danger with a warped piece is that it can split if you simply screw a brace across its back, although this is a remedy that works when the warp is only a minor one.

With badly warped pieces of wood, first wrap the wood in damp sawdust, rags, or newspapers for four or five days to moisten the wood fibers and make them pliable. Then clamp the warped board every 10 inches along its length and allow it to dry in a warm, dry place for several days. The most effective method of clamping it is to cut 2″ × 4″ stock that is wider than the board to be clamped. Drill 1/4″ holes in the ends of the 2″ × 4″ to receive stove bolts. The board is sandwiched between the 2″ × 4″ clamps, and the bolts are alternately tightened two or three turns until the board is flat.

During the drying period, loosen, then immediately retighten, the bolts several times a day to prevent cracks from shrinkage in the wood. When the board is dry, refinish it as soon as possible to seal it against moisture.

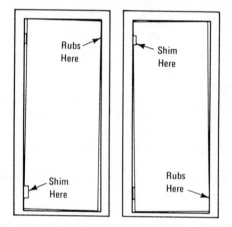

Figure 15-9.   To repair a sticking door.

Reviving Old Finishes

Having devoted hours upon hours of labor and skill to creating a piece of furniture, it is placed in view and becomes a useful part of your daily life. But sooner or later that hard-earned finish may become marred, scratched, or somehow damaged. There are a number of ways to eliminate minor scratches, blemishes, burns, and stains:

White spots usually come from heat. If commercial cleaners fail to remove them, dip a cloth in wax, lubricating oil, vegetable shortening, lard, or salad oil, and then into cigar or cigarette ashes. Rub the stain until it disappears. Wipe immediately with a dry cloth.

Candle wax. Hold an ice cube against the wax until it hardens. Break off as much wax as you can with your fingers. Scrape the remaining wax with a *dull* knife and rub the area with a clean cloth soaked in liquid wax. Wipe the spot dry; repeat rubbing until the wax is gone.

Alcohol and milk spots. If milk or any product with milk or cream in it is left on furniture for long, it acts like a mild paint remover. Wipe up spilled milk as quickly as possible. There are two methods which will clean alcohol or milk stains: (1) dip your finger in a paste wax, silver polish, linseed oil, or moistened cigar or cigarette ash, and rub the spot; (2) sprinkle a few drops of ammonia on a damp cloth and rub the spot until it disappears; polish the area with tung oil.

Water marks can be removed by dampening a pad of fine steel wool with furniture polish or wax. Rub the spot until it disappears. Or place a blotter on the spot and press with a warm iron. Repeat until the ring disappears.

To hide *minor scratches,* use a shellac stick to match the color of the finish and fill in the blemish. Rub the wax in well, then wipe with a soft, dry cloth.

Cigarette burns, if they are not too deep, can be removed by applying a solution of oxalic acid (1/2 cup of crystals to one quart of hot water). If that fails, try rubbing them with lighter fluid or benzene.

Deep cigarette burns require scraping and refinishing the area.

To Repair or Refinish?

Before deciding whether or not an old finish should be completely removed and replaced, thoroughly clean it with benzene (which will safely clean any wood finish). Soak a soft cloth in the benzene and wipe the finish. Use clean cloths and more benzene until the surface is absolutely clean.

Now examine the surface for extensive cracks, flakes, crazing, alligatoring, or blisters. If it does not have any of these, give it a coating of fine furniture cleanser-cleaner to restore the natural grain of the wood, then apply a coat of good furniture polish.

If you decide the surface cannot be revived, your next step is to determine whether the top coat is shellac, varnish, or lacquer. Pick an inconspicuous place in the piece and apply one drop of denatured alcohol and another drop of lacquer thinner on the surface. A lacquer finish will be mildly affected by the lacquer thinner; the alcohol will not affect lacquer at all. But the alcohol will dissolve shellac and the thinner will blister varnish.

New Topcoats

If the wood surface has minor blemishes but is adhering well, remove its gloss with #4/0 steel wool or a very fine grit sandpaper, and apply a fresh coat of finish.

Should the topcoat seem to lack luster, is pale, or uneven, coat it with a glaze made of equal parts stain and gum turpentine. Allow to dry for at least 24 hours before putting on the topcoat.

Minor Scratches

Shallow scratches that do not penetrate the finish can be repaired once you have determined what the finish is. Use the appropriate solvent for the finish (turpentine for varnish, alcohol for shellac, lacquer thinner for lacquer) and apply it to the scratch with a small brush, feathering it out along the edges. The thinner will dissolve the finish, permitting it to blend over the scratch; allow it to dry for 24 hours before rubbing with a clean, lint-free cloth. Then rub the area with a good furniture compound and buff with wax.

Deep Scratches

Stick shellac, which comes in a variety of colors that can be melted and mixed, will fill most deep scratches in wood finishes. If they are *really* deep, fill them almost to the top with wood putty and top off with a shellac wax that matches the surrounding color. Then carefully scrape off any excess wax and rub the repair with rottenstone or an extra fine steel wool. Apply a fresh topcoat to protect the wax.

Checks

Checks are a crazed pattern of minute surface cracks that occur in varnish. They can be corrected by first scrubbing them with a stiff brush and mild detergent. When the surface is dry, apply a solution of 2 parts turpentine, 3 parts varnish, and 4 parts boiled linseed oil. Rub the mixture into the checked surface and if all of the checks have not disappeared when it is dry, give them another coating.

Hairline Cracks

These can be filled with shellac sticks or if the wood is dark enough, with iodine applied with an India ink pen.

Dents

As you would do during the prefinishing stage of a project, place a damp blotter or cloth over the dent and press it with a warm, dry iron. The steam should expand the wood fibers and cause them to expand and fill the dent.

Going Back to "Square One"—
Applying a New Finish

When the finish cannot be revived; when the checking is too broad, and the scratches too deep; when the stain is uneven and the water rings so many they overlap each other, it is time to take off the old finish and put on a new one.

Make no mistake about it, removing any finish is a long, messy, sometimes dangerous, always ungratifying chore. Your best bet is to use one of the commercial chemical strippers—not the type you find on the shelves of your neighborhood hardware store—but one of the *secret* brands. Professional strippers are available to contractors and other professionals, but are not on the open market because they are too caustic. If the paint store you frequent is large enough, the owner will sell you a 5-gallon can of professional stripper, but he won't unless you specifically ask for it. What it will do for you, aside from burn your skin off, is cut through any finish in about half the time as other strippers.

The chemical strippers, commercial or otherwise, should be patted or flowed on the finish surface with a nylon brush that you are not planning to ever use again. Wear rubber (not plastic) gloves and a long-sleeved shirt; and do not brush over the stripper once it is on the wood. Now wait for 15 or 20 minutes (or as long as the instructions indicate) and start scraping. The finish will have blistered and peeled and should come off fairly easily. But there will be spots that remain and these must be given a second, third, or fourth coating of chemical. When scraping flat surfaces, you can use a dull putty knife, scraper, piece of cardboard, or wood. If the surfaces are curved or ornate (as on legs or scroll-work), use a toothbrush, can opener, steel brush, or old burlap to scrape whatever bubbles appear.

One trick the professionals use is to cover large areas at a time, much larger areas than they can scrape off before the stripper dries. Then they scrape for a while and stop to redampen the areas they have not covered. The technique is to keep everything wet until you get around to cleaning it off. The result is that a professional paint stripper can clean off a hundred square feet of heavily painted molding and trim in a day's work.

It should be noted that if the finish you are removing happens to be shellac, use denatured alcohol, rather than a chemical stripper. It works faster.

Once the piece is clean, you are ready to begin the process of applying a new finish (see Chapter 13).

1. Fill all gouges, dents, scratches, and blemishes in the wood.

2. Sand the entire piece of furniture, beginning with coarse-grit abrasives and working down to the very fine grits.

3. As soon as you are finished sanding, sponge the wood with clean, warm water. Allow it to dry thoroughly and then use fine grits to level any grains or fibers that may have been raised. At last, you are ready to apply a new finish.

Review Questions

1. Why are dowels preferred in furniture repair over nails or screws?
2. What types of glue would you choose for repairing furniture? Why?
3. What are the advantages of using epoxy and hot-melt glue when replacing a dowel?
4. What is the procedure for replacing a dowel in a table frame?
5. Why should you bother making a "dry run" before regluing a piece of furniture?
6. When examining a sticking drawer, what defects should you look for? How would you correct each of them?
7. How would you straighten a badly warped cabinet door?
8. When would you glaze an old piece of furniture?
9. What are the advantages of hand-screw clamps?
10. Suppose you were mending a chair with loose legs and had no strap clamp. How would you improvise holding the legs together while the glue dried?
11. Name two ways of removing a broken dowel from its socket.
12. If a cabinet door rubs at the top, which hinge do you shim?

Glossary

Abrasive Any substance which is rubbed against a surface for the purpose of smoothing it.

Adhesive Any bonding agent used to assemble materials.

Adjustable shelf standard A track with multiple slots or holes in it to hold supports for a shelf.

Air dried The removal of moisture from green wood by exposing it to air.

Alcohol A thinner and solvent for shellac.

Alligatoring A finish resembling alligator skin, usually caused by old age.

Aluminum oxide A man-made abrasive, formed by purifying bauxite.

Backing In veneering, the backing material can be a man-made product (plywood, particleboard, hardwood) or a thin sheet of mahogany, sycamore, poplar, or other wood. The backing is glued to a veneer sheet giving it stability and strength.

Bark The outer layer of a tree composed of the *inner* bark which is living and the *outer* bark which is a corklike layer made up of dead tissues.

Base coat The first coat of a final finish. Often the basic color coat applied before a final glaze.

Beading Convex molding.

Benzene A cleaning fluid and solvent made from tar.

Beveled crosscut A right-angle cut across the grain with the saw blade at any angle other than 90°.

Beveled-edge cut A slice with the grain at any angle other than 90°.

Beveled-end cut A slice across the grain at any angle other than 90°.

Beveled-rip cut A right-angle cut with the grain but with the blade held at any angle other than 90°.

Bill of materials A list of materials needed to construct a project or projects.

Bleach A caustic chemical used to lighten the color of wood.

Bleeding Stains and natural wood dyes which dissolve in solvents, then spread into other finish layers.

Blueprint Architectural plans printed as white lines on a blue background.

Board feet A cubic measurement used in the lumber industry. One Bd. Ft. = 144 cubic inches.

Book match The butt joining of two or more consecutive sheets of veneer so that their figures meet at the joint and give the appearance of an open book.

Box frame A completely enclosing solid frame around a drawer.

Butt A rectangular hinge consisting of two leaves attached by a pin.

Butt joint The joint made when two pieces of wood are brought flush together.

Cabinet drawing A drawing that outlines the shape of an object; usually the front view is shown in exact scale and proportion.

Cabriole leg Characteristic of eighteenth century Traditional furniture. The cabriole leg incorporates a double curve in which the top part of the leg is convex and the bottom part concave.

Cambium The layer of cells between the bark and the new wood which grows during each year's growth cycle.

Caster A wheel used under each leg of a piece of furniture, rarely over 6″ in diameter. Makes it easy to move.

Cell (tree) A fundamental structural compartment, microscopic in size, differentiated in composition, structure, and function, containing wood fibers, vessel segments, and other elements of a treee and surrounded by a cell wall.

Centi Prefix meaning hundredth.

Coarse-grained Wood with wide annual rings in which there is a marked difference between the springwood and summerwood.

Compound crosscut A cut across the grain with neither the direction of the cut nor the angle of the blade at 90°.

Concealed loose-pin hinge A hinge used in open-frame door construction.

Contemporary style Usually squarish in form with a minimum of carvings and ornamentation. Contemporary furniture tends to be functional, space saving, and versatile.

Core Any less expensive material placed between two pieces of veneer to form a unit of plies.

Corner block A large piece of wood fitted diagonally across the inside of a corner to brace and support it.

Cove A concave molding.

Crazing A network pattern of fine cracks sometimes found on aged finishes.

Crosscut A right-angle cut across the grain with the blade at 90° to the wood surface.

Cup The distortion of a board when its long edges curve upward, causing it to be curved along its width.

Dado A slot cut across the grain of a piece of wood.

Deca Prefix meaning ten.

Deci Prefix meaning tenth.

Density The weight of wood per unit volume.

Dishing To cut a concave section out of the middle of a board.

Distressing A method of antiquing wood by scarring and gouging it with such objects as chains and coral.

Dovetail A joint made from interlocking tenons. Most often used in drawer assembly.

Dowel A peg or pin inserted between two pieces of wood to hold them together in a joint.

Dressed lumber Wood that has been planed, or surfaced.

Dry lumber Wood containing 19 percent or less moisture content.

Dust panel The plates positioned horizontally above and below a drawer. They may be made of solid material or have a frame and panel construction.

Early American (Colonial) style Usually simple in design and sturdy in construction with less ornamentation or complicated joinery than other styles.

Edge banding To cover the edge of a core and veneer with veneer or some other material.

Edge bonding Gluing the edges of two or more boards or veneers together.

Edge cut A slice with the grain into the side of a board.

Ellipse A flattened circle.

End cut A slice into the end of the board, across the grain.

Epoxy A strong, hard, synthetic resin used in adhesive glues and finishes.

Feathering Bleeding sanded edges to achieve a smooth, indefinite blend.

Fiber Any long, narrow wood cell.

Figure The pattern in a wood surface produced by coloration, rays, knots, and deviations from the regular grain pattern.

Filler A material used to fill cracks, holes, or crevices in woods before finishing or painting.

Finish Any chemical or paint used to cover a surface, such as polish, wax, varnish, shellac, lacquer, or stain.

Flint Silicone dioxide (quartz). Used as an abrasive.

Flitch A section of log to be pelled into veneer.

Flush door A door which fits inside its frame with no more than 1/16" of space between the frame members and the door.

Flush drawer A drawer which fits completely inside its frame with no more than 1/16" space between the edges of the front and the frame.

Fluting A series of convex divisions cut in a leg or post as a decorative feature.

Frame and panel construction A way of making a door by inserting a thin panel in the center of a frame made of thicker wood.

French provincial style Characterized by cabriole legs, scrollwork, flutings, and carvings; it often has a distressed finish.

Garnet (almandite) Used as an abrasive.

Glaze A shiny finish coat sometimes used to cover a color base coat.

Glazing A liquid or paste used to fill the pores of wood prior to the application of a finish coat.

Glides A metal disk nailed or screwed to the bottom of a piece of furniture.

Gloss (glossy) A smooth, silky, highly reflective surface.

Glue block A triangular or rectangular piece of wood glued behind a joint to give it added support.

Golden mean rectangle The ideal rectangle proportions in which the short and long sides have a ratio of 1:1.618.

Grade The amount of defects (or perfection) in a piece of wood.

Green   Newly sawed lumber which has not been seasoned.

Green lumber   Wood having in excess of 19 percent moisture content.

Grit   The size and amount of abrasive mounted on a backing for the purpose of smoothing surfaces.

Groove (plough)   A slot cut with the grain of a piece of wood.

Growth layer   A layer of wood or bark produced during a single growth period.

Hardboard   A manufactured wood product made from refined wood fibers and adhesive.

Hardwood   Any broad-leaved, flower-bearing tree.

Heartwood   The innermost wood of a tree extending from the pith to the sapwood. Heartwood is no longer growing and is the primary wood used commercially.

Hecto   Prefix meaning hundred.

Hexagon   A six-sided figure.

Inlay   A strip of decorative veneer pieces assembled in a repeated design. Inlay is normally 1/28" thick.

Isometric drawing   A drawing having all of its angles equal, usually 60° each.

Italian provincial style   Featuring a simplified version of ornamentation popular during the Roman Empire, together with the ample use of simple straight lines, veneering, and inlay work.

Kerf   The width of a saw blade.

Kerfing   The cutting of several kerfs in a piece of wood, usually for the purpose of bending it.

Key   A small piece of wood inserted in grooves between matching pieces to strengthen a joint.

Kiln   An oven used for drying wood.

Kiln-dried   Wood that is dried in a kiln.

Kilo   Prefix meaning thousand.

Laminated wood   A "piece" of wood made by joining layers of wood together with all of their grains placed in parallel position.

Lap joint   The joint made when two pieces of wood overlap each other.

Latch   A mechanism for holding a door closed.

Layout   A drawing or general plan for making a project.

Leg brace   A metal or wooden brace fitted into the corner of a project to strengthen the leg.

Linseed oil   An oil made from flaxseed used in paints and stains.

Lipped door   A door which overlaps its frame on any one or all sides, when closed.

M   The Roman numeral meaning 1000.

Milli   Prefix meaning thousandth.

Mineral spirits   A thinner and solvent that will do all of the things turpentine does, but that is less odorous and less expensive as a paint and varnish thinner than turpentine. Made of distilled petroleum.

Miter joint   The butting of two pieces of wood at any angle other than 90° or 180°; the miter is most usually cut at 45°.

Mitered crosscut A crosscut made at an angle across the grain, with the blade held at 90°.

Moisture content The weight of water in a piece of wood; normally expressed as a percentage of the wood's weight.

Mortise and tenon joint The mortise is a rectangular hole. The tenon is an oblong peg cut from a matching piece that fits into the mortise to form one of the strongest possible joints.

Multiview drawing The plan of a project presenting several views drawn in different styles.

Nail A slender piece of metal, pointed at one end, broadened at the other, used to drive into or through wood so as to hold or fasten one piece to another. There are over one hundred different types of nails.

Nominal size The dressed measurements of a piece of wood.

Octagon An eight-sided figure.

Oil stain Made of penetrating oil and pigments; used to color wood by saturating its fibers.

Open frame The frame around a drawer made out of strips of wood, rather than solid walls.

Overcoating Completely covering a surface or previous finish.

Overhead The costs of running a shop or factory, including clerical costs, machinery, rent, etc.

Padding Using a pad or wad of material to wipe on a finish.

Perspective drawings A "photographic" drawing of a project showing how it will look when finished.

Pith The minute, soft core in the center of a tree, surrounded by heartwood.

Plastic laminate A man-made product with high resistance to water and wear. Plastic laminate is thin, hard, brittle, and sold in panel-sized sheets.

Plywood An assembly of odd-numbered plies of wood which are glued together with each grain running at right angles to the layer or layers adjoining it.

Pores Small holes or pits in wood which are actually the open ends of sap vessels in a tree.

Profit The amount of money earned over and above the cost of labor, materials, and other overhead costs.

Pull A small handle for opening doors or drawers.

Pumice Made from lava ground into a white powder which is mixed with oil and rubbed on the top coat of a finish to heighten its sheen.

Rabbet An L-shaped notch cut along the edge of a piece which conforms to the thickness of a matching piece that fits into it.

Rays Strips of cells which extend radially within a tree and serve to store food or move it horizontally across the tree.

Reeding A series of concave divisions cut in a leg or post as a decorative feature.

Rip cut A right angle cut in the direction of the grain, with the blade held at 90°.

Rollering The act of pressing veneer against its core or backing with a roller after it has been glued.

Rottenstone Made from shale, a gentler form of pumice, reddish to grey in color.

Rough-cut lumber Lumber that is squared but not surfaced.

Sap Most of the fluids found in a tree.

Sapwood That part of a tree which is living wood containing cells. Sapwood is always found between the heartwood and bark.

Scale A fixed proportion used in determining dimensions—a ratio of small to large—a scale of one inch to the foot—as in a scale drawing.

Screw A threaded metal shaft used to join pieces of wood or metal.

Seasoning To remove the moisture from green wood.

Shaper A machine used to cut various shapes in wood using different cutters.

Shellac Made from the secretions of the insect, the lac, used as a furniture finish.

Shop sketch A rough drawing of a project to be constructed that includes accurate dimensions.

Shrinkage As wood is seasoned and gives up its moisture content, it shrinks or becomes smaller.

Silicone carbide A tough, sharp, man-made abrasive.

Softwood All conifer, or cone-bearing trees having needle or scalelike leaves. Pine is a common example.

Solvent A liquid which will dissolve a particular material.

Spanish (Mediterranean) style Tends to be massive in appearance with heavy ornamentation reflecting a Moorish influence.

Specific gravity The ratio of the weight of a wood to an equal volume of water.

Spline A thin strip of wood inserted in grooves, cut in matching pieces of wood to strengthen a joint.

Springwood The part of the annual growth ring that is formed at the beginning of the growing season.

Stain A pigment or dye used to color a wood surface. A discoloration in the wood.

Stiles Any members of a frame.

Stock billing The procedure followed when developing a bill of materials.

Summerwood The portion of the annual growth ring formed during the later part of the growing period.

Surfaced lumber Wood that has been planed smooth.

Tack rag A piece of cheesecloth or any lint-free material used to wipe dust and debris from a surface.

Tacky The point in a drying process when the sticky surface will grab or pull at anything that touches it. Also when the new surface cannot be easily removed from the old.

Thinner Any liquid used to reduce the consistency of a compatible liquid finish.

Topcoat Usually refers to the final coat, however it could mean a coat of finish covering another coat.

Tongue-and-groove An open mortise and tenon with one piece having a groove to accept a tongue cut out of a matching piece.

Traditional style Heralded by the well-known eighteenth century English designers, Chippendale, Sheraton, Hepplewhite, and the Adams brothers. Traditional design is noted for its intricate carvings, delicate curves, and finite moldings.

Tree A perennial woody plant that attains at least 10' in height, has a single self-supporting trunk with branches and foliage growing at some distance above the ground, and a specific shape to its crown.

Turning The shaping of wood by turning it against different knife blades, usually done on a wood-turning lathe.

Turpentine A solvent for paint and enamel, made from the resin of the pine tree.

Twist The distortion of a board when its edges wind so that the four corners of any face are no longer on the same plane.

Urethane A synthetic varnish resin which is durable, plastic-like, and moisture-cured.

Veneer Any sheet of wood that is between 1/100" and 1/4" thick. Any wood sliced into thin sheets. Veneer is glued to the face of other materials for decorative purposes.

Veneer press Composed of a bed and frames which contain screws that can be tightened to put pressure on glued materials while the glue is drying.

Warp Any variation of a board from its true plane. A warp can include bowing, crooking, cupping, or twisting.

Wash A very thin sealing or shielding coat of any finishing material.

Wax Made of beeswax, paraffin, carnauba wax, and turpentine; used to protect the top coats of a finish from water and weather.

White print The plans of a project to be constructed, printed as black on a white background.

Wood The major strengthening and water-conducting tissue of a tree.

Workability The degree of ease with which wood can be cut, smoothed, and joined.

Index